Praise for Martin Dillon's
25 YEARS OF TERROR

'Dillon's skill is his remarkable ability to get
the terrorists and their intelligence and army
opponents to talk to him'
Independent

'The great value of Martin Dillon's carefully
researched and readable work is that it enters a
world few journalists have been inclined or able
to penetrate'
The Listener

'Martin Dillon is the greatest living authority on
Irish terrorism. He is our Virgil to that Inferno
in all the varieties of its torments'
Dr Conor Cruise O'Brien

'The product of a working lifetime's brave and
persistent effort to get information of a kind
which, as he frankly says, can be perilous
to possess, let alone to reveal . . .'
Times Literary Supplement

'Lively and interesting . . . timely and
easy-to-read . . . I recommend it'
Irish Times

'The inside story on the IRA's terror trail . . . Without
losing objectivity, [Dillon] maintains a clarity in his
writing that makes a vastly complex subject easier to
understand'
Daily Express

'Required reading for all those who wish to understand
the English establishment's long-term plans for
Ulster . . . This is a serious study, well-researched and
very competently written'
Sunday Telegraph

Also by Martin Dillon

THE SHANKHILL BUTCHERS
THE DIRTY WAR
KILLER IN CLOWNTOWN
STONE COLD

25 YEARS OF TERROR

MARTIN DILLON

BANTAM BOOKS

TORONTO • NEW YORK • LONDON • SYDNEY • AUCKLAND

25 YEARS OF TERROR
The IRA's War Against the British
A BANTAM BOOK : 0 553 40773 2

Originally published in Great Britain as *The Enemy Within* by
Doubleday, a division of Transworld Publishers Ltd

PRINTING HISTORY
Doubleday edition published 1994
Bantam edition published 1996
Bantam edition reprinted 1997
Bantam edition reprinted 1998

Set in 11/13pt Monotype Bembo by
Phoenix Typesetting, Ilkley, West Yorkshire.

Bantam Books are published by Transworld Publishers Ltd,
61–63 Uxbridge Road, London W5 5SA,
in Australia by Transworld Publishers (Australia) Pty Ltd,
15–25 Helles Avenue, Moorebank, NSW 2170,
and in New Zealand by Transworld Publishers (NZ) Ltd,
3 William Pickering Drive, Albany, Auckland.

Printed and bound in Great Britain by
Cox & Wyman Ltd, Reading, Berkshire.

I dedicate this book to Linden Stafford,
for her editorial expertise and clarity of thought,
and to Mike and Mary Rose Cooney
for their kindness and support.

Acknowledgements

During the preparation of this book there were many people in the intelligence and security organizations in both Ireland and Great Britain who gave me their time and insights into the war against the IRA. They asked me to protect their identities, yet I feel I must pay tribute to them for the assistance they provided because they will each recognize their individual contributions in this work. There were also people within the British and Irish diplomatic communities who were willing to assist me because they believed I was making a genuine attempt to unravel complex issues which have relevance to both Ireland and Britain.

I thank Linden Stafford for her editorial expertise and her words of encouragement during the writing of this book. My publishers, Doubleday, through Marianne Velmans and Jennie Bull, believed in the project and gave it their energy and support. Doubleday's representative in Ireland, Philip MacDermott, had confidence in me. I am indebted to my wife, Kathy, and our children, Nadia and Crawford, for their patience and understanding at all times; and to my parents, Gerard and Maureen Dillon, who constantly remind me of their commitment to my books. Maureen Bannon is not only my mother-in-law but a friend whose eighty-three years have enhanced the world around her.

Tim Pat Coogan, writer and historian, demands special mention for providing me with documents and insights into the history of Irish republicanism. His published works are essential reading for students of twentieth-century Irish history. Gill and Simon Hess worked tirelessly to promote my work, as did Gill's wife, Nolene, who died tragically and is a great loss to many Irish writers. Professor Paul Bew at Queen's University, Belfast, was always ready to help, and his published works on Northern Ireland offer important perspectives for writers of that conflict.

In the media world there were many people who gave me their time and expertise. They include the writer and journalist Eamon Mallie, who makes the news as often as he writes about it; Tabitha Troughton and Leslie Anne Van Slyke, who supplied much-needed research material and valuable perceptions; television producer John Slater, and television directors Alex Sutherland and Moore Sinnerton, who were listening posts when I needed to publicly express some of my theories. Don Anderson, writer and ITC executive, never ceased to remind me of the value of what I was trying to achieve in writing about the IRA. Ed Curran, editor of the *Belfast Telegraph*, and Martin

Lindsay, editor of *Sunday Life*, both recognized the importance of encouraging the public to a greater understanding of the real nature of conflict. Jim Campbell, formerly editor of *Sunday World*, was an important source when I required detail which only his extensive journalistic experience could provide.

There are those who are an important part of my life, and by their very presence constitute a valuable source of creative thought. They include Dr Conor Cruise and Maura O'Brien and their son, Patrick; Ian Kennedy whose friendship and professional collaboration are central to my life; my former agent, Christine Green who worked hard to ensure this book was published; the writer Frank Delaney and his wife, Susan, who were a source of encouragement when I was writing other works; my agent, Anthony Harwood of Curtis Brown; Brian and Ursula McLaughlin; Michael and Imelda Fienberg; Brendan and Mary Hanley; my brothers, Damien and Patrick Dillon; Michael Lynch of Elliott Duffy Garrett; Mike and Mary Rose Cooney and their family, Aidan, Alex and Georgina; Alain and Patricia Pillaud, and Christelle; Bruno Cramarejas who is ploughing an important furrow in life; Bruno's grandparents whose generosity knows no bounds; Isabelle Pertuls; Stefan and Francine Chabiron; Tom and Josephine Tickner and their daughter, Nicola; Dr John Casey of Clifden and his wife, Brenda, who remind me of fond days on the Ballynahinch; Ronald and Soshana Appeleton, and their son, Michael, who works with me on television projects; cousin, Frank Dillon, Patricia and their children; Colin Baker, a fine television reporter of international standing who spent many hours with me in dangerous situations in the 1970s; Philomena O'Neill and her family; Christiane Fontaine, a friend and companion who knows how to enjoy the natural world; Francois Bouan, friend, poet and philosopher; John Gingell and his wife, Anne; Lorrie Leeson, an artist who recognizes the intrinsic value of hard work, and his wife, Heather; Jacinta Noble; Bruce and Marie-Claire Hockings; Patrick Weil and his family; Peter and Valerie Aris; Tom Armour and Crispin Avon; Stephen Bailey of DL Taffner; Liam Clarke of *The Sunday Times*; Martin O'Hagan of *Sunday World*; Avril Barker of BBC Belfast; Geoffrey Beattie, a friend and fellow writer who understands the complexities of political life in Ireland; Marc Hosquet; Lise Boussarie who keeps us all sane; David Malone, Susie, and their family in Donaghadee; Roger and Angie Sarsby; Chris Warren and his son, Jay; Richard Walker; Chris Moore and Paul Robinson of UTV who have always been courageous in their handling of news and current affairs; Dr James White, writer and art historian; Karen and Paul Stockman; Ivan Mac Michael, a veteran journalist who cradled all of us in the early days of difficult news reporting; John Taylor and his brother, Patrick, at the Taylor De Vere White Gallery in Dublin; Dr A. T. Q Stewart, writer and historian; Barry Cowan, a media presenter interviewer with few equals; Colin Lewis worked with me in BBC Northern Ireland and understood that publishing the truth is not always achievable. Other friends include Alain Bernard, a highly respected journalist with the *Sud-Ouest*, the photographer Giles Fouquet, Professor Simon and Patricia Lee, Cecilia Kennedy, Chad and

Judy Paine, Jane Lewis, Siobhan Sinnerton, Greg Darby, Brian and Anne Turley and their daughter, Paula, Elaine Draper and her son, Martin. David and Vanessa Hewitt kindly supplied me with a bolt-hole when I was writing this book. David Lloyd and Fiona Chesterton of Channel Four Television were supportive when I was making the documentary *The Last Colony*, which was broadcast while I was completing this book. Jean-Marie and Françoise Trarieux, Michèle and Madeleine Goldenberg, David and Monique Aylward, Victor Shephard – all helped my family while I travelled to Britain and Ireland to research this work. I owe special thanks to Gilles Peyronnet and his family for their kindness to me when I was in need.

Colin and Jane Fulthorpe gave me fascinating perspectives on Shakespeare when the problems of Ireland were closing in. The artist Ken Henderson, his wife Kathy, their daughter Rebecca, and Bob Gilchrist reminded me that there is more to life than writing; as did Robbie Ross at the Hôtel de France; Erique and Astride Thimon; Jean-Pierre Thimon; Tom Milner; my friends at the Café Colonnes; Claude and Marie-Claude Lambert and Elsa; Nigel Charker at Cidaris; Anne and Albert Curran and their daughter Barbara Anne; Paddy and Patsy Hunt; Mary and Peter Johnston and their daughter Emma Louise; Fidelma McVeigh, BBC Northern Ireland; Sean Rafferty, who is a thoughtful and sensitive man; Tony Rowe; Michael Appleton; John Nicholson; John Kennedy at Stormont; Roy Bradford, writer and former cabinet minister, BJ; Elish Hogg; Geordie and Tess Anderson; John Bach, a fine conversationalist and criminologist; David Dunseith, a skilled presenter and seeker of the truth; and David Sykes, who understands the problems of non-fiction.

I would like to pay special tribute to Field Marshal Lord Michael Carver, whose autobiography, *Out of Step*, offers penetrating insights into the period when he was Chief of the General Staff; and to General Sir Anthony Farrar-Hockley for his directness and clear thinking.

Contents

Author's Note   xv

Foreword   xxiii

1 THE S PLAN   1

2 THE PURSUIT OF THE BOMBERS   23

3 DEATH IN THE AFTERNOON   41

4 A BITTER LEGACY   60

5 THE WILDERNESS   86

6 THE ARRIVAL OF THE TROOPS   106

7 GOVERNMENT AND THE GENERALS   127

8 ECHOES OF THE COVENTRY TRAGEDY   146

9 CLOSE ENGLAND   163

10 THE MOST DANGEROUS MEN   178

11 THE IRA'S ENGLAND DEPARTMENT   210

12 THE INTELLIGENCE WAR   237

13 A TRAIL OF TERROR   264

14 TALKING AMID THE CARNAGE   300

Epilogue   343

Appendix: The Green Book   353

Index   385

Author's Note

After I had completed this book and it was going through the press, the IRA leadership made a formal statement, published in the newspapers on 1 September 1994, that 'as of midnight, August 31, there will be a complete cessation of military operations. All our units have been instructed accordingly.' Saluting 'our volunteers, other activists, our supporters and the political prisoners who have sustained the struggle against all odds for the past 25 years', the IRA proclaimed their 'desire for peace based on a just and lasting settlement'.

The first response of the British Prime Minister, John Major, was to say he was encouraged by the statement but insisted that discussions regarding the possible entry of Sinn Fein into constitutional talks could not begin until the IRA made it clear that the ceasefire was permanent. On the other hand, the Irish government acted swiftly to bring the IRA in from the cold: on 6 September the Sinn Fein president Gerry Adams was welcomed in Dublin by Prime Minister Albert Reynolds. President Clinton's administration supported Reynolds's view that the IRA had finally renounced violence; US contacts had already met with various parties and held out the promise of US aid to Northern Ireland in the event of a peaceful settlement.

Meanwhile the Ulster Unionists expressed fears of a 'sell-out' by the British government. Loyalist paramilitaries bombed Sinn Fein's offices in Belfast on 4 September, exploded a device on a Dublin train, and threatened attacks on other targets both north and south of the border.

Just over two weeks into the ceasefire, John Major, speaking at Stormont Castle on 16 September, announced the immediate lifting of the broadcasting restrictions on Sinn Fein and all the paramilitaries. Declaring that there was now an unparalleled opportunity for peace, he reiterated his decision that as soon as the IRA proved by their words and actions that the ceasefire was 'lasting and genuine', and stated 'unambiguously' that there would be no resumption of violence in any circumstances, Sinn Fein would be allowed to enter the talks process. At the same time the British Prime Minister made a specific undertaking that the outcome of constitutional talks between the various political parties would be put to a referendum of all the people of Northern Ireland.

Clearly it was difficult for the IRA to use words such as 'permanent ceasefire' and 'never again' without knowing the future shape of politics in Ireland, particularly at a time when Catholics in the North were being targeted by loyalist gunmen.

It wasn't long before loyalist paramilitaries, who had watched the political success of the Provisionals, also declared a ceasefire. It was clear their decision was motivated by a recognition that they were at risk of being politically isolated if they continued their campaign of violence. That decision, coming close on the heels of the IRA ceasefire, generated a wave of optimism throughout Ireland and encouraged many commentators to declare that a political breakthrough was a reality. The people of Northern Ireland were resolute that after two decades of war, peace was finally achievable. However, by the summer of 1995, those who had carefully studied the conflict knew that a lasting peace was going to be difficult to achieve. The guns on both sides were well-oiled in underground dumps and there were plenty of people willing to use them if called upon to do so.

It should have been clear to astute observers of British–Irish politics that even in the early months of 1995, the British Government was preoccupied with matters other than the peace process. John Major was busy devoting his energies to keeping himself politically afloat while members of his own Party plotted his downfall. The Ireland Question was once again moved down the agenda, illustrating a feature of British political life which has consistently negated the efforts of those who have sought a peaceful solution in Northern Ireland. Respected politicians and journalists pointed an accusing finger at the British Government and warned that the peace was fragile.

In order to distance himself from the charge that he was guilty of moving too slowly, John Major and members of his Cabinet contrived to place obstacles in the way of Sinn Fein in order to demonstrate that Sinn Fein was the intransigent element. The British insisted that the Provisionals apply the word 'permanent' to the ceasefire and demanded that the IRA surrender its guns. Behind the scenes, the Irish Government, under the leadership of a new Taoiseach, John Bruton, warned British negotiators that their posturing was counterproductive. One source close to the Irish Government told me that there were stormy scenes between British and Irish negotiators, the latter accusing their counterparts of using 'stalling tactics'. 'We told the British side that John Major was playing with fire by constantly placing obstacles in the way of Sinn Fein. It was obvious that he didn't want to be seen to be conceding too much to the Catholics because he needed the support of the Unionists in Parliament to guarantee his political survival. It was the historical impediment of Britain playing the Unionist card. Major and his Cabinet did not wish to be seen to move too quickly or to bring Sinn Fein directly into talks. The British increased the stakes for Sinn Fein participation in talks by demanding that, as a precursor, the IRA surrender its weapons. The Brits knew the IRA would not agree to that until there was a framework for a political settlement. We all know that in conflicts throughout the world the handover of weapons follows a settlement. It's a bit like saying to the kidnapper, "Give us the hostage and then we'll do a deal". It was a ploy to slow down the peace process and to demonstrate that the IRA was being unreasonable. We knew what the British were at and so did the American element who were pressing Major to take advantage of the IRA's willingness to find a peaceful settlement. It's the old British thing of playing politics with Ireland at the expense of the people of the island.'

That assessment was shared by the IRA who told Sinn Fein in the spring of 1995 that they were not convinced the British Government was sincere about brokering a settlement which would radically change the shape of British–Irish politics. They made it clear to leading Sinn Fein figures such as Martin McGuinness that the decommissioning of weapons would not take place while the RUC remained an armed force and large numbers of British troops were stationed in the Province.

The fragility of the peace process was starkly symbolized by two events at the beginning of the summer of 1995. First was the release on warrant of British paratrooper Lee Clegg, the convicted murderer of a female joy-rider. The Catholic community and the Irish Government were angered by the move because Clegg had served only four years of a life sentence imposed by a British court and was permitted to return to his Regiment. In contrast, many Republican and Loyalist prisoners guilty of firearms offences which did not constitute murder were serving long sentences and there was no reciprocal gesture to offer them terms similar to Private Clegg. Following the outcry and street protests about Clegg's release, the peace process was again placed in jeopardy at the beginning of July 1995 when Orangemen took to the streets of Northern Ireland to assert a triumphalist right to march wherever they chose. They argued that they had marched through Catholic areas for 188 years and were still entitled to do so. It presented the British Government and the RUC with a choice of whether they should confront tribalism or capitulate to the Orange Order. For decades, the playing of anti-Catholic songs by Orange bands strutting through Catholic districts was a source of sectarian strife. In the light of the peace protest, many Catholics, and the Irish Government, hoped that the provocative role-playing of the Orange Order would not be permitted. If Orangemen wished to march, they argued, they were free to do so in their own areas. Considering the nature of such a divided society, that was not an unreasonable alternative but it was one which did not please the Orange Order and many of the Unionist politicians who were among its members.

The crunch came in Portadown with a three-day confrontation between the RUC and loyalists who insisted that they had an historical right to parade through a part of the town which was predominantly Catholic. The stand-off culminated in a compromise which permitted Orangemen to march through a Catholic enclave without their bands and the 'Kick the Pope' songs which might have led to a serious confrontation. The compromise was applauded by some as a by-product of the peace process but the majority of Catholics resented the capitulation. In Belfast, the RUC sealed off a Catholic district to permit the Orangemen to march through it. It demonstrated the fragile character of the peace process and the need for a political settlement which would erase the tribalism which has permitted some to believe they have a right to impose their culture on others.

In August 1995 there was a startling revelation from the former Taoiseach, Albert Reynolds, who was co-signatory with John Major to the Downing Street Declaration which had signalled a new beginning and a search for peace. With the anniversary of the IRA ceasefire imminent, Albert Reynolds addressed the British demand for decommissioning of IRA weapons as a precursor to talks. He told the media he would never have signed the Downing Street Pact if the British had made that an issue. He went on to say it was not on the agenda when he was negotiating with John Major. Reynolds's comments served to illustrate the gulf between the two Governments and he was supported in his public revelation by his successor, John Bruton. Many observers were left in no doubt that the British side was once again placing obstacles in the way of peace and a settlement was going to be difficult to achieve.

It is impossible to determine whether loyalist and republican communities will reach an accord which will take the guns and tribalism out of their society, or whether the British Government has the moral courage to place the issue at the top of its political agenda, irrespective of the internal problems in the Conservative Party or the need for the support of Unionist Members at Westminster. The opportunity exists at the time of writing, to move towards a full dialogue with all parties without preconditions which the British Government knows will only serve to stall efforts towards a lasting peace. Many of those close to the secret talks which have taken place between all the parties unanimously point the finger at the British Government for failing to provide the momentum for an inclusive dialogue.

Perhaps it is inevitable that any British Government with a slim Parliamentary majority of nine will be more concerned about political survival than grasping the nettle of Irish politics. That is an explanation, but hardly a position which is morally defensible.

Martin Dillon
September 1995

Foreword

The assertion that history is only valuable if we remember it creatively seems not to apply to Northern Ireland, yet those of us who write about it should do so with that proposition in mind. All of us who were born there share the guilt, but until we recognize our complicity in the making of the history, and learn tolerance and a recognition of each community's uniqueness, the war will continue.

It is difficult to remember a time when Northern Ireland was at peace. The fabric of its society has been disintegrating for twenty-five years; the innocent have suffered. The conflict has spread into Britain and the continent of Europe, while other seemingly irreconcilable disputes have been settled elsewhere. The tragedy is that the victims have no voice and the shadows are monopolized by men who cynically believe that God sanctions the actions of their individual tribe.

When I was born, in 1949, Northern Ireland was

at peace with itself, and Europe was recovering from the Second World War. I was born into the Catholic nationalist community where the inherited instinct was to be anti-British, anti-State and pro-republican. Ironically, the paradox in my history was the presence of a British Army tradition which was at variance with the natural inclination of the nationalist-republican ethos. My grandfather, Patrick Dillon, had fought at Dunkirk and on the Normandy beaches. Like his brother, John, who was a professional soldier in the British Army, he was proud of the part he played in the defeat of Nazism. Patrick went to Normandy with his tommy-gun and a fishing-rod; he knew the Germans would be defeated. If he had lived to see the last twenty-five years of violence he would have disapproved of terrorism, the killing of soldiers and the bombing of British cities. After all, he had fought to protect the British Isles between 1939 and 1945. He would have been dismayed if he had seen the British soldiers rampaging through his neighbour-hood, the Lower Falls, in 1970. The nationalist tradition found its way into my formative years when I was under the tutelage of the De La Salle Brothers. It is hard for a child to shatter that refracting lens of life. The Christian Brothers were the shock troops of Catholic nationalist Ireland, and I learned a narrow, prejudiced history of the British Isles.

The tribalism in my society was in the separateness of the two religious traditions. It was clearly visible in the geography of my native city, Belfast. My childhood was not inhabited by friendly Protestants, or an intimate knowledge of their traditions. The communities were divided by the shibboleth of religion, genuine fears and contradictory symbols. My earliest memory of Protestants relates to shopping forays with my mother into the Shankill district known as the heartland of loyalism. I remember thinking that Protestants looked very much like Catholics. They were dressed like us and, according to my mother, sold cheaper vegetables. The significant differences were the wall paintings of King William on a horse and Union flags fluttering from lamp-posts. My mother's apparent apprehensiveness about being in 'enemy' territory probably conveyed itself to me.

'Fuck the Pope' was not a slogan which attracted me to the Protestants of the Shankill. It was painted in big letters on the walls for me to decipher when I reached a reading age; but it did not interrupt my mother's shopping or prevent my father from taking me for long walks through that neighbourhood. My mother clearly thought that Protestant doctors were professionally more competent than their Catholic counterparts. Our family GP was on the Shankill Road. In the early 1950s it was not uncommon for Catholics to shop or buy fish and chips in Protestant territory. It was accepted that Protestants honoured their dead in the city's main cemetery in the heart of the Catholic Falls district. Every Sunday, Protestants worshipped in their church, 20 yards from my family home at Albert Street in the Falls. There were no men in paramilitary uniform waiting to abduct Catholics or Protestants who wandered into each other's ghettos. Phrases such as 'sectarian murder', 'proxy bomb' or 'another atrocity' did not find their way into the columns of the local newspapers.

Nevertheless, it was a divided and unequal society in

which everything from schooling to hospital treatment had a separateness which reinforced division. It was a place which the sovereign Parliament at Westminster preferred to ignore in the mistaken belief that all was well with devolution. They did not understand that by abdicating responsibility they were allowing dangerous elements to germinate into discontent and finally a long war.

Fifteen years after my childhood trips to the Shankill, I returned there with a pen and notebook and discovered that the wall painters had forged new images: men in combat jackets with automatic weapons beneath a slogan 'For God and Ulster'. In the streets of my birthplace, the Lower Falls, similar images adorned the walls but the slogan was different: the Catholics preferred Ireland to Ulster. In both areas of the city, a process of atavism was reinforced with newly built walls ringed with barbed wire. They were there to keep people in the ghetto as much as to keep others out of it. British soldiers, with bayonets fixed, looked perplexed because it was not Aden or Cyprus, and the enemy was difficult to define.

As the years passed, I became one of those journalists with purely reflex instincts shaped by events on the streets. There was no time to examine the roots of the conflict because the words 'today' and 'yesterday' were the controls on all journalism. I saw the victims in the gory detail which celluloid could never fully convey. They were Protestants, Catholics, men, women, children and the elderly. There were young soldiers among the dead; although the place and the people resembled home, death was the price of peace-keeping. But the majority of the victims were non-combatants. I talked to those who inspired, planned and perpetrated the violence. They were also victims of the history of the place but they did not suffer. In each community they were the inheritors of their individual traditions, and the siege mentality was not exclusive to either tribe.

Those who inspired the violence were often cold, cynical men and women whose vision was narrowed to exclude compromise. Their foot soldiers were the naïve, and not so naïve, young men and women who had 'God' writ large in their justification of violence. The politicians on both sides were skilled in their expressions of indignation; negotiation had no place in their vocabulary. British Army officers did not understand a troubled Irish history, and would have preferred a real colonial situation in which the General Officer Commanding did not have to answer to local politicians, the media and the Home Office. The clergy, Catholic and Protestant, were quickly discovering they had no mandate, and God was being hijacked by those who controlled what the IRA referred to as 'the hearts and minds' of a generation.

When I began to seek another way, rather than journalism, to analyse the conflict, I found it difficult to overcome the reflex instinct that characterized my profession. I was fortunate that others, like Robert Fisk, the *Sunday Times* Insight Team reporters, and such local journalists as Jim Campbell, were also stepping outside the confines of news reporting to discover the roots of the violence. Sadly, the Northern Ireland story became a tired one for the media in Great Britain and was replaced by reports of other conflicts. It is understandable that by the early 1970s the British public, never well educated about the Irish problem, felt battered by daily coverage of killings that did not affect them directly. Only when IRA outrages occurred in England was the spotlight firmly focused on Ireland. The IRA kept that spotlight directed at Ireland when they began to devote their energies to major acts of terror in Britain from 1989. Coverage of the renewed onslaught was accorded considerable space in the newspapers and given increased television time. The knee-jerk media response highlighted the tendency in the 1970s and 1980s to ignore the problem as long as it resided within Ireland.

I have always believed that the British public need to be constantly informed, beyond the news, about the roots of the problem: the reasons why this recent conflict is not the only one which endangered Britain, the ineffectiveness of British and Irish policy-making, and the nature of the people who threaten British lives. Few people in Britain know the history of IRA activity on the mainland, or the mind-set of the perpetrators of violence. Part of the media tends to depict them all as 'mad evil psychopaths' and to ignore other issues such as the failure of the intelligence apparatus to defeat the Provos, the grievances (real or imaginary) of the combatants in this war and the inability of politicians to find a solution.

In writing this book I decided to concentrate mainly on the IRA in Great Britain, in order to expand the knowledge of people on the mainland about the organization which threatens them. I hold no brief for any of the protagonists in the conflict, but I contend that we should know why they wage war. I have confined myself to the period since 1938 during which the seeds of the present conflict were sown, and when real opportunities to find a settlement were lost and ignored. The politicians in Ireland have failed their electorate. They have constantly left a vacuum which has been filled by the men who espouse and perpetrate violence. Politicians in Britain have been ignorant of Irish history, and many have cared little about Northern Ireland. The 'bog of Irish politics' is a phrase that has haunted British politicians and acted as a deterrent to any British prime minister who sought to intervene in that part of the United Kingdom. The fear of being immersed in that political 'bog' is what characterized the lack of serious policy-making from Westminster in the decades before the present conflict began in earnest. The two governments, British and Irish, are inextricably linked to the problem, yet they have spent twenty-five years vacillating between outright resentment of each other and trying, unsuccessfully, to bring an end to the war.

This book will also examine the IRA bombing campaign in Britain before and during the Second World War; the IRA's flirtation with Nazism and Eire's wartime neutrality, and how that conditioned subsequent British policy towards Ireland; the failure of the security forces and the intelligence community to eradicate the present-day threat, particularly in Great Britain; how the IRA sustained a campaign in England; why the British Army was once convinced it could win the war; the problems faced by the majority of Irish people living in England; the internecine rivalry between elements of the security apparatus in Britain, and how the IRA benefited from that problem; the tactics and type of personnel employed by the IRA on the mainland; and why the British government held secret talks with IRA/Sinn Fein amid the carnage of Warrington and other atrocities.

1

The S Plan

Disturbing though the truth may be, the country today must face the fact that terrorism has reared its ugly head in city and town, and now openly threatens human life and menaces the great public services.

Police activities usually associated with a state of Martial Law and not with the peaceful ordered life of Britain are in unmistakable evidence, especially in London.

Mobile cars carrying armed detectives scurry through the streets of the Metropolis; the gates of Scotland Yard are for most of the day bolted and barred against all callers; a guard is thrown round every police station; the Houses of Parliament are closed to the public, and uniformed police posted at the gates. The Royal residences have all become places of special protection.

Sensational bomb outrages and acts of sabotage

in the Tottenham Court Road and Leicester Square Tube stations have convinced the authorities that a ruthless campaign of terrorism is now in the process of execution in Great Britain. Scotland Yard has ten thousand men engaged in the most extensive and intensive round-up in London's history.

That could have been the front-page story of many newspapers in the last twenty years. It was the front page of the *News of the World* on 5 February 1939.

While Britain was facing the prospect of the Nazi menace in Europe, the IRA was engaged in a campaign of violence in London and other British cities. There are striking parallels between that period and the present. The IRA of the late 1930s was an organization divided by internal disputes after the 1921 Treaty with Britain which led to the partition of the island of Ireland. In 1938 the Irish Prime Minister, Eamon de Valera, was trying to restore good relations with Britain. While he recognized that the IRA could pose an obstacle to the talks, he hoped that an improvement in Anglo-Irish relations could start a process which might lead to the ending of partition.

As part of the 1921 Anglo-Irish Treaty, Britain had retained the right to use three ports in Eire for the defence of Great Britain and Ireland. One was at Lough Swilly in County Donegal and the others were at Berehaven and Cobh in the southern part of the island near Cork. De Valera viewed the British possession of the 'Treaty Ports' as an obstacle to his intention to keep Ireland neutral in the event of a war in Europe. He had long been aware that if Eire owned the ports unconditionally, with no facilities available to the British, Eire would not be regarded as a combatant on the side of the Allies. In April 1938 he successfully negotiated the unconditional return of the ports to Eire as part of a new Anglo-Irish Agreement which was perceived by Neville Chamberlain's government to be a step on the road to better relations between the two countries.

It was a disastrous step for British interests, and this quickly became apparent with the outbreak of the Second World War. Yet de Valera refused to listen to pleas from the British to allow Allied shipping to use the ports. They were sufficiently important for the British government to commit itself to the principle of the reunification of Ireland if de Valera would make the ports available and join the Allied war effort. De Valera, however, was not prepared to compromise his policy of neutrality. The significance of the Treaty Ports became important after Germany invaded and occupied France. Allied shipping had to be re-routed via the headlands of County Donegal and into the North Channel, where German U-boats found sanctuary before going in search of their prey. The failure of Eire to permit access to the port of Lough Swilly for the defence of merchant shipping left Allied vessels at the mercy of the enemy. The ports of Berehaven and Cobh would have been strategically important as bases from which naval vessels could quickly reach convoys in the Atlantic; but Allied protection vessels were forced to make much longer trips from ports such as Plymouth.

In the political climate of 1938, however, it seemed more important to Chamberlain's government that

British relations with Eire should be improved by means of the new Anglo-Irish Agreement. As well as handing over the Treaty Ports to Eire, the 1938 Agreement provided a settlement of longstanding economic and trade difficulties between the two countries. But no concessions were made on the ending of partition.

By the 1930s the IRA seemed to be a spent force, content to hold annual parades with public appearances by the older veterans. However, there were others in IRA ranks who harboured ambitions to return to 'the armed struggle'; among these was Sean Russell, whose influence was to prove crucial in the IRA's future attitudes towards violence in mainland Britain.

Sean Russell was a cradle-to-grave republican. He was born in 1893 and joined the Irish Volunteers in his late teens. During the 1916 Rising against the British he was interned and was one of many IRA men who later opposed the 1921 Treaty with Britain which gave British dominion status to the twenty-six counties in the South. He supported de Valera until the latter established the Fianna Fail party in 1926 and chose constitutional politics ráther than the gun. In 1926 he went to Russia to ask for arms for the IRA and was a rising star in the organization, becoming its Quartermaster-General in 1936. Alongside Russell, Tom Barry and Sean MacBride had opposed the 1921 Treaty and found themselves confronting the forces of the new Irish Free State in what became a bitter civil war in 1922–3. Barry was a renowned guerrilla leader who, like de Valera and MacBride, rejected the Treaty because it left unfinished business, namely the reunification of Ireland. They wanted to continue the war with the British and remove the partition of the island which was enshrined in the 1920 Government of Ireland Act. The new State knew it could not afford to continue the war and the IRA had to be crushed. It was a brutal period, with both sides prepared to indulge in swift executions and retaliation. By the end of the civil war there were over 12,000 IRA personnel in gaol. The Irish authorities executed 77 IRA men and were deemed to have been more brutal than the British. The IRA surrendered by declaring a ceasefire on 24 May 1923, but men like Russell, MacBride and Barry did not relinquish their dream of uniting the country by force of arms and by confronting the British in Northern Ireland or, as Russell believed, on mainland Britain.

Russell and his supporters, many of them younger members of the movement, began to deride the veterans such as Barry and MacBride in the late 1930s. The conflict between the older and younger elements, between the hardliners and the men of caution, typified the IRA. Then and later the IRA has often been riven with dissent because of the historical imperative to drive the British out of Ireland at any cost. As early as 1937 Russell and his allies at home and among organizations in the United States were advocating a campaign of bombing and assassination in Great Britain. They discussed harebrained schemes including one using a plane to drop a bomb on the Houses of Parliament in London which they eventually decided was impractical: their logic, which emanated from discussions with American sympathizers, was that if they hired a plane in the United States it would only have enough fuel to cross the Atlantic and drop

5

the bomb but not to make the return journey and would therefore have to crash-land on the coast of France. The Russell camp also proposed that a major campaign of sabotage be directed at Britain. They maintained a hatred of everything British, and their argument won the day at an IRA General Army Convention held in April 1938.

Tom Barry, on the other hand, was prepared to consider attacking Britain, but not through a campaign of sabotage that could kill civilians. He favoured a 'selective strike': taking an IRA unit into the House of Commons to kill the Prime Minister and his cabinet. He wanted IRA targets to be British politicians and not the British people. Barry, MacBride and many other veterans resigned, leaving the way open to Russell to reform the command structure of the IRA and pursue his ambitions.

De Valera watched the split in the IRA, the departure of the experienced and intelligent rump, and assumed that the organization was so depleted of men and resources that it no longer posed a threat to his government or to the British. Police Special Branch in Dublin calculated that the IRA would vanish into the obscurity of its own past. De Valera could not have been scrutinizing events too closely; he was preoccupied with British–Irish relations. The cynic might argue that, since he was a former IRA leader, de Valera should have known the IRA was still a threat and should have taken measures to neutralize it. Sean Russell could have reminded de Valera that after the Civil War he had recommended that the IRA should not part with its weapons until the whole island was free of the British. It is arguable that his personal antipathy to Britain deterred him from acting against his former comrades.

Although Irish Special Branch and their counterparts in Britain did not see the danger, the view in Northern Ireland was different. The Unionist government and Ulster Protestants preferred to believe that the IRA was capable of subversion even when it was a moribund force. The Northern State was built with repressive legislation to deal with republicanism, and it was convenient for successive Unionist leaders to warn that the IRA was forever present within the Catholic population. The threat of a fifth column allowed Unionist leaders to control and shape Protestant attitudes and politics. When Northern Ireland Protestants moved away from the doctrine that the State was 'a Protestant parliament for a Protestant people', they were quickly brought back into line with the dire warning that the IRA was plotting to overthrow 'Ulster'. The Royal Ulster Constabulary, and particularly the Ulster Special Constabulary, were shaped for confrontation with the IRA, and it was their alertness which mattered in the late 1930s.

Sean Russell co-opted his followers into the senior posts within the IRA, creating in the process a virulently anti-British organization. The arrival of Russell as the IRA supremo pleased republicans in Northern Ireland who had long argued for a renewed campaign. They felt cheated by partition, and by de Valera's refusal to fight to end it. Russell and other members of the IRA's Army Council regarded their Northern comrades as hotheads, and were content to see them merely fulfil the role of protectors of the Catholic population in cities such as Belfast and Derry. That view of the role of the IRA in the North was to persist until 1969 and led to the formation of the Provisionals.

However, while he was happy to rely on the organization south of the border, Russell had no master plan, nor the money and resources to mount a successful campaign in Britain. Some writers have argued that Russell embarked on his project because he was convinced de Valera would turn a blind eye to it, since he would benefit politically should it lead to the British capitulating and delivering the six counties of Northern Ireland. Russell was naïvely confident that the British could be bombed into submission. The IRA's General Headquarters Staff were given the task of planning and co-ordinating a sabotage campaign to be carried out in English cities. Scotland and Wales were exempted because their people were Celts. The IRA were not deterred from their objective even though they knew a war in Europe was imminent; on the contrary, they believed it would be opportune to strike while Britain was building its war industries.

Today the callousness of such a course of action is difficult to comprehend, and it left a memory of bitterness which was to have harmful political conse-quences for Northern Ireland. Yet in 1938 republicans did not perceive Germany as the enemy. Flirting with the Nazis was an IRA preoccupation which, if it had not been so ludicrous in its intent and reality, could have posed a serious threat to Allied interests during the war. The Army Council discussed whether they should seek German help; but in the initial stages of Russell's take-over IRA requests for assistance were directed instead towards sympathizers and fellow travellers in the United States. GHQ began its preparations for sabotage believing that a campaign in English cities should be aimed at disrupting the British economy. Its members casually accepted that there would be loss of innocent lives. It was a return to the physical-force politics of romantic nationalism, and did not anticipate that the British people would not capitulate to a terrorist organization, and that their anger would be greater because they were being attacked while they prepared for a war in Europe. No consideration was given to the impact of such a campaign on the majority Protestant population in Northern Ireland, and the dire consequences for Northern Catholics if the Unionists thought Britain might cede their State to a republican Ireland. The IRA held the view that the Protestants were really Irishmen who were being conned by the British. Russell and his followers knew little of the intricacies of Ulster politics, and were blind to the inherent links between the Unionist hierarchy and the British establishment. Although the IRA leaders were not acting on behalf of the people of Ireland, they were arrogant enough to claim that right, believing they knew better than the public at large, and arguing that popular support would flow from their actions once they attacked the old enemy, the British.

While Irish Americans filled the coffers, IRA General Headquarters Staff in Dublin selected the bombers. Most of the younger men did not possess a knowledge of explosives. Jim O'Donovan, a veteran IRA officer, was persuaded to come out of retirement to deliver lectures in bomb-making. Dublin was the centre of a great deal of activity in the months following the General Army Convention of April 1938. GHQ recognized that when bombing teams were placed in English cities they would require a courier service to provide volunteers with money for lodgings, details of possible targets and information about the movement of guns and explosives. The people chosen for those tasks were mostly members of the IRA's women's organization Cumann na mBann. Women would be less likely to attract the attention of English police and Special Branch. Ferries were to be the vehicles for moving personnel and materials, and IRA staff were despatched to liaise with republicans resident in England. There were units in England but they were poorly equipped, many of their members were known to Special Branch and they had no bomb-making skills. Under the noses of the security forces in both islands, IRA personnel slipped backwards and forwards across the Irish Sea, trained volunteers in bomb-making and transported gelignite and other materials to English cities. The IRA lacked large quantities of commercial explosive but devised ways of manufacturing bombs from fertilizer products.

In the summer of 1938 Russell and his henchmen made speeches declaring their intent to return to 'the struggle' and made reference to the IRA's British units. Warning bells should have rung in Dublin and London but many people regarded the threats as IRA bluster. Although IRA members were supposed to maintain a strict level of secrecy, they held bomb-making lectures in St Stephen's Green, a public park in the centre of Dublin. Russell felt so confident that secrecy was being maintained that he was able to travel to England and inspect IRA units as if he were an officer examining the passing-out recruits at a military ceremony. He talked to the graduates of the bomb classes, who were trained and in place by the late autumn of 1938. The majority of IRA personnel sent to England were from the Southern counties, with approximately five from the North.

At the outset of the bombing campaign about a dozen trained personnel were sent from Ireland into England to join up with IRA members who already lived there. During this period, altogether there were no more than two dozen hard-core operatives who remained in Great Britain or made trips in and out of the country. The IRA also asked sympathizers in England to act as couriers, to store materials or to provide shelter for operatives. As there was a huge Irish population in the country and many were constantly on the move in search of work, IRA volunteers were able to travel around freely without arousing suspicion. However, since there were so few men and women in Great Britain who were actually bound by the IRA's oath, the critical factor was the support of people sympathetic to the IRA cause.

In December 1938 the IRA Army Council met in Dublin to give final approval to the plan, and to declare itself the legal government of Ireland. It decided, for the sake of correctness, to present the British with a formal declaration of war. If the consequences of the IRA's actions had not proved to be so shocking, their decision to declare war on Britain would even now appear farcical. An IRA ultimatum, demanding the removal of British troops and personnel from Ireland, was delivered to the British Foreign Secretary, Lord Halifax, on 12 January 1939. The British government was given two days to reply but Lord Halifax and, undoubtedly, Scotland Yard Special Branch treated the matter with contempt, believing it was an idle threat. Two days later the people of Ireland were afforded an opportunity to scrutinize the ultimatum from those who claimed to represent them. The text was printed on walls in Dublin and in Belfast, but, like the British government, most people paid little attention to it.

On 17 January at 6 a.m. eight bombs exploded simultaneously in London, Manchester, Birmingham, Liverpool and Alnwick in Northumberland.

The largest bomb, heard two miles from the seat of the explosion, was at the Central Electricity Board's premises at the junction of Guildford Street and Park Street in Southwark, London. It caused extensive damage, but no-one was injured. A witness, Arthur Lee, was on his way to work when he saw two men emerge from a taxi and plant the bomb; he remembered the time as 5.47 a.m. exactly: 'I remember it was thirteen minutes to six because I signalled the time to a workmate by holding up my fingers. The inside light of the taxi was on and in all I saw three men well dressed.' Lee was able to provide police with detailed descriptions of the three bombers and his evidence confirmed that the terrorists did not fit the archetypal image of dishevelled figures in shoddy clothes.

In Harlesden in north-west London a bomb went off at the cable bridge over the Grand Union Canal but caused little damage. In Birmingham the IRA target was a huge power station, Hams Hall, and the device was placed at the base of one of the massive cooling towers. Fortunately the explosion blew outwards rather than upwards and major damage to the system and electricity supplies was averted. Another explosion, at the Brimstown power station in Enfield, did not have the desired effect of damaging the transformer but put cables out of service. At Alnwick an electricity pylon was blown up.

In Manchester the IRA planted a bomb under three manholes leading to electricity cables. That attack resulted in the death of twenty-seven-year-old Albert Ross, a native of the city, who was on his way to work when the bomb tore a 12-foot-square crater in the roadway. Albert Ross was found unconscious at the side of the crater and died in hospital.

The following day the main story in the London *News Chronicle* claimed that Scotland Yard detectives were 'working on the theory that at least some of the eight explosions were the work of Irish Republican Army terrorists': 'Telephone talks between London, Belfast and Dublin to check recent movements of known agitators revealed that many members of the illegal IRA have forsaken their usual haunts in Eire for England. Traces of many have been lost.' The *News Chronicle* reported that Scotland Yard had for some time suspected that England would be a target if no solution was found to the politics of Ireland; but in reality Scotland Yard had been outmanoeuvred by the IRA and was trying to convince people otherwise. Ironically, during the past twenty years, Scotland Yard has employed similar public relations tactics when faced with mounting criticism for failing to catch London bombers.

The *News Chronicle* also carried an article revealing that, on the day of the blasts, posters were displayed in London declaring the IRA's intention to bomb English cities. These posters — at St George's Church in Southwark, outside other places of worship and in centres with large Irish communities — reproduced the IRA Army Council's proclamation that as the government of Ireland they were calling on England to capitulate:

Withdraw her armed forces, her civilian institutions and officials and representatives of all kinds from every part of Ireland as an essential preliminary to arrangement for peace and friendship between the two countries. Ireland is still tied, as she has been for centuries, to take part in England's wars. The time has come to make a fresh fight — that is, a fight to make effective the 1916 Proclamation which sets up the Irish Republic.

The document was signed by Stephen Hayes, Peadar O'Flaherty, Lawrence Grogan, Patrick Flemming and Sean Russell. The *Chronicle* quoted a source who described Sean Russell as 'the big noise of the Irish Republican Army'.

Scotland Yard sources neglected to tell the media that two months earlier they had ignored what was the clearest warning of things to come. On 19 October 1938 two men had been arrested at Green Lane in Ilford. They had been stopped while driving a van containing explosives. They had been committed for trial and sentenced to nine months' imprisonment. No-one had been sufficiently alert within Scotland Yard to follow such an obvious lead.

The immediate outcome of the bombings of January 1939 was that the Irish communities throughout England suddenly became the focus of considerable police attention and animosity. As we know from the recent conflict, the majority of Irish people living in Britain detest IRA violence and resent the tendency of some British people to brand them as co-conspirators with the IRA. The IRA had anticipated that police and Special Branch would seek the perpetrators among the Irish communities; the bombers were not found because they were living outside those communities in the role of sleeper agents. GHQ in Dublin now selected the majority of targets, although they had allowed English units some freedom in choosing targets in the early days of the campaign. While Dublin controlled the pace of events, IRA personnel in Britain remained inactive for the rest of January. Arrests were made by the police, but the people were released when it became clear that the real culprits were still at large.

In the two weeks following the first onslaught, there was a gradual feeling in Britain and Ireland that the explosions were a one-off effort by the IRA. That view was dispelled in February when the IRA exploded bombs at Tottenham Court Road and Leicester Square Tube stations in London. The explosives were concealed in the left-luggage offices and were detonated by timing devices. Seven men were injured, two of them seriously.

The *Daily Telegraph* of 4 February reported that, coincident with the latest spate of bombings, police in Northern Ireland had seized IRA documents outlining plans for a widespread campaign of violence in England. The blueprint for the England campaign was known as the 'S Plan', the letter 'S' indicating sabotage. It was an ambitious plan to attack electricity grids, centres of communication, and economic and military targets. De Valera publicly attacked the IRA for claiming to be the government of Ireland, and for their physical-force politics, but he made no specific mention of the bombings in England.

Between 5 and 24 February 1939 there were explosions at Walton gaol, Liverpool; in the LNER coal bays at King's Cross Station, London; on board the steamer *St David*, berthed at Liverpool; at the LMS railway goods depot at Somerstown, St Pancras, London; and in a motor truck in Aberdeen. Bombings continued every month including an explosion in the charge room of a Lancaster police station. The IRA did not rely simply on gelignite or a fertilizer mix but on incendiary devices which went off in eight hotels throughout the country; the incendiaries were detonated by delayed-action timers. On 9 June the IRA's bombing units turned their attention to the postal service, and exploded a large number of incendiary devices in mailboxes in London, Manchester, Birmingham and Leicester.

The newspapers vied with each other in assessing the number of IRA operatives in Britain. Their calculations varied from two to twenty thousand, but the true figure was closer to fifty, including ancillary courier personnel and sympathizers who were not IRA members but provided safe houses or transport. The exaggerated estimates had the effect of making every

Irish person living in England the object of unnecessary scrutiny. That did not concern the IRA, who were oblivious to the hardship caused to many families by nightly police raids. The *Daily Telegraph* and *The Times* reported exceptional police activity and the cancelling of all police leave. Guards were placed at all major centres, military and political, and a constant watch was maintained on all ferry sailings between the two islands.

The mailbox explosions of 9 June galvanized de Valera into action. Police in Britain were proving incapable of containing an IRA threat which originated in Ireland and therefore jeopardized relations between the two countries. De Valera and the Irish government may well have begun to suspect that their plan to keep Eire neutral in a European war could be compromised by a resurgent IRA which did not recognize the constitutionally elected government of Ireland. Worried that British patience was being eroded, de Valera calculated that an IRA threat to Britain at a time when war seemed imminent might present the British with a genuine excuse for invading Southern Ireland. The British were not going to tolerate an Eire-based organization which might be capable of inflicting serious damage to Britain's war industry. On 14 June 1939 the Government in Dublin introduced the Offences Against the State Act which provided for the setting up of military tribunals to deal with the IRA. This was de Valera's gesture to Britain that he was prepared to confront the IRA. But the new legislation had no deterrent effect, and the IRA stepped up their campaign by attacking the heart of London.

For those of us who have watched the horror of London bombings of the 1970s, 1980s and 1990s it is difficult to believe similar scenes were part of the life of the city in 1939. On Saturday night, 24 June, six IRA volunteers entered the West End, each man carrying a small bomb wrapped neatly in brown packaging. An IRA officer later told a reporter that the plan was to place the bombs in the night safe deposit boxes of various banks, and that IRA personnel posing as businessmen had rented keys for the night safes. That was patently untrue because the ensuing series of explosions indicated a move away from sabotage to terror.

The *Daily Telegraph* later printed details of the timing and location of the bombs:

10.00 p.m. Piccadilly Circus. Severe damage to premises of Westminster Bank, Van Raalte & Sons, tobacconists, Etam Shop. Plate-glass windows shattered.

10.05 – Bomb burst in pillar-box opposite Madame Tussaud's. Three incendiary bombs later found in Madame Tussaud's and fires extinguished with damage to wax figures. Another bomb found in a pillar-box at Nottingham Place W.

10.50 – Strand and Aldwych. Masonry and nine plate-glass windows of Lloyds Bank smashed. Damage affecting Strand and Wellington Street.

10.55 – Lloyds Bank, Piccadilly, Sackville Street corner. All windows shattered and premises of Italian Tourism Organization damaged.

> Midnight – Midland Bank, Park Lane–Aldford
> Street corner. The most serious damage
> here. The bomb is thought to have been
> put through the letter-box.

The bombs contained gelignite with short time fuses and in one or two instances were simply shoved through letter-boxes. No consideration was given to the throngs of people in the area and it was fortunate that only thirteen were injured, though two young boys suffered severe eye damage.

Next day Cardinal Hinsley, the Catholic Archbishop of Westminster, condemned what he described as 'cowardly and atrocious outrages':

> There evidently exists a secret organization, call
> it what you will, army or lodge or cell, which is
> plotting against the peace and order of this country
> and, by its insane methods, exposing innocent
> persons to bodily injury, and even, perhaps, loss of
> life. Such barbarism is in itself a crime, no matter
> how specious the pretext advanced to make it
> appear less savage. The Church strongly and clearly
> condemns those who plot against the Church or
> State. The members incur excommunication, and
> until they repent and completely renounce their
> participation in such societies, they cannot be
> admitted to the Sacrament. All simple and sincere
> Catholics, of whatever nationality they may be,
> should be deterred by this warning, and should
> not allow themselves to be made the tools of
> designing extremists.

Unfortunately, the cardinal's denunciation was not met by a similar unequivocal statement from the Catholic hierarchy in Ireland. His anger was nevertheless timely and demonstrated his desire to protect his English flock, particularly its Irish members, from being tainted by IRA violence.

In London there was a sudden realization that the IRA had changed tactics to a point where there appeared to be a casual if not deliberate attempt to endanger human life. Journalists described the aftermath of the bombings with phrases such as 'panic and terror in the West End'. The British government was left with no choice but to introduce Draconian legislation to deal with a problem that seemed beyond the resources of the police forces throughout the country. On 24 July the Prevention of Terrorism Bill was presented to the Commons, allowing the authorities the right to deport, to detain suspects and to register all Irish people living in Britain. The IRA's answer to the Commons debate was already in place.

At King's Cross Station a Scots academic and his wife were waiting to board a train to take them on holiday. A bomb exploded without warning, sending slivers of glass and debris hurtling through the station. The force of the blast tore off the academic's legs, and he died later in hospital. Fifteen other people were injured, two of them seriously.

While the Commons was still debating the new legislation, another bomb, concealed in a suitcase, exploded in the cloakroom at Victoria Station. The blast was so violent, it blew out the windows of a train parked on the edge of the station. Seven persons, five of them railway porters, were injured.

The House of Commons was kept informed of the carnage and the remaining stages of the Prevention of Terrorism Bill were rushed through the House in five minutes.

While bombs exploded during the first six months of 1939, detectives and Special Branch personnel at Scotland Yard were compiling dossiers on every known republican sympathizer in Britain. The most important room at the Yard was 40B, where Chief Constable Canning and Superintendent A. G. Foster masterminded security. According to press reports, thousands of policemen were tasked to defeat the IRA in 1939; some of the national newspapers put the figure at 10,000 in the London area. The level of panic throughout the country was so high that the police and public were constantly on their guard. Then as now, however, it was not easy to defeat terrorists; they are rarely caught perpetrating an attack.

At the end of 1939 the body responsible for monitoring the manufacture of explosives in Britain, HM Inspectors of Explosives, produced their 64th annual report, part of which dealt with the IRA campaign:

During the year, 242 outrages or attempted outrages were reported to us from various parts of the country. Forty-one cases of illegal possession of explosives were also detected. These outrages caused the deaths of seven persons and ninety-six people were injured. The police made 128 arrests, 62 in London and 66 in the provinces. There were 96 convictions, 55 in

London and 41 in the provinces. There is not the slightest doubt these outrages were part of a thoroughly well-organized conspiracy, and the various persons taking part in it had received instructions of a very comprehensive nature.

2

The Pursuit of the Bombers

In recent times, just as in 1939, there are often no clues available to those involved in tracking down terrorists. Often such clues are revealed only when terrorists become careless, or when a vigilant member of the public is alerted by something unusual. Only then can the real job of intelligence gathering, analysis and detection begin.

In early 1939 Charles Heap, a plumber in Manchester, was curious about the type of people responsible for the recent IRA bombing there. Some of his friends later described him as a busybody, but it was his natural curiosity that led him to uncover an IRA cell. On 19 January he was called out to a house in Dryden Street in a drab district, Chorlton-on-Medlock. The house comprised both a dwelling and a shop, and he noticed that the dwelling part was heavily curtained, suggesting that the occupants were preoccupied with privacy. When he entered the shop he found it was furnished with advertisements for sauces, mustard and cigarettes but there were no goods on sale. While he was pondering the absence of merchandise, a young woman appeared, and introduced herself as Mary Glenn. She explained that she had only just taken up residence there and intended turning the premises into a millinery business.

Charles Heap asked if she was the owner; she replied that two men had rented the place to set her up in business. Then he told her the landlady had sent him to repair some pipes that ran through one of the upstairs bedrooms.

After he had begun work in the bedroom, his attention was drawn to a wardrobe door which was slightly open. He looked inside and saw several barrels and bags.

Before he left the building he said to Mary Glenn: 'Are you on the level?' (He later told police that he had copied this question from a detective in a film.) Mary Glenn simply answered 'Yes', and Heap went on his way.

The next day, Heap, the amateur sleuth, returned to the shop and entered the same room on the pretext of examining his handiwork. This time he observed that the wardrobe doors were nailed tight to the frame. Heap then went to the local police and informed them of his discovery, and they contacted Scotland Yard. A few days later police raided the building.

Detectives removed the nails from the wardrobe and discovered that the sacks and barrels contained chemicals for making bombs. There were also detonators, alarm clocks and cable. The police were about to leave the room when an alert detective spotted the glint of a nail from one of the floorboards. He remarked to his colleagues that the nail had obviously been hammered in more recently than other nails in the flooring. Several boards were prised apart, to reveal a hoard of fifty sticks of gelignite. One of the policemen placed his hand beneath the explosives and withdrew a sheet of paper. It contained the layout of Bristol Central Electricity Board control room.

Under interrogation, Mary Glenn, who was a twenty-two-year-old servant girl, provided detectives with the names of the two men who rented the house and they were quickly arrested. In one of their homes, police found a receipt bearing the name of a lorry driver from Old Trafford. The receipt read: 'For going to London and bringing back a cargo of stuff to be used on January 16, paid £6 10 shillings'.

The lorry driver was traced, but he protested that he had moved a quantity of beeswax from London to Manchester in his van and, as far as he was concerned, it was to be used to polish a dancehall floor. Police asked him to give a date for the journey and he replied that it was on 31 October 1938. Unfortunately, the driver could not remember the address in London from which he had collected the beeswax but believed it was in the area of Kilburn; he had met an Irishman there who had guided him through a maze of backstreets to a garage. Special Branch and CID now hoped to trace the link between the IRA unit that had carried out the bombings in Manchester and the suppliers of explosives in London. For three days detectives toured north-west London with the lorry driver until the afternoon of the third day, when he pointed to a garage at Fordington

Road, Highgate, as his pick-up point. The garage was in a tiny crescent just beyond Highgate Wood, off Muswell Hill.

The information was relayed to Room 40B at Scotland Yard. Once detectives had identified the owner, they checked his name against the files of known activists and republican sympathizers. The owner's name was John Healy, a man who allegedly dealt in beeswax. Enquiries were slow at first; then it was discovered that Healy had bought large quantities of potassium chlorate over a period of years. Explosives experts knew that potassium chlorate mixed with sugar or types of wax produced a volatile explosive. In fact, some time earlier a consignment of potassium chlorate had been discovered at Camden Town goods station. Packages marked 'soda', bearing an address in Manchester, had accidentally been torn, revealing crystals of potassium chlorate. But police had failed to follow up that lead. Healy made his purchases from an agent in the City of London on the pretext that the substance was to be used in the making of textiles. He also introduced 'friends' to the same supplier and they had bought sulphuric acid. He had also bought a ton of oxide of iron and aluminium from the dealer. When police arrested Healy, they discovered he bore no relation to newspaper characterizations of terrorists. He was forty years old, with a wife and two children. In his youth, he had played Gaelic football in his native Kerry before moving to England, where he became a furniture dealer and a club owner.

Scotland Yard relentlessly pursued leads provided by the arrest, but at that stage the detectives did not know they were close to netting the 'big fish', the IRA's Commanding Officer in Britain. They got their first break with a tip-off from another alert member of the public. A signwriter called Peter Stuart, who had a small workshop in New Oxford Street, had been asked to make a sign for a barber's shop in Oxford Street. Stuart told the barber it would cost him ten shillings, a sum which surprised the man, who had expected to pay at least two pounds. Intrigued, the barber visited the signwriter's workshop on numerous occasions, to be told he was busy and unable to complete the commission. When it was finished, the barber, who by now was curious about Peter Stuart's lifestyle, was appalled by the shoddiness of the workmanship. He convinced himself that Stuart was a fraud, if not a terrorist, and informed the police. When detectives searched Stuart's bedroom, they found articles which testified to his role as an IRA intelligence officer. There were uniforms which would have allowed him access to RAF bases, and overalls which were worn by workers in power stations. In a drawer they found a chemistry book and in the wardrobe a quantity of explosives. One of the most interesting finds was envelopes and writing paper bearing the Whitehall stamp. The IRA had used these to send communications through the normal postal service without attracting the daily scrutiny given to all mail between Britain and Ireland.

While the police were applauding their success, fingerprint experts at the Yard were piecing together parts of a thumb-print found on an unexploded bomb at an electricity pylon in St Helens, near Liverpool. Other detectives were puzzling over the name Michael Joseph

Mason. It had appeared on two suitcases at Paddington Station which were emitting a foul smell and were opened by porters and given to the police. Inside were bottles of sulphuric acid used in the manufacture of bombs. The suitcase labels with Mason's name also gave a Manchester address. When Mason was arrested, detectives were grateful to their colleagues in the fingerprint section, who matched the thumb-print found on the St Helens bomb with Mason's right thumb.

The Yard did not know the full significance of these arrests until one other piece in the puzzle fell into place. Documents discovered in the raid on Healy's house bore the signature 'G. Kane, O.C. London'. Eventually, as dossiers on potential IRA activists expanded, police found the name George Brendan Kane. He was a twenty-three-year-old butcher's apprentice, and enquiries revealed that he was a pleasant, hard-working young man often seen making deliveries on a bicycle. When police moved in to arrest him they discovered he was the IRA's Officer Commanding for Sutton, Cheam and Ewell. He delivered in London suburbs, and made notes of targets during his journeys. In his flat there was a four-page document containing details of bridges, power stations and post-boxes.

When Kane appeared at the Central Criminal Court in London he was in the company of eight other men: Michael Joseph Mason, aged 29; Peter Stuart, 25; Charles James Casey, 23; Michael Preston, 23; John Healy, 40; James Michael Lyons, 26; Joseph Walker, 26; and Michael O'Shea, 24. Kane pleaded guilty; Walker, O'Shea and Healy pleaded not guilty. In keeping with the IRA policy of not recognizing a British court,

Casey, Mason, Stuart, Preston and Lyons, who represented the hard core of the group, refused to plead. The
judge described this action as absurd and said the men
had made statements 'glorifying what they'd done'. Mr
Justice Humphreys was determined to put their actions
into perspective in his address to the jury. His words
could easily have applied to IRA cases in recent times:

> There is complete freedom of thought in this
> country and anybody who takes the view that
> Ireland or Scotland, or the Isle of Man, or the
> Isle of Wight ought to be severed from the British
> Crown and become a republic is entitled to that
> view. Moreover, there is here complete freedom
> of utterance of thought and such a person is
> entitled to express his views and, by writing, or by
> speech, to induce others, if he can, to be converted
> to his views. All that is permissible and that is what
> is called political propaganda. But when a person
> ceases to employ these constitutional methods of
> altering the position of part of a British Dominion
> and employs methods of terrorism, incendiarism,
> causing explosions and rendering the life of law-
> abiding citizens impossible, then it is the Crown,
> in this case represented by the Attorney-General,
> that steps in and invites those who are responsible
> for the administration of the Criminal Law . . .
> juries included . . . to act firmly in doing what they
> can to suppress such illegal and dangerous acts.

The jury took less than two hours to reach its verdicts,
and found all but Walker guilty of conspiring to cause

explosions. Walker was found guilty of a lesser charge and sentenced to eighteen months' imprisonment with hard labour. It was only when sentences were about to be imposed that details of the history of some of the accused provided fresh revelations.

A Detective Inspector Thompson said that under questioning Mason had refused to give any information about his past, but Scotland Yard was convinced, from documents discovered in house raids, that he was the IRA's Officer Commanding Great Britain. The detective inspector was correct in his assertion because Mason had been sent by GHQ to Liverpool in the autumn of 1938 to replace a former OC who had been killed that summer while testing the type of bomb the IRA hoped to use in its S Plan. Mason was an engineer, and his father had fought and been imprisoned by the British during the 1916 Rising in Dublin.

The judge asked Mason if he wished to respond to DI Thompson. Mason replied: 'My name is not Mason. I wish to be sentenced in my real name, which is Cleary.'

Michael Preston followed Mason's example by revealing his true identity as Michael Flemming. Peter Stuart was Peter Joseph Walsh, a native of Glasgow; his father was a retired police constable, and there was nothing on his record to associate him with republicanism.

In sentencing Mason, Mr Justice Humphreys described him as 'an incendiary' and 'the worst of the men in the dock'. He gave him seventeen years' penal servitude. The judge described Casey as the explosives expert and 'a very bad case indeed'. To this Casey responded: 'The fight will go on, history will justify us and the Irish people will vindicate us.' After this outburst, Casey was sentenced to fourteen years' imprisonment. Healy tried to plead his innocence as he was given a ten-year sentence. Lyons unapologetically announced that he had 'done his duty' and shouted, 'God Save Ireland!' He received a ten-year term, while a period of twelve years was handed out to Michael Flemming, alias Michael Preston. O'Shea was given five years after the judge consulted the jury foreman, who confirmed that the jury believed he had played a minor role. The only one of the nine who behaved respectfully in the court was Healy, who thanked the judge.

In a separate hearing, Mary Glenn, who was seen in newspaper photographs wearing a demure pearl necklace, was sentenced to seven years' penal servitude. Her case was heard separately because the authorities believed she played a lesser role. It was rumoured that she co-operated fully with the police, and her sentence seemed appropriate to the role of a conspirator who was naïve and exploited by more unscrupulous individuals.

The trial revealed something of the nature of IRA planning and co-ordination. IRA personnel used aliases and had no previous connections with each other. Detective work won in the end, but only because a few members of the public were able to provide vital clues. It was difficult for the police to deal with an organization which had put sleeper agents in place with new identities. Some of them were seemingly respectable figures such as Healy, while young men like Kane employed the apparent ordinariness of their regular jobs to cloak their activities. In a later chapter I will show how the IRA of recent years returned to the tactics of that period.

Cases such as the one I have described can become highly charged politically. Mr Justice Humphreys presided over the next IRA trial, which opened on 3 April 1939 at the Old Bailey. Before him were five men and two youths charged with possessing explosive substances and conspiring to cause explosions. Evidence against them had been gathered in house raids, but the police did not have the information to charge any of them with a specific explosion. In the dock at the Old Bailey were Gerard Francis Wharton, 35, a rigger who lived in Camden Town, London; Daniel Fitzpatrick, 21, a labourer from Camden Town; John Mitchell, 28, a garage attendant from Brentford; Daniel McCarthy, 21, a labourer from Manor Park in the East End; John Ryan, 31, a labourer from Ashmore Road, Paddington; Jack Logue and Francis James Burns, both 17, from Mornington Crescent in Camden Town.

During the trial, Detective Inspector Thompson said Fitzpatrick had connections in Belfast, where police regarded him 'as a vicious member of the IRA'. He also claimed that McCarthy was connected to the IRA explosives expert Charles James Casey, who had been sentenced to fourteen years at the earlier trial. The detective inspector said Ryan had co-operated with the police in trying to trace the IRA contact 'who left stuff with him'; he described Ryan as 'simple-minded'.

A piece of evidence which could have had an immediate bearing on the case against Wharton was withheld from the court. During police interviews, Casey had admitted that Wharton had been fooled into taking possession of suitcases containing explosive substances; he maintained that Wharton was innocent of any involvement and did not know the contents of the suitcases.

The jury found all of them guilty; the judge sent the two youths to borstal, and handed out sentences totalling thirty-four years. Mr Justice Humphreys reserved his venom for Wharton, whom he sentenced to ten years in prison. Wharton had pleaded not guilty, and had handed the court a document detailing his history in the IRA. He admitted that he had taken part in the capture of several places in Ireland from the British during the War of Independence, and had later fought against the 1921 Treaty with Britain. In Ireland he had been sentenced to two and a half years' imprisonment by a district court martial for Offences Against the Realm. He was caught tunnelling out of prison, and was interned in the military camp at the Curragh until his release in 1924.

Wharton took the opportunity to make a statement from the dock. 'I want to say that I abhor these bombings as much as anyone else,' he began. 'I had never known the IRA contemplated these actions. As for my past record, many cabinet ministers in the government of Eire have the same record. These things happened twenty years ago.'

The judge contemptuously dismissed Wharton's denial, and his direction to the jury was tainted by his own interpretation of Irish history. 'You are a rebel against all constituted authority,' he pronounced. 'You were a member of that gang which committed murders of British officers in 1922. There was then constituted a different government in Ireland. You

33

rebelled against that, and fought against that . . . You are a hypocrite, and in my view you are the most dangerous of the gang that is now before me.'

Mr Justice Humphreys's remarks about gangs who murdered British officers during the War of Independence caused outrage in Eire. Questions were raised in the Dail (the Irish Parliament) and de Valera was obliged to state: 'My attitude, and that of the Government, is that we regard the judge's remarks as insulting and grossly partial.' When asked if the Irish government had referred the matter to London, de Valera replied that a protest had been lodged through the High Commissioner in London. Nevertheless, he was not prepared to oppose all the sentences passed by Mr Justice Humphreys, since he would thereby risk being perceived as a defender of the IRA bombings in Britain.

However, the British government acted quickly through the Attorney-General, who passed the case to the Court of Criminal Appeal in May. The conviction was quashed and Wharton was released. Lord Chief Justice Hewart said that at the trial Wharton claimed that he had unknowingly had in his possession (in his flat) potassium chlorate, oxide of iron and 103 rubber balloons, and that he had never associated these items with explosives, thinking the powders were 'cement and stuff for pointing walls'. The Lord Chief Justice remarked that Wharton swore he possessed no knowledge of the alleged activities of the IRA. Documents were, nevertheless, found in his flat, and it could not be disputed that there was a case against him for the jury to consider. What the appeal judges were concerned about was the alleged misdirection of the jury by

Mr Justice Humphreys and his use of the words: 'You don't want evidence because it is a matter of history what the IRA was when this man belonged to it before 1927 and, in fact, before 1922. It was an illegal conspiracy, formed for the purpose of committing crimes against this country. It was a rebellion and that was what he was engaged in.' Lord Chief Justice Hewart, sitting with Justices Singleton and Hilbery, described as 'unfortunate' the trial judge's reference to 'illegal conspiracy' and 'rebellion':

Such a reference tended to show that the appellant had committed crimes against this country. It is difficult to see that the statement could have served any purpose in helping to determine the guilt or the innocence of the appellant on the charges against him. If there was to be any such reference, it might well have been followed by the reference to the Amnesty, or the act of oblivion, and, still more, it ought to have been pointed out that the fact that the appellant was connected with that movement years ago did not show that he was a party to the conspiracy alleged at the trial. In the absence of any such clear direction, the danger of prejudice arising in the minds of the jury is tolerably obvious. The appellant had given evidence that he had nothing to do with these plots or schemes to cause explosions, that the first he heard of them was on the radio, and that he had no knowledge of the activities of others in regard to explosions. In a case such as this, it appears to us that the jury ought to have

35

been reminded of that evidence. But they were not so reminded. Nor were they reminded of his evidence of what he thought the substances to be. In the opinion of this court, these matters were the essence of the Defence. Failure on the part of the Judge to refer to them, coupled with the reference to rebellion, compels us to express the view that there was misdirection and non-direction on essential matters in the case . . .

We are unable to say that, on a proper direction, the jury must inevitably have come to the conclusion that the appellant was guilty.

The substances that Wharton said he thought were 'cement and stuff for pointing walls' were the essential ingredients for bomb-making. There was no reference to his view on the presence of 103 rubber balloons. In fact the IRA used 'balloon bombs' in London and Liverpool cinemas. An explosive mixture of potassium chlorate and oxide of iron was put inside a balloon; a wax cover was placed over part of the balloon, and the amount of wax roughly determined the amount of time required for a small container of sulphuric acid to burn through the wax and into the rubber of the balloon. It was a dangerous way of igniting the materials because the bomber could not always be sure of how long it took for the acid to burn through to the explosive mixture.

In a house raid, police had found an exercise book with several missing pages. Dr Roche, a Scotland Yard scientist, used oblique lighting – the process of shining light at an angle on indentations – on the page below those which were missing. He discovered indentations that suggested someone had written on the missing sheets. Photographs of these indentations showed the words 'Jerry Wharton, Camden Road – N.W.1, Waterford City Unit'.

It was the same scientist who was summoned to a house by detectives to determine the truth of an allegation by a suspect that the smell in his flat derived from materials he used in his work as a plasterer. At one of the trials a Detective Inspector Lynch stated that he had asked Dr Roche, 'Should we believe this man that this smell comes from oil used in his work?', and Dr Roche had replied: 'The smell comes from sulphuric acid, which is used in connection with explosive substances. No man, in my experience, would dream of washing his hands in sulphuric acid.'

By the time of the trials, Scotland Yard detectives and explosives experts were examining a range of documents discovered at the homes of all those sentenced by Mr Justice Humphreys. Notebooks were found in the possession of many of those charged with handling explosives, and each contained detailed advice on how to make what the IRA dubbed 'Paxo'. This was constructed from basic materials using home-made apparatus, so that bombs could be made at home without arousing suspicion. The IRA's GHQ knew that once gelignite was stolen the British police would place heavy security on quarries. Gelignite also deteriorated if kept in warm humid conditions and could become so unstable that it exploded without the use of a detonator. It also exuded a strong smell which was difficult to disguise. The process of blending easily acquired chemicals presented less risk and bombs could be constructed very quickly. Small quantities of gelignite were, however, used to detonate the fertilizer devices.

The notebooks of the graduates of the Dublin bombing school also contained descriptions of fuse and electric detonators, and included the rate of the burning of the various fuses. There was information on the application of Ohm's law to the firing of electric detonators in series or parallel, when firing three charges at one time, or in the general case where numerous charges were fired. There were instructions on the battery voltage necessary to fire the charges. All the calculations illustrated an accurate knowledge of the current needed to fire an electric detonator making due allowance for the resistance of the leads to the charges and the internal resistance of the battery. Formulae were recorded for calculating the weight of explosives needed to demolish walls and bridges, and examples were given of how to achieve those objectives. There were diagrams of how explosive charges should be placed to demolish a section of railway line and the composition of materials for the manufacture of incendiary devices. One document provided a detailed outline of the electricity transmission in Great Britain and the control rooms and control equipment of the grid system.

Most of those involved in the acts of bombing were men, but as mentioned earlier there were also women who acted as couriers, moving explosives or carrying messages and money to the various units.

When eighteen-year-old Molly Gallagher appeared at the Old Bailey, in April 1939, she was described by her defence counsel as a respectable young woman who was employed as a clerk and lived at Thornhill Square,

Islington. She was highly attractive, with auburn hair and a tall shapely figure. Molly Gallagher was a friend of several of those sentenced with Cleary, the Officer Commanding Great Britain – namely James Casey, Peter Walsh (alias Peter Stuart, the Glaswegian) and the IRA officer George Brendan Kane. She also knew Jimmy Joe Reynold, the former OC Great Britain who was killed when a bomb exploded prematurely on the Ulster border. Under police questioning, she denied membership of the IRA, and claimed all those men were simply friends, Casey being her sister's fiancé. Her sister lived in Dublin, and was sacked from her government job when Molly was arrested in London.

Molly's denials did not deter the police, who had in their possession a photograph of her with a young Dublin woman, Margaret Edgeworth, carrying rucksacks. In Molly's flat police found two rucksacks, each containing seven 4lb bags of potassium chlorate.

The judge was informed that Margaret Edgeworth had returned to Dublin on the day Molly Gallagher was arrested. She was there with Molly's brother, to whom she was engaged to be married. A police inspector told the court that Molly was born and educated in London, but her family were known to Special Branch as ardent IRA supporters. He added that she was indeed a respectable girl. Obviously she had been exploited by her IRA friends. Mr Justice Humphreys accepted her denial of IRA membership, and sent her to borstal for three years for her involvement with the explosive subtances. Her Dublin friend, Margaret Edgeworth, did not return to England; Justice Humphreys pointedly remarked that she was 'At large in Dublin and likely to remain at large'.

He was again in the limelight when he observed: 'The police have shown very great diligence and very great intelligence, without very much assistance from any other body, in bringing to justice these dangerous people.' His criticism of 'other bodies' was hardly subtle – he was obviously referring to the lack of co-operation from the Dublin authorities – but he was making a point which pleased Scotland Yard's Special Branch. He was aware that Special Branch officers made numerous trips to the Irish capital with warrants for IRA suspects who had fled England, but their police counterparts in Dublin, and the Irish government, made little or no effort to hand over wanted terrorists. It is perhaps ironic that this very problem should have taxed British governments over thirty years later and yet again soured relations between London and Dublin.

British security forces were hampered by this lack of co-operation, but by the end of July 1939 they had achieved considerable success in their pursuit of the bombers. A casual observer might have been inclined to think the IRA campaign was over when, in fact, the worst was yet to come.

3

Death in the Afternoon

At 2.30 p.m. on 25 August 1939 Broadgate in the centre of Coventry was crowded with shoppers and people returning to their places of work. It was a sunny Friday afternoon, and the weather forecast for the weekend promised two days of sunshine.

Twenty-one-year-old Elsie Ansell was gazing through a jeweller's window. She was due back at work but her mind was probably on her forthcoming marriage. In one week she would be walking down the aisle with Harry Davies, her childhood sweetheart. Twenty yards from where Elsie was standing, John Arnott, who had recently celebrated his sixteenth birthday, was leaning against the wall waiting for a bus. James Clay, a retired pensioner, was walking home after a quiet pub lunch. Near by, George Rowlands was making his way to the council depot, and a thirty-three-year-old clerk, Rex Gentle, was walking briskly to his workplace.

Only one person in the vicinity had found her attention drawn to anything unusual. Earlier that afternoon Mrs Ada Clarke was standing in her house at Kingsway looking towards a passageway which led to a row of houses at the end of Clara Street. At 12.30 she noticed a new bicycle standing against the kerb at the top of the passageway. It was of the type used for transporting goods, described as a carrier cycle. It was customary for such a bicycle to have a name-plate, but this one bore no markings to indicate its owner or the company for which it was used. Mrs Clarke logged the episode in her mind and began preparing lunch.

Two hours later a military plane flew over the city, and simultaneously a massive bomb exploded.

Elsie Ansell was closest to the explosion and was killed instantly; her injuries were so horrific that her clothing would later have to be used to identify her. James Clay, George Rowlands, Rex Gentle and John Arnott lay dying on the nearby pavements. Windows for several hundred yards shattered, sending swathes of glass splinters through the tightly knit streets, thronged with people. As the smoke cleared, the dead, the dying and the injured were strewn across pavements and roads. Fifty-two men, women and children required medical assistance.

A crowd chased three men running from the scene. There were shouts of 'Lynch them!' The police reached them first, to discover they were fleeing in horror from the carnage. In the confusion, many people thought the blast had been caused by a German bomber plane passing overhead. Others talked of having seen a lorry marked with the letters 'TNT'. But it was later established that a government lorry carrying explosives had driven through the area hours earlier, and the plane was an RAF transport.

It was an hour before police identified the seat of the explosion as the alleyway close to Mrs Clarke's home. She told them about the carrier cycle with no name-plate. Enquiries were made at every cycle shop until one proprietor revealed that he had recently sold a new bicycle of that type; one man had paid him a £5 deposit and another had collected the bike. Within hours the police possessed descriptions of both men, but no real leads to their identities. By coincidence, five hours after the massacre, Scotland Yard Special Branch received a tip-off about an explosives hoard and searched the flat of an Irishman living at Westbourne Terrace in London. After finding a quantity of potassium chlorate, they arrested Peter Barnes, a thirty-two-year-old labourer from County Offaly who had been in England since the spring of 1938. In his jacket was a letter to a friend dated 24 August, the day before the explosion. Part of the letter read: 'I am after coming back from Coventry tonight, 11.30, so by the time you get this the paper should have some news.' That was enough to convince detectives they had their man. He was taken to Coventry and at an identification parade was picked out as the man who had paid the £5 deposit for the carrier cycle.

Police moved quickly and, with information provided by Barnes, arrested another Irishman, twenty-nine-year-old James Richards. He lived in Clara Street, less than 50 yards from where the explosion occurred. Three other occupants of the house, James Hewitt, his wife Mary (both in their late twenties) and forty-six-year-old Brigid O'Hara, a cleaner, were taken into custody. Yet neither Barnes nor Richards had planted the bomb. The culprit was in Dublin the day after the bombing. According to IRA sources, he was a psychopath and was still receiving psychiatric treatment in the early 1980s.

Those arrested were charged with conspiring to cause the explosion and murdering five people. The Hewitts and Brigid O'Hara were later acquitted because the jury believed they did not know that Richards was in the IRA. James Richards (who used the alias James McCormick) was a committed member of the IRA, while Peter Barnes was a courier who transported explosives for the bomb-makers. He never knew the bombers' targets. Barnes tried to construct a defence, claiming that he had visited Coventry because a casual acquaintance called McMahon had suggested there were better prospects of work in that area. McMahon, said Barnes, had told him to go to an address at Clara Street and ask for Norman, but on the first visit no-one 'seemed to know Norman'. He returned a second time and that was how he met Richards. He said he had bought the packets of potassium chlorate from a girl in Oxford Street who told him the substance was shampoo. He alleged that the letter found in his jacket belonged to the mysterious Mr McMahon, who had asked him to deliver it personally to someone in Dublin. At the trial, which opened on 11 December 1939, Barnes was asked to explain evidence that he had been carrying a suitcase when he went to Clara Street the day before the explosion. Barnes replied that it contained his hat, overcoat and pyjamas. Police officers testified that they had made considerable efforts to trace the person referred to as McMahon, but their enquiries had been fruitless.

Richards made the bombs at the Hewitts' home, but it is probable that, like Barnes, he did not know the nature of the target on that fateful Friday. He was robust, dark-haired, with flashing dark eyes. When he addressed the jury he made no attempt to hide the fact that he knew he was heading for the scaffold. Explaining his attitude to violence, he stated: 'I am a soldier of the IRA. My job was to store explosives until they were needed by men who would call on me and ask for them. I did not know it was intended to place the bomb in the centre of Coventry in the daytime. I would never have been a willing party to that, for the instructions of the IRA are that lives are not to be endangered.'

I spoke to a veteran member of the IRA who was involved in the bombing campaign, and asked why the bomb was placed in a crowded area and no warning given. He told me:

None of us ever found out the truth. Barnes was really a courier of sorts and Richards was a kind of quartermaster and bomb-maker. There were lots of stories that the guy who planted it panicked, that the bomb was about to go off and he had to dump it. There were those of us who wanted him court-martialled and shot but GHQ in Dublin would hear none of that. My belief is that he decided to kill people because the delay between the bomb being left at the kerb and a passage of two hours before it exploded suggested to some of us that it was deliberate. Maybe we'll never know. It certainly wasn't policy, otherwise we could have killed a lot more people during that campaign. I always had the feeling that there were some people at GHQ who didn't mind that kind of tactic. Anyway, after Barnes and Richards were sentenced to be executed, nobody in the IRA would have dared suggest an internal inquiry to deal with the real culprit. From our point of view, the way they dealt with Barnes and Richards was pure revenge and not justice. A lot of people at the time said 'this is war' and people get killed in a war but I don't think it's that simple.

The jury found Barnes and Richards guilty, and they were sentenced to be hanged. Before the sentences were formally passed, Barnes addressed the court, saying: 'As I am going to meet my God, condemned to death, I am still innocent. Later, it will come out that I had no part in it.' Richards steadfastly maintained his political commitment to the end: 'I am not afraid to die, because I am dying for a just cause . . . God save Ireland and the men who are prepared to fight and die for her.'

Both men were taken to Winson Green prison in Birmingham with the instruction that they be hanged side by side. The night before his execution, Richards wrote to his sister, Mary Casey:

Well, Mary, this is my last farewell letter to you as I am just after being told that we have to die in the morning. I knew that I would have to die so the news did not come as a shock to me, but thank God I am prepared, as I know I am dying for a good cause. So, Mary, I shall walk out in the morning sunshine smiling as I shall be thinking of my God and the good men who went before me fighting for the same cause.

As an IRA activist Richards knew that dying on the scaffold would transform him into a hero and martyr. But Barnes was a minor player, and nationalist Ireland regarded his execution as a travesty. The British government rejected numerous pleas for clemency from Irish politicians and churchmen. The executions, which took place on 7 February 1940, left a legacy of bitterness in Ireland.

The Home Office refused permission for the bodies to be removed to Ireland. A Home Office spokesman claimed the decision was taken on the advice of Special Branch, who said such a transfer 'would stir up anti-British feeling in Ireland and create martyrs'. Yet the fact is they were martyrs from the moment they were hanged, and the bodies should have been returned. The authorities in Britain were acting on the basis of two precedents: in 1916 Sir Roger Casement, who had consorted with the Germans, was hanged in Pentonville gaol and buried in 'the murderers' cemetery'; and Alderman Terence MacSwiney, the Lord Mayor of Cork, was buried in Brixton prison when he died after seventy-four days on hunger strike in 1920. When Barnes and Richards were executed and buried in England, there were major demonstrations in Ireland and threatening letters were sent to English families and to Irish Protestants. Thirty years later, when the 1970s bombing campaign began, those who called for capital punishment were ignorant of the history of Irish politics. Similarly, the British refusal to transfer IRA men to prisons in Ireland to serve their sentences was a vital ingredient of IRA mythology. The IRA used the pending execution of Barnes and Richards as a pretext for placing bombs in London, Manchester and Birmingham. At Euston Station in London, four porters were injured when balloon bombs hidden in luggage exploded as parcels were being transported to a train heading for Birmingham.

Before the execution of Barnes and Richards, de Valera had already begun to implement his strategy for stopping the IRA in its tracks. In June 1939 the Dail had introduced the Offences Against the State Act which proscribed the IRA and provided for military courts to try suspected members of the organization. Nevertheless, he still had good reason to fear a deterioration in Anglo-Irish relations and the risk of provoking the British into invading Eire. In 1937 the Germans had told de Valera they would respect Eire's neutrality in the event of a war between Germany and Britain; a reciprocal statement from Dublin confirmed that Ireland would observe a neutral position towards Germany. However, Irish neutrality was being jeopardized by the IRA's flirtation with the Nazis and in particular with the German intelligence network, the Abwehr.

From the start there was potential for confusion in relations between the Nazis and the IRA. The Nazis knew little about the complexities of Irish politics, and the IRA was not a sophisticated organization capable of liaising effectively with German intelligence.

There were internecine struggles within the German intelligence network, and for a time the Abwehr were forbidden to traffic with the IRA. The German ambassador in Dublin believed the IRA should not compromise Irish neutrality and should support de Valera. At times the Abwehr failed to understand that the IRA could not give their backing to the Prime Minister of Eire because, although de Valera was a republican, he had turned from the armed struggle to constitutional politics. But for the IRA it was a case of 'Britain's enemy is our friend', and IRA leaders regarded the Nazis as a useful ally because funds were drying up, and weapons and explosives were in short supply.

In February 1939 a German intelligence agent, Oskar Pfaus, using the alias 'Eion Duffy', arrived in Dublin to make contact with the IRA. He met members of the GHQ staff, including Sean Russell and the bomb instructor, Seamus O'Donovan. This was essentially a meeting to establish a working relationship, and to discover whether the IRA could be used as a fifth column within Great Britain in the event of a war. German intelligence wanted to confirm that the IRA would be prepared to attack British war industries. GHQ was pleased with the progress made at the meeting and despatched the bomb instructor, O'Donovan, to Germany for further talks with the Abwehr. From an IRA standpoint, here was an opportunity to set up a supply route for munitions and cash which would enable them to continue and to upgrade their campaign in Britain. O'Donovan's first trip produced nothing, however, and he returned to Germany in April 1939 with suggestions for a route for weapons, money and transmitters. Whatever the Germans' reasons, the second visit too was a futile exercise for the IRA.

On 23 August 1939, nine days before German tanks rolled into Poland, O'Donovan was on his third visit to Germany, again with no tangible results. Britain's declaration of war on 3 September gave de Valera an urgent reason for striking against the IRA and ensuring that Irish neutrality was no longer threatened from within. Irish intelligence and Special Branch moved quickly. In Dublin in September they seized leading officers of GHQ, and a large sum of money in dollars. They also found documents outlining the German connection.

The IRA Chief of Staff who had been masterminding the campaign in Britain was stranded in the United States, where he had gone to raise funds. The organization was not leaderless, but arrests increased and military tribunals led to a depletion in IRA ranks. The process of attrition was slow at first, and the potential of the bombers to operate in Britain remained a real threat as 1939 came to a close. There was a grave risk that, if the link with the Nazis was properly developed, the IRA would be able to cope with the disruption caused by the policies of the Irish government. One month after the Second World War began, the IRA finally made radio contact with the Abwehr and again asked for supplies of guns, explosives and transmitting equipment, but again the IRA request was ignored. The sheer scale of the threat to the Irish State was brought home to de Valera in December 1939 when the IRA raided the Irish military installation known as the Magazine Fort in the Phoenix Park, west of Dublin, and seized over one million rounds of ammunition. The Irish Army, police and Special

Branch responded swiftly and thoroughly. Within ten days most of the ammunition had been recovered and, with it, many IRA weapons and personnel. One of the successes of the follow-up operation was the discovery of the radio transmitter the IRA was using to contact the Abwehr. The Royal Ulster Constabulary also aided the search for the Magazine Fort ammunition; they seized crates of it in the North and returned it to the Dublin authorities. For once the enemy within had become the enemy in both parts of the island.

Neutrality in the European war ruled all de Valera's actions against the IRA at this time. One other important feature of neutrality was that Britain must be prevented from imposing conscription in Northern Ireland. He sternly warned the British against such a step, and made representations to the USA. De Valera's central argument against conscription in the North was that it would be a breach of Irish neutrality because the Irish Constitution claimed jurisdiction over the six counties of Northern Ireland. He believed that it would be opposed by Northern Irish Catholics, and Eire would be obliged to support them. In any case, the Unionist government of Northern Ireland and its security forces were not happy about the prospect of conscription either, since it would reduce their ability to deal with the IRA. Reluctantly, the British government agreed not to impose conscription. Many Northern Irish Protestants were glad to avoid conscription; and many Catholics both north and south of the border joined the British Army.

Meanwhile in Britain people were faced both with the awful fact of war and with a continuing IRA bombing campaign. On 22 February 1940, under cover of the blackout, the IRA planted devices in London at Marble Arch and in Oxford Street. The bomb at Marble Arch exploded while men from HMS *Ajax* were in the vicinity, and they were able to help the injured. In Oxford Street the bomb went off in a waste-bin near a bus stop. Terrified crowds ran screaming from the scene. A piece of flying metal tore off a woman's leg, and twelve other people were injured, though none of them seriously.

In Eire hundreds of republicans faced a bleak winter in the Curragh military camp as the Government inexorably moved towards the ultimate weapon, internment without trial. The military tribunal was doing its job, but the IRA had a history of evading the most stringent laws. De Valera and his ministers believed that internment was the only weapon that could defeat the IRA. The legislation contained in the new Offences Against the State Act provided the means for detention without trial as well as the power to arrest on suspicion anyone advocating, maintaining or raising a military force. Mere suspicion of membership of the IRA was sufficient to permit an arrest and the person's subsequent appearance before a military court. After the raid on the Magazine Fort, the Emergency Powers Act was amended to allow the internment of Irish citizens as well as aliens. The IRA's own tactics of refusing to answer questions or recognize the courts made it much easier for the authorities to remove those men they considered the greatest threat. As Mountjoy and Arbour Hill prisons filled to overflowing, a concentration camp was hastily constructed at the Curragh military camp.

Like the Long Kesh camp of the 1970s in Northern Ireland, the Curragh of 1940 was composed of Nissen huts ringed with barbed wire. There was no heating and only poor washing facilities. The Irish always found it easier to deal brutally with their own terrorists.

The IRA developed its own command structures within the camp and the prisons and tried to confer prisoner-of-war status on its people. The Irish military had a 'punishment block' at the Curragh where the more truculent prisoners suffered a harsh diet and even harsher conditions. As at Long Kesh in the 1970s, there was an attempt to burn down the Curragh. The culprits were brutally punished by the soldiers, sometimes using methods later employed by British military personnel in the early days of internment in 1971. For example, prisoners were made to run a gauntlet of lines of soldiers armed with batons and guns. Perhaps one could argue that the actions of the Irish soldiers in 1940 were more extreme than those of their British counterparts thirty-one years later. In the Curragh, the IRA ringleaders were subjected to further physical ill-treatment and kept in solitary confinement in the stark surroundings of the punishment block for nearly three months. One incident which left a bitter legacy in IRA history occurred several days after the failed arson attempt. Prisoners were lined up outside their huts and soldiers opened fire indiscriminately. Five IRA men were shot, one in the back.

The Government in Dublin was determined that the IRA would not be granted any special privileges or special-category status. There was a policy to criminalize the IRA. Those who had been gaoled for possession of firearms or explosives were transferred to the Curragh as soon as their prison sentences were completed. The Irish government planned to maintain internment until the end of the war in Europe, in the hope that by then the IRA would be finished as a military and political force. Ironically, the British government found itself dealing with a similar situation in the 1970s but was not as effective in dealing with the problems. Also during the war the IRA used the hunger-strike tactic, and de Valera, like Margaret Thatcher in 1981, was unrelenting in his response. Two IRA men died on hunger strike, and their 'sacrifice' did not have the desired outcome of forcing the Government to concede to demands for the ending of the criminalization of IRA prisoners. Press censorship and control of other information outlets effectively led to a mere public acknowledgement of the episode. After calling off the hunger strike, the IRA ordered a revenge attack for the deaths of the hunger strikers, and planted a bomb at Special Branch headquarters in Dublin. Two detectives and a woman were injured in the explosion, and the Government seized the opportunity to denounce the IRA. It received support from the Opposition in the Dail, and de Valera made it clear that the IRA was jeopardizing Eire's neutrality. He warned both of the danger of civil war and the risk of invasion if the IRA was permitted to continue its campaign to unseat a democratic Irish government. The public, watching the course of war in Europe, supported his contention and the IRA gradually began to disintegrate.

Neutrality was secured, yet de Valera did not tell the Irish people that the British government, both in its fear of a German invasion of Ireland and in its determination to protect shipping from the German U-boats, had made overtures to him. Britain's Foreign Secretary, Lord Halifax, had proposed that if Britain could offer guarantees on the prospect of a united Ireland the Treaty Ports might be released for use as staging posts in the defence of shipping. Churchill, who in May 1940 replaced Chamberlain as Prime Minister, sanctioned an approach to de Valera and the British Cabinet discussed the matter during the summer. The plan was to make a declaration that Britain in principle favoured a united Ireland; in return Eire would make available the ports for the duration of the war, and take the side of the Allies.

When Lord Craigavon, the Unionist Prime Minister of Northern Ireland, learned of these developments he was shocked, and demanded to know how Britain could consider sacrificing the loyalty of Ulster. Neville Chamberlain, who was acting as an intermediary, reminded the Unionists that Britain was in grave peril and a deal with Dublin was vital. The Unionists were unmoved by assurances that Ulster's position would be protected, and accused Britain of treachery. They need not have been so concerned: in the event, de Valera rejected the offer, simply because he did not trust the British. He felt that when the war was over such a declaration would be meaningless, since the proposal had not been formally put to the Unionists. What de Valera failed to recognize, possibly because of his single-mindedness about preserving neutrality and his deep mistrust of the British, was that Chamberlain and Churchill had been prepared to do such a deal without Unionist consent. The initial approaches made to de

Valera from Downing Street were not conditional on a Unionist agreement to the principle of Irish unity. This whole issue left Churchill feeling bitter and believing that his only friends and allies in Ireland were within the Unionist community.

As the war progressed, the IRA campaign in Britain came to an end and the fortunes of the IRA in Eire steadily declined. The prison experience sapped IRA morale. Treated as common criminals, denied free association and rarely provided with reading or writing materials, they responded by refusing to wear prison attire, sat naked in their cells clothed only in blankets, and suffered solitary confinement. As the organization grew weaker in Eire, and the campaign in Britain ground to a halt, the IRA began to exploit the vulnerability of the British in another part of the United Kingdom, namely Northern Ireland.

The IRA's Northern Command had lost few people to the campaign in Britain and only a small number to the internment process in the Republic. One of those involved in reshaping the IRA into an effective organization was a veteran of the bombing campaign in England. The Northerners preferred a separate command, believing that they alone understood the precise problems and objectives in areas such as Belfast and that the leadership in Dublin was out of touch with the situation in the North. In 1941–2 they were better equipped and had more men at their disposal than the IRA in the South. Accordingly they planned the sabotage of war industries and the killing of members of the Royal Ulster Constabulary (RUC) and the Ulster Special Constabulary, better known as the B Specials.

The latter was a majority Protestant force with a history of anti-Catholic sentiment, while the RUC, though mainly Protestant, did have a small number of Catholics in its ranks. At the creation of the RUC, the Government declared its intention that 12 per cent of policemen should be drawn from the Catholic community but the proportion never exceeded 5 per cent.

While the IRA planned a new campaign, the Luftwaffe marked Belfast and Derry as important targets. Belfast housed the massive Harland & Wolff shipyard which was given over to the war effort. The ports of both cities were employed partly to fulfil the role intended for the Treaty Ports, denied to Britain by de Valera. Neither city was prepared for the war: Belfast had only four bomb shelters and an inadequate supply of anti-aircraft guns. In April 1941 Belfast experienced one of the worst bombings of British cities, in which 900 people died. German bombers raided the city again in May, and a further 200 were killed. Almost half the buildings in Belfast were razed to the ground and the majority of the population moved into the countryside.

The IRA was prepared to inflict additional suffering on its own people, but internment hindered them, and the Northern Ireland government also denied IRA members political or prisoner-of-war status. Although the IRA still managed to kill policemen and members of the B Specials and to bomb police barracks, they did not succeed in attacking war industries and were reduced to broadcasting anti-British propaganda from a secret transmitter. Many of the IRA volunteers were young men, some of them in their teens.

When six volunteers who had shot dead a police constable were sentenced to death, the Catholic Church in Ireland made representations to the British government, which was determined to hang the six as a warning to the IRA not to hamper the war effort. The British relented and the sentences of five were commuted to life imprisonment; the hangman's rope was reserved for eighteen-year-old Tom Williams. To avenge his death, the IRA killed a police constable and a member of the B Specials. The Northern Ireland government at Stormont responded by interning several hundred suspected IRA activists, and imposed a curfew in nationalist areas. IRA men who used the border as an escape route were often captured by the Irish military and interned at the Curragh. Random shootings and gun-battles continued, but gradually the IRA lost its momentum and most of its personnel on both sides of the border. In Northern Ireland, where most Catholics sympathized with the IRA, it was possible for activists to seek sanctuary in nationalist homes, whereas in Eire the majority of the people refused to harbour them. By 1945 the IRA no longer posed a threat in both parts of the island, mainly because of the Draconian measures adopted by de Valera's government. If Eire had not taken a firm stand against the IRA, Northern Ireland could have faced a major terrorist campaign after 1939. It was also the Irish military and Special Branch who succeeded in neutralizing the IRA flirtation with German intelligence agents, many of whom were dropped off from U-boats. All the German agents were arrested, some before they could contact the IRA, and they were held until the end of the war.

In August 1940 Sean Russell, the IRA chief responsible for the bombing campaign in England, met German military leaders, including Joachim von Ribbentrop, the Foreign Minister, and Admiral Canaris, the head of the Abwehr, to request guns, explosives and transmitting equipment and to emphasize the IRA's willingness to attack British war industries. Ribbentrop sanctioned the use of a U-boat to return Russell to Ireland. The vessel, under the control of Commander von Stockhausen, left Wilhelmshaven, the major U-boat base, on 8 August. Seven days later Russell, after suffering severe stomach pains, died and was buried at sea. The U-boat was due to reach the west coast of Ireland the same day. No-one knows the cause of death: some reports suggested stomach ulcers, others that he was poisoned. Maybe the Germans did not wish to compromise de Valera and Irish neutrality by allowing Russell to return and organize a new campaign.

4

A Bitter Legacy

Churchill's bitterness towards De Valera and the Irish government remained constant throughout the war, but with Hitler's death on 30 April 1945 a new ingredient was added to an already simmering resentment. When the Irish newspapers reported Hitler's suicide on 2 May, de Valera responded by paying a visit to the German legation in Dublin 'to express condolence'. To most people it was the action of a man with no sense of decency or humanity, and to future Irishmen it was an act that would taint their history; by this stage the full horror of the Nazi extermination camps was being revealed to the outside world. De Valera's 'condolences' drove a wedge between the two communities in Northern Ireland and between both parts of the island, and isolated Eire from Britain and many of the other Allies, including the USA. No amount of rhetoric can ever erase that event, and it is regrettable that many Irish people, particularly republicans, have explained his actions in terms of Irish political bias and naïvety.

On 13 May 1945 Churchill used a world radio broadcast to condemn de Valera:

> The sense of envelopment, which might at any moment turn to strangulation, lay heavy upon us. We had only the north-western approach between Ulster and Scotland through which to bring in the means of life and to send out the forces of war. Owing to the action of Mr de Valera, so much at variance with the temper and instinct of thousands of southern Irishmen who hastened to the battlefront to prove their ancient valour, the approaches which the southern Irish ports and airfields could so easily have guarded were closed by the hostile aircraft and U-boats. This was indeed a deadly moment in our life, and if it had not been for the loyalty and friendship of Northern Ireland we should have been forced to come to close quarters with Mr de Valera or perish for ever from earth.

The end of the war gave the Unionist population the chance to express their Britishness; they enjoyed the praise heaped on them for their contribution to the war effort. Yet the archetypal Unionist portrait of de Valera as an Irish leader who aided the Nazis is far from the truth. British aircraft frequently used Irish airspace without hindrance or complaint. British servicemen who were forced to land by air or sea were generally given safe passage to Northern Ireland, unlike Germans, who were interned in harsh conditions.

During the Belfast blitz, fire crews in Eire went north to assist firefighters in Belfast, and the Irish military often had discussions with their British counterparts about the mechanics of co-operation in the event of a German invasion of Eire. The Irish supplied weather reports, reported submarine sightings and created an air corridor for planes to fly in towards the Atlantic. They monitored German nationals in the country and at the German legation in Dublin.

Nevertheless, Eire's neutrality did create a sense of isolation, particularly for the Catholics of Northern Ireland. It reinforced the subsequent British commitment to maintain the status quo in Ulster, to the point where the sovereign Parliament at Westminster allowed the Unionists to run the province without proper scrutiny. It was, essentially, the price that British postwar administrations paid to the Unionists for their support of the Allies. Had de Valera chosen the alternative course, British–Irish relations after the war would have been conducive to discussions aimed at solving the political problems of a divided country. There was to be no prospect of that for another twenty-eight years.

As the postwar reconstruction began, with Northern Ireland and other Allied territories receiving generous financial subvention, Eire sank into economic decline in its isolation, and Northern Ireland began to prosper. The IRA men who emerged from the prisons and internment camps were disillusioned. The world had changed; events had passed them by, and Catholics in Ireland had forgotten them. It seemed their rhetoric no longer had a place in either part of the island. Within the

IRA in Eire, there were bitter rivalries, recriminations and internecine strife which left the organization so divided that the Justice Minister claimed that he had 'killed them off'.

In the North, the Unionist government adopted the policy put forward by Lord Craigavon in 1934 – that 'appointments made by the Government are made, so far as we can manage it, of loyal men and women'. This meant that the majority of government posts went to Protestants. Religious discrimination was central to the maintenance of the State. It was considered dangerous to employ Catholics whose community ethos was nationalist and republican. It was not only in government posts and the civil service that doors were closed to Catholics; in the private sector, employers were encouraged to make Protestant workers their first choice. For example, advice given to employers by Sir Basil Brooke, a Unionist minister (who later became Prime Minister of Northern Ireland), was reported in his local paper the *Fermanagh Times* as follows: 'There were a great number of Protestants and Orangemen who employed Roman Catholics. He felt he could speak freely on this subject as he had not had a Roman Catholic about his own place. He appreciated the great difficulty experienced by some of them in procuring suitable Protestant labour, but he would point out that Roman Catholics were endeavouring to get in everywhere. He would appeal to loyalists therefore, wherever possible, to employ good Protestant lads and lasses.' The basic and unapologetic thesis of Unionism was articulated by Sir Basil Brooke in these words: 'I recommend those people who are loyalists not to employ Roman

Catholics, 99 per cent of whom are disloyal.' He reminded Protestant employers that they 'had the ball at their feet', and if they did not act decisively they would be a minority rather than a majority.

Many statements of that kind were uttered and published in the 1920s and 1930s and they went unnoticed at Westminster. Such remarks were more confidently repeated in the postwar period, when the status quo in Northern Ireland was unimpeachable because of the total ignorance at Westminster that Northern Irish Catholics did have grievances. When in 1948 Eire declared its intention to become a republic, Clement Attlee, the British Prime Minister, spelled out in a memorandum Britain's commitment:

Now that Eire will shortly cease to owe any allegiance to the Crown, it has become a matter of first-class strategic importance to this country that the North should continue to form part of HM Dominions. So far as can be foreseen, it will never be to Great Britain's advantage that Northern Ireland should form part of a territory outside HM's jurisdiction. Indeed it seems unlikely that Great Britain would ever be able to agree to this even if the people of Northern Ireland desired it.

It was the clearest statement of British intentions, an affirmation that partition of Ireland would remain in place, even if a majority of Catholics ever emerged to democratically challenge the status quo.

The Unionist government got on with the job of reconstruction. They began building houses for the first time in twenty-four years, and the majority of those homes were allocated to Protestant families, leaving Catholics to languish in sub-standard accommodation. Westminster was prepared to pay the bills, and reforms began in housing and education. House building and allocation provided Unionist-controlled councils with the opportunity to maintain power in areas where they held slim majorities at the polls. Occupancy of a house carried with it the right to vote in council elections, since the franchise for local government elections was restricted to householders and their spouses in Northern Ireland. Many councils in areas with a majority Catholic population were controlled by Unionists through the process of gerrymandering – that is, manipulating electoral boundaries to ensure that a particular party has a majority. The Unionist Party encouraged both the undemocratic gerrymander and the unfair allocation of housing to Protestants in the effort to deprive Catholics of real power; there was also a deep-seated fear that Catholic rejection of birth control would enable them to 'outbreed' their Protestant counterparts. It was in these areas of life that the Unionists in the 1950s, particularly at council level, and with the acquiescence of the Stormont government, fuelled the discontent that would be highly flammable twenty years later. The need to deny Catholics votes was central to the Protestant siege mentality, and they believed that in their midst was a fifth column, the IRA, which was bent on destroying the State with the support of the whole of the Catholic/nationalist population. They saw themselves surrounded on the island of Ireland by the constant threat of subversion from a Catholic-led Republic which had flirted with Hitler. Protestant fears were not imaginary: few Catholics in Northern Ireland accepted partition, and the majority of people on the island believed it was an unhealthy political solution. However, the strengthening of Unionism encouraged renewed activity from the Protestant extremists, the Orangemen, who historically had organized since the eighteenth century for Protestant political ascendancy in Ireland.

At the outset of partition, Britain had introduced proportional representation to provide a fair electoral system for minorities – the Catholics in Northern Ireland, and the Protestants living in Eire. British political strategists had recognized that, without PR, Catholics in the new state of Northern Ireland would suffer electorally. The initial result of PR was that Catholics took almost one-third of all council seats in 1920. Two years later Stormont scrapped PR and redrew the electoral boundaries. The effect was to reduce the proportion of Catholic-controlled councils to only 3 per cent of the total. In some council areas where Catholics had claimed victories in 1920, they suddenly found themselves in the minority, their constituents under-represented.

In education there were parallels to the problems of housing allocation. Many Unionists were bitterly opposed to the implementation of the British Education Reform Bill, introduced in 1944. It was only after three years of intense debate within both communities that the 1947 Education Act became law. The Catholic Church, with separate schools where it controlled the religious upbringing of its flock, felt that the new legislation would give funding for the reform of State schools to the detriment of the Catholic institutions. The Catholic hierarchy also argued that the ethos of the State school system was Unionist and would therefore lead to a corresponding bias in the educational process in those schools. Yet, equally, the Catholic Church was the Catholic Church in Ireland and as such provided an education with a nationalist political character. The Catholic schools were known as 'voluntary schools' and, unlike their State counterparts, did not receive full capital grants; they were maintained by the Church, which claimed that a Unionist proposal to increase the capital grants from 50 per cent to 65 per cent would still deny the voluntary schools parity and was thus a way of coercing Catholics into using the State education system. If the Stormont government had problems with the Catholic hierarchy, those difficulties were minor compared with the upsurge in Protestant anger at another element in the Bill. The legislation proposed ending compulsory Bible classes in State schools and introducing religious teaching and group worship at morning assembly. This was deduced by many to be an attack on the Protestant heritage and a concession to Catholics. The attempt to move the schools gradually towards a multi-denominational system collapsed under public pressure. It also fuelled sectarian arguments that Catholic schools should not receive any increase in capital funding.

The Act did not have full impact for almost twenty years, though it provided the opportunity for second-level and third-level education for working-class Catholics. Many of those who benefited from the legislation were later prominent in the civil rights movement and nationalist politics. Bernadette Devlin (later McAliskey) and many other radicals went through first-level education with the prospect of opportunities that would take them into university and the age of protest. Yet every aspect of social reform carried with it the baggage of a divided society and the separate cultures of the two communities.

In the postwar era, Irish Catholics became disillusioned with de Valera's failure to end partition. Sean MacBride, a former Chief of Staff of the IRA, was among those who believed there was a constitutional way to attack partition. His credentials as an intellectual with a republican history provided the dynamic for the creation of a new political party, Clann na Poblachta. Sean MacBride was a twelve-year-old schoolboy in Paris in 1916 when he was told that his father, Major John MacBride, had been executed by the British for his part in the Easter Rising. His mother was Maud Gonne, revered by the poet W. B. Yeats, and herself a republican activist in Ireland. The young Sean MacBride returned to Ireland but retained his French accent for the remainder of his life. Having fought in the IRA before and after the 1921 Treaty, spending time in prison and on the run, he was made Chief of Staff in 1936; however, he resigned from the IRA in 1937 because he opposed Russell's plan to bomb Britain. In the 1970s he won the Nobel and the Lenin peace prizes. In 1946, despite his earlier association with de Valera, he became leader of the new party, which drew support from many of the republicans who had been imprisoned in the Dublin gaols and the Curragh camp during the war.

Clann na Poblachta advocated the creation of a republic comprising the twenty-six counties of Eire, thus breaking the final political link with Britain. It argued for a renewed campaign against partition, employing constitutional methods – a divergence from the traditional republicanism of physical-force politics. Clann na Poblachta demanded the right for Catholic representatives from Northern Ireland to be admitted to the Southern Irish Parliament, the Dail Eireann, but this was later ruled to be unconstitutional by the Irish Attorney-General. In by-elections they won enough support to worry de Valera and in February 1948 a general election was called. De Valera and his Fianna Fail party did not have sufficient seats to remain in power. There was a general feeling that he was too dictatorial and the country was going into a steady social and economic decline. Clann na Poblachta and other Opposition parties including the Irish Labour Party formed a coalition with Fine Gael, the old Free State party which had accepted partition. MacBride was made Minister for External Affairs. The new government, though concerned to end the link with Britain by creating a republic, was also preoccupied with economic issues which often took priority over MacBride's republican aims.

While MacBride faced the problems of governing, de Valera, released from those constraints, embarked on an international tour to campaign for a united Ireland. The irony of de Valera suddenly devoting so much of his energy to carrying the republican message to an international audience was not lost on the republicans who had opposed him. In Northern Ireland the IRA saw his actions as opportunistic – an attempt to steal the republican mantle from MacBride and the Clann. Meanwhile, MacBride, as Minister for External Affairs, put forward his proposal to the Unionist government in Northern Ireland for a reunification which would contain guarantees for the Unionists. The response was that 'Ulster was not for sale' (echoing de Valera's reply before the war when he was told the British wanted to negotiate an end to Irish neutrality: 'Ireland is not for sale'). MacBride and de Valera were wrong to think they could influence international opinion on the issue of partition. The Western Allies were now facing a new enemy, communism; yet Eire still persisted with its policy of isolation. After the war there was a special relationship between Britain and the United States which guaranteed that the US would not interfere in British–Irish politics, nor advocate a policy that could be construed as supporting the Irish republican position. It could be argued that the Second World War had proved that Northern Ireland was an adequate base to protect Western interests, and that Irish neutrality had revealed Eire neither to be critical to the defence of Western Europe nor to constitute any tangible threat to the Allies. Consequently, Britain had no need to make any political concession to Eire or the Republic of Ireland, since the Dublin government offered no strategic advantage to NATO.

In 1948–9 the defence of Europe became an issue once again as the Cold War began. The USA and Britain invited the Irish Republic to join the North Atlantic Treaty Organization and abandon the principle of neutrality. The Republic responded that while partition was in place it could not join the Allies. Once again the Republic chose the wrong option, because NATO did not need the whole island of Ireland, but membership of NATO would have guaranteed a favourable response from the United States and placed Anglo-Irish relations on a better footing. It might even have had the effect of allowing the Republic to place Northern Ireland on the British political agenda. The Irish refusal of the invitation to join NATO reinforced the British view that Northern Ireland was strategically important to Britain and Europe; and it increased the Republic's isolation internationally.

In June 1949, one month after Eire formally became the Republic of Ireland, the British Parliament passed the Ireland Act, which confirmed that Northern Ireland was constitutionally part of the United Kingdom and stated that Northern Ireland would not cease to be part of His Majesty's Dominions or the United Kingdom without the consensus of the Stormont Parliament. The issue of consent went further than the Republic or the Catholics in Northern Ireland had considered possible. Nationalists in both parts of the island had always argued that some day Catholics would outnumber Protestants and vote themselves into a united Ireland. The terms of the Ireland Act gave the Unionists the power of veto over the decisions of any future Catholic majority.

Unionist leaders rallied their supporters with anti-Catholic slogans when a Northern Ireland election was called in February 1949. There were serious outbreaks of violence, as Orangemen marched through Catholic areas announcing their triumphalist right to march anywhere in 'their country'. The slogans were familiar – 'No Surrender', 'No Pope Here', 'A Protestant Ulster for a Protestant People' and 'Dublin Rule is Rome Rule' (referring to the Protestant claim that the Vatican was conspiring with Ulster's enemies in Dublin). The Northern Ireland Labour Party, a Protestant-dominated organization founded in 1924, fielded candidates who were attempting to move the community away from sectarian politics and towards social issues, but they were decisively defeated in the election, while some of them were also physically beaten by loyalist mobs. The election left the province with a small Catholic parliamentary Opposition – an ideal result for a Unionist leadership which controlled its own people by feeding them anti-Catholic rhetoric. What Unionism did not need was a growing Labour movement which might dilute the tribal politics and thereby provide a credible opposition to the monolith at Stormont. Catholics felt isolated, betrayed by the politicians in Dublin and fearful that Unionist triumphalism would continue unabated. The stage looked set for the return of the IRA.

If we are to learn anything from the history of the IRA, it is that when its enemies claim they have defeated the IRA it reappears in a more dangerous form. When there is a political vacuum, when British–Irish relations are at a low ebb and when nationalist Ireland gives vent to the republican ideal, the IRA finds fertile ground for recruiting and reorganizing. Until 1950 the IRA was incapable of attracting much support, or dealing with the schisms within its own ranks. There were recriminations over the bombing campaign in Great Britain and the leadership during the war, and disagreement over the organization's strategy for the future. Many of those released after being interned at the Curragh or held in the Dublin prisons joined MacBride's Clann, convinced there was a constitutional way forward, and disillusioned with the politics of the gun. Others argued for a reform of the IRA's executive structure, and a return to the basic ideal of ridding the island of partition by means of the armed struggle.

It was in the newly formed Irish Republic that the republican ideal was given its most vociferous expression, not by the IRA but by the coalition government, by de Valera and the general public. The presence of Sean MacBride, a former IRA Chief of Staff, in the Cabinet reinforced republicanism, albeit in the new framework of a constitutional campaign against partition. Nevertheless, it was a sudden boost for IRA fortunes, revitalizing an organization which the previous Irish government claimed to have 'killed off'. The most significant development was a hardening of attitudes towards Britain, with the prospect of bitter Anglo-Irish relations. When the Attlee government introduced the Ireland Act in June 1949, the move was seen as a riposte to Eire's formal inauguration of the Republic of Ireland on Easter Monday 1949. The British had not told the Irish that they were preparing to introduce the Act; but British diplomats pointed out that the Dublin government had not consulted London before it decided to repeal its External Relations Act in 1948 as a prelude to declaring Eire a republic. MacBride interpreted the relevant clauses of the Ireland Act to mean that the British government intended, for all time, to coerce Catholics in Northern Ireland to live under partition, even if they were to become a majority. The Irish Prime Minister, John A. Costello of the Fine Gael party, condemned the British for giving permanence to partition, and de Valera was vitriolic in his denunciations of British intransigence. Costello and MacBride vowed to continue to raise the issue internationally, particularly in the United States.

The IRA, however, knew the rhetoric of Costello and MacBride would prove futile, and believed the only way forward was through physical-force politics. Elated with the political acrimony and the new gulf dividing Ireland and Britain, the IRA leaders told their followers the climate was right and insisted they were the only people prepared 'to force the issue'. Their immediate objective was to reorganize the army structurally, beginning at the top. The task was not an easy one because imprisonment and internment had decimated the ranks and left many of the leaders disillusioned.

Yet the IRA had learned some very harsh lessons during de Valera's premiership. The Army Council decided that violent action in the Republic was counterproductive because it had justified de Valera's use of military tribunals and internment during the Second World War. The raid on the Magazine Fort in 1939 and other wartime acts of violence against the forces of the Irish State had isolated the IRA in the South and deprived it of popular support. In 1949 the IRA formally declared that it would never again undertake operations against the security forces of the new Republic. The organization would require bases in the Republic for any future campaigns in the United Kingdom, and it was important not to antagonize the Irish authorities. A policy of non-aggression in one part of the island would encourage Dublin to turn a blind eye to the use of Irish territory for launching attacks in Northern Ireland. This policy owed much to the IRA's belief that Irish governments would privately support any IRA action aimed at achieving the republican ideal, provided that action did not threaten the sovereignty or security of the Irish State. The IRA instinctively knew that if it kept the violence out of the Republic it would not be threatened with extinction. This was the genesis of a doctrine which is still in place today. According to 'The Green Book' (see Appendix) General Army Order No. 8 states:

1 Volunteers are strictly forbidden to take any military action against 26 County forces under any circumstances whatsoever. The importance of this order under present circumstances, especially in the border areas, cannot be over-emphasized.

2 Minimum arms shall be used in training in the 26 County area. In the event of a raid, every effort shall be made to get the arms away safely. If this fails, the arms shall be rendered useless and abandoned.

3 Maximum security precautions must be taken when training. Scouts must always be posted to warn of emergency. Volunteers arrested during the training or in possession of arms will point out that the arms were for use against the British forces of occupation only. This statement should be repeated at all subsequent court proceedings.

4 At all times Volunteers must make it clear that the policy of the Army is to drive the British forces of occupation out of Ireland.

The start of a new decade saw the re-emergence of IRA politics in the form of Sinn Fein, which had virtually disintegrated in the 1920s when de Valera left and formed Fianna Fail, after the split over the 1921 Treaty with the British. Now there was debate about whether the IRA controlled its political wing and its news-sheet, *The United Irishman*. In Northern Ireland the IRA capitalized on the republican rhetoric emanating from Dublin and began to attract younger men into its ranks.

Throughout the island of Ireland, the IRA talked of another campaign, but there was an unspoken recognition that Great Britain could not be a target. The IRA did not have enough money or military hardware to include England in its plans, and many felt that the Russell campaign of 1939–40 was a failure not to be repeated. There were few guns in IRA dumps, and the reconstruction of a secret army was a slow process. In Northern Ireland, however, there was a greater urgency to proceed with unfinished business, and in 1951 the Derry Unit proposed a raid on the British naval base at Ebrington. The Derry IRA men knew many Catholics who worked at the base and were familiar with all its security arrangements. They claimed they could enter without hindrance and steal a large quantity of guns. The raid was successful and put the IRA back on centre stage. They seized a large quantity of ammunition and approximately fifty weapons, including .303 rifles, sub-machine-guns and machine-guns. It was the kind of operation that made for colourful stories and heroes; and it perpetuated the cult of the gunman. An IRA that suddenly possessed weapons and could provide proper training for volunteers was a much more attractive proposition for potential recruits. However, the raid offered the Unionists the opportunity to re-equip the RUC and improve its intelligence structure. With the IRA bogeyman back in Ulster politics, the Stormont government felt justified in using repressive measures. RUC training took on a military dimension to deal with the commando-style raid.

Meanwhile in 1951 a general election was held in the Republic; the main issues were social and economic, and republicanism was relegated to little more than sloganizing. The coalition government fell; Fianna Fail was returned to power with a small majority and stayed in government until 1954, with de Valera as Prime Minister again. MacBride's party was damaged by internal wrangling and won only two seats. It was unclear whether the new Republic could survive economically. Levels of emigration were rising: within six years almost a quarter of a million people would leave the Republic for the United States, Australia and England. The IRA in the South opposed the setting up of a welfare state, supporting the Catholic Church view that it was a by-product of 'communism'. It ignored social and economic issues, and concentrated its attention on acquiring guns and ammunition for a renewal of conflict.

In 1953 information reached IRA GHQ in Dublin about an officer training barracks at Felsted, near Braintree in Essex, which could be easily penetrated by a small but determined group of men. Manus Canning from the Derry Unit which had successfully raided the Ebrington naval base was sent by Dublin to England to participate in a new operation. There he was joined by Cahal Goulding and Sean Stephenson.

Goulding, born in 1922 into a staunch republican family, had been interned during the Second World War and was prominent in the revival of the IRA in the late 1940s and early 1950s. He was small, energetic and good humoured, a house painter by trade, and knowledgeable about IRA history. In 1953 while working in England he came into contact with Sean Stephenson, who was five years his junior. The latter's real name was John Edward Drayton Stephenson; he was born in 1928 in Leytonstone, London, and later adopted the name Sean MacStiofain. Although he was English by birth and had never been to Ireland, he had acquired an Irish accent and claimed his mother was a native of Belfast. He had been a corporal in the RAF; after National Service, he mixed with Irish groupings in London, where he joined the republican movement.

Canning, Goulding and Stephenson set out for Felsted Barracks on the evening of 25 July 1953 in a battered old van. When they reached the barracks they entered unhindered, breaking a window at the side of the building. They loaded the rear of the van with scores of rifles, machine-guns and ammunition, but as soon as they set off they discovered that the weight of the weapons prevented the van from moving forward more than a few yards. After removing many of the weapons they were left with 108 rifles and eight Bren machine-guns. Years later Goulding admitted that the situation was farcical: 'The van would hardly move when we had it loaded. The tyres wouldn't take the stress.' Their journey was interrupted at

Bishop's Stortford in Hertfordshire when a police patrol car noticed the dilapidated vehicle, heavily weighed down, with three scruffy-looking men on board. The van made its way past the patrol car, but a bobby on a bicycle was the first to reach the vehicle when it came to a halt.

The three IRA men were each sentenced to eight years in prison for what, on the face of it, was an absurd operation which had been foiled by unarmed policemen. Goulding recounted to me in an interview a few years ago how GHQ sent one of its trusted men to England with orders to plan his escape from Pentonville prison. According to Goulding, there were two unsuccessful attempts to extract him from the prison exercise yard. 'On one occasion they threw a rope-ladder over the prison wall. I was supposed to run across the yard and climb onto the rope-ladder. Nobody had taken account of my height and the ladder was too small, so here I was running at this wall but I couldn't reach the fuckin' ladder.'

As recruitment and training increased, the IRA in Belfast and Dublin harboured the dream of raiding a barracks in the North and seizing enough guns to equip a large number of units for cross-border attacks. The dream began to become reality when an IRA member who was a former British soldier, Leo McCormack, observed that the sentry on duty at Gough Barracks in Armagh did not have a magazine attached to his Sten gun. There was elation at GHQ when they learned that the sentry at one of the largest barracks in Northern Ireland was essentially unarmed. The idea of a quickly executed hit-and-run operation was discounted.

If a raid was expertly planned, they could expect to seize a large haul of guns. They would require hard intelligence on the size of the British garrison and the whereabouts of the armoury.

GHQ decided that the only way of preparing a successful operation was to have a 'man on the inside'. A Dubliner, Sean Garland, was ordered to go to Gough to enlist in the Royal Irish Fusiliers. Garland encountered no obstacles and soon supplied detailed drawings of the layout of the barracks, and information about the size of the garrison and where the soldiers were billeted. He arranged for an IRA colleague and a member of the women's organization Cumann na mBann to enter the barracks as his guests. Garland gave the female volunteer a guided tour of the compound.

On 10 June 1954 IRA preparations were complete. Armed volunteers assembled south of the border in Dundalk, where they boarded a cattle truck that had been commandeered at gunpoint from a local farmer, and were driven to Gough Barracks. The cattle truck was parked opposite the front gate. They disarmed the sentry and replaced him with an IRA officer dressed in a British military uniform. Eighteen soldiers were taken at gunpoint to the guardroom and tied up. They seized over 300 weapons, the majority of them rifles, a small number of sub-machine-guns and nine Bren guns. The truck, with the guns and IRA men on board, travelled back across the border without hindrance. The weapons were quickly moved to different locations and stored in dumps. Republican speeches hinted that the guns would soon be used against 'the forces of occupation in Ireland'.

The IRA was back in business, and everyone was pleased, but for differing reasons. Catholics in Northern Ireland were impressed by the expertise and daring of the raiders; while the Unionist government could claim it had been right to warn people of the IRA threat, and used the opportunity to announce further spending on the security apparatus and to test out new anti-Catholic legislation. When Sean MacBride appeared at a rally in Omagh in 1954 along with thousands of nationalists and republicans and a riot ensued, the RUC, under the orders of the Minister for Home Affairs, decided to remove an Irish tricolour carried by the marchers. It was explained that the presence of the tricolour was in defiance of the recent Flags and Emblems Act, which permitted the RUC to remove any flag or emblem displayed on private or public property, if its display might lead to a breach of the peace. In effect the legislation was designed to prevent Catholics from displaying any flag or emblem which signified their political aspirations, in particular the Irish tricolour.

In the autumn of 1954 the IRA demonstrated what an amateurish guerrilla organization it really was. In an attempt at repeating the success of the Armagh operation, it planned a raid on the military barracks at Omagh. This time GHQ despatched a larger group of men, armed with guns taken in the Gough Barracks operation. As before, an IRA volunteer had enlisted at the barracks, but he was not as perceptive as Garland. The entire logistics of the raid proved disastrous. Transport problems faced the raiding party even before it left the Republic – illustrating that the IRA seemed to find it easier to steal guns than to commandeer vehicles and ensure that the volunteers arrived at the barracks on time. At Omagh, the sentry and a boilerman refused to be subdued by guns and knives; the ensuing commotion led to the barracks being placed on immediate alert, and a gun-fight forced the IRA men to flee. Eight IRA volunteers were caught, but over twenty escaped across the border. The failure of the operation showed that large and highly complex military exercises were still too difficult for the IRA. Nevertheless, the IRA extracted as much propaganda value as possible from the failed operation, publicly applauding its members in the language of the 'romantic tradition'.

In the general election of May 1955 two Sinn Fein candidates won the Westminster seats of Fermanagh/ South Tyrone and Mid-Ulster and between them polled 152,000 votes. This was a statement of the Catholic support for an end to partition; to many Unionists, it was also an endorsement of IRA violence in Ulster. In fact the large poll for republicans was as much a Catholic protest at Protestant Unionist triumphalism as a vote for the IRA. Two months later the Stormont government offered a clear indication of its political perception of the way ahead.

It was the summer marching season, which tradition-ally expressed Protestant cultural and political bonding, but which was also an opportunity for Unionists to demonstrate that Protestant triumphalism was alive and well in Ulster. Orangemen accompanied by bands play-ing racist and sectarian songs marched through Catholic districts watched over by the RUC and B Specials. The claim that the July parades were simply a wonderful car-nival was patently untrue. An occasion for anti-Catholic songs with 'Kick the Pope' phrases in them did not exactly resemble a fun day for Catholics. They were forced to endure the abuse because the State declared that Orangemen could march wherever they chose. It was proof that it was a Protestant country for a Protestant people. Any attempts by liberal Unionist politicians to defuse the yearly sectarian parades by pleading for the marches to be re-routed was resisted. Throughout the 1960s and 1970s and into the 1990s the problem remained, providing a focus for conflict and discontent.

In 1955 Brian Faulkner, a leading Member of Parliament at Stormont, took part in a display of triumphalism on a grand scale. There was a long-running and bitter dispute about Orange parades in the tiny enclave of Longstone Hill in the Mourne Mountains. Each year Orangemen insisted on marching along the Longstone Road, despite protests on behalf of local Catholics. Faulkner marched into the area along with 15,000 Orangemen, protected by large numbers of policemen and the paramilitary B Specials. It was the Unionist riposte to the Sinn Fein vote and to the Catholic community. The Orange Order and the Stormont government failed to acknowledge the sectarian nature of the parades and the offence they caused, and refused to recognize that Catholics had a right to ask that the parades be re-routed from their areas. As always in Northern Ireland, the bigots won the day and Orangeism, which represented a valid and colourful historical dimension of Unionism, became merely a vehicle for crude sectarianism. Faulkner's actions in 1955 conferred on him the persona of the archetypal bigot who fed and nurtured sectarianism for political

83

gain. But the climate was right for promoting hatred: the IRA was about to start another campaign of violence.

At midnight on 11 December 1956 the IRA launched 'Operation Harvest', the code-name for the campaign which it believed would take Northern Ireland out of the United Kingdom. It was a grand scheme, but too grand for the IRA. The plan was to use flying columns of five to twenty men to attack targets in the North, liaising at times with Northern units and returning to bases in the Republic. GHQ believed constant attacks would wear down the morale of the RUC and B Specials. Instructions from the Dublin leadership stressed that civilians were not to be shot at, but it was open season on members of the B Specials. The main problem facing IRA units striking at police stations along the border was that they did not possess anti-tank weapons or mortars. Units were ordered not to take action in Belfast, where IRA violence would be met with a loyalist reaction which could not be contained. The IRA strength was 150 active service volunteers, with other personnel and sympathizers offering logistical support.

The opening of the campaign took the RUC by surprise but it did not achieve its objectives. A courthouse was damaged by fire, a BBC transmitter was blown up, a hut belonging to the B Specials was set alight and a mine damaged a Territorial Army establishment, but two bombs failed to demolish two border bridges. An attempt to blow up a radar station failed when an RUC patrol surrounded an IRA team of three volunteers and arrested them without sustaining a scratch. Later, on 12 December, the IRA issued a proclamation employing grandiose phrases to describe the launch of its campaign. 'Spearheaded by Ireland's freedom fighters, our people have carried the fight to the enemy,' the IRA announced, and went on to claim that a new Ireland was about to be born: 'For this we shall fight until the invader is driven from our soil and victory is ours.'

The IRA printed this proclamation in *The United Irishman* the following month, January 1957, by which time most people knew a campaign of violence was under way. No-one knew whether this latest IRA offensive would lead to major political change on the island or whether it would result in the ultimate defeat of the politics of the gun and the bomb.

5

The Wilderness

The IRA campaign continued with an abortive raid on a police station in the mainly Protestant town of Brookeborough in County Fermanagh in Northern Ireland. As the failure of military operations was nothing new to the organization, they transformed the event into a propaganda success, and it soon found a prominent place in republican folklore.

The raid began on New Year's Eve 1956, when Sean Garland, famous for his role at Gough Barracks, led a flying column from the Irish Republic across the border. From the moment the IRA gunmen left the Republic it should have been clear to Garland that the escapade was going to be a fiasco. His men were armed with home-made grenades, and had only a limited supply of ammunition for some of their weapons. During the attack on the police station, the home-made grenades and the mines failed to explode, and the assailants ran out of ammunition during a furious gun-fight. It was like a scene from the Wild West, with half of Garland's men positioned in and around a lorry, in front of the heavily barricaded RUC station. The rest of the IRA team acted as lookouts on the edge of the town. The real hero of the night was Police Sergeant Cordner, who singlehandedly held off the attackers, and wounded six, two fatally.

Garland and his men were forced to abandon the operation, and fled towards the Irish Republic with RUC reinforcements and B Specials in hot pursuit. The IRA column was hampered by the presence of the two badly wounded men, who were in a critical state. They were left to die in a barn while the others reached the safety of the Irish Republic. According to the RUC, when its men reached the barn they fired into it, but by that time the two IRA men were dead. That did not prevent the IRA from claiming that the police had executed the two.

In the Irish Republic the flying column hid its weapons before the men were arrested by the Irish police. The wounded were conveyed to hospital but not placed under armed guard, while Garland and the others were taken to prison. Although they were all held under the Offences Against the State Act, they only received short terms of imprisonment for failing to answer questions. The bodies of the dead IRA men, twenty-year-old Sean South and nineteen-year-old Fergal O'Hanlon, both from the Republic, were conveyed to their native counties and massive funerals took place. Nationalist Ireland went into mourning, and South and O'Hanlon were depicted as heroes who had sacrificed their youth for Ireland, good-living Catholics who had met their deaths at the hands of RUC executioners. The British government was appalled by the overwhelming expression of grief which followed their deaths, and Unionists warned that it represented tacit support for the IRA.

The Brookeborough raid summed up the subsequent character of the 1950s border campaign. The IRA did not have the weaponry or expertise to threaten the security forces in Northern Ireland seriously. For their part, the RUC and the B Specials were well armed and grew increasingly adept at dealing with IRA offensives.

The IRA leadership considered returning to the 1939 tactic of targeting Britain, but it had neither the resources nor the will. Memories of the failure of that campaign weighed heavily on the minds of some of the leaders. They believed it had provided the justification for the Irish government of the time to destroy the organization, leading to its demise for almost fifteen years. Some of them warned that a re-enactment of the 1939–40 bombings in Britain would re-create a similar downturn in the fortunes of the movement. Perhaps more significantly, by the mid-Fifties, the republican structure in Great Britain was in decline. After the war no attempt was made to reorganize cell structures in English cities. Republicans in Great Britain had bitter memories of the round-up of Irish citizens and the anti-Irish feeling generated by events such as the Coventry bombing. By 1956 they were merely sympathizers, not activists. Visits by members of the IRA to Great Britain in 1955 confirmed republicans' unwillingness to support bombings on the British mainland.

A veteran IRA man of that period told me that

the character of republicanism in Britain had significantly changed by the mid-1950s:

Maybe it was the war which changed our people in Britain. After all, they experienced the Blitz and also the anti-Irish feeling which left many of them ostracized after the '39 campaign. Those of us who languished in the internment camps in Ireland were consumed with our own struggle and the Blitz didn't matter to us. Maybe a new generation of Irish in Britain was also emerging. Many of them still held republican values but they did not have the cutting edge of republicanism in Ireland. Many of them were living in an alien environment, trying to get by, and they didn't have the stomach for it. They still sang republican songs and held the ideal of a united Ireland but the fight to achieve it was not going to be at their expense. I can understand that because the '39 campaign was a disaster and in '56 we did not have the resources to send teams into Britain the way Russell did. It has to be said that he was a good organizer.

I think we knew our limitations in the mid-Fifties. I suppose, if we had possessed the manpower, the weaponry and the money, we would have moved towards a bombing campaign in Britain despite the fact that some of our leaders felt it was counter-productive. If we had been able to do it, those republicans in Britain would have provided back-up even in terms of safe houses or acting as couriers. There would have been no way they could have refused to help their own people. The only way we considered operations in Britain was as a source of weapons. In several instances we sent in our own people and used only a limited number of sympathizers. The '39 campaign provided an opportunity for the police and Special Branch in Britain to target the Irish communities and to build significant dossiers. They were successful in penetrating the IRA structure. After that we were always going to be wary of the security of our people in Britain.

One of the IRA projects in Britain was a raid on a large army base at Blandford in Dorset. A seven-man unit was put into England and arrangements were made with sympathizers to hide the anticipated weapons haul. In a daring operation on 16 February 1958, sentries guarding the armoury were subdued, bound and gagged. However, the operation began to disintegrate when the IRA team came across a group of soldiers near the armoury who refused to be intimidated by threats, and one of the IRA men felt obliged to fire shots over their heads. This alerted the base commander, who rushed to the scene and was then held captive. Fearing the sound of gunfire would lead to a general alert, the senior IRA officer decided to abandon the operation, and the IRA unit returned safely to Ireland, despite a massive police hunt throughout Britain.

In its search for arms, the IRA made contact with the Greek Cypriot EOKA terrorists, with Russians and with sympathizers in Spain, but these approaches proved futile. Apart from gelignite stolen from quarries in Ireland, the IRA was forced to rely on small quantities of weapons smuggled in from the United States. The organization was reduced to cross-border raids on police stations, the bombing of customs posts and the use of booby-trap devices to kill policemen. Nevertheless, it was not the lack of military hardware that wrecked the campaign but the one mechanism which had always destroyed the IRA in the past, namely internment throughout the island. In the North internment was enshrined within the 1922 Special Powers Act and was used from the outset of the campaign. Much to the Unionists' dismay, the Irish coalition government of 1954–7 did not respond in a similar fashion; after all, in 1949 the IRA had promised there would be no future military operations within the territory of the Republic. That promise meant nothing when, to the delight of the Unionists, de Valera was returned to power in February 1957, and he swapped his republican rhetoric of the postwar period for a robust policy against the IRA.

De Valera was a patient man and he waited for an opportune event to allow him to act decisively. He knew it was inevitable that the IRA would commit some atrocity which would offend sensibilities in the Republic and offer him the moral climate in which to act. On 4 July 1957 reports of the killing of an RUC constable and the wounding of another made grim reading throughout the island. Within three days Irish Special Branch arrested scores of IRA activists and most of the GHQ leadership. Internment was back, and so was the Curragh military camp which had housed internees during the war. IRA personnel who were released after serving prison sentences were immediately rearrested and sent to the Curragh. Internment on both sides of the border was not a quick solution, but it gradually forced the organization underground. Its men were constantly on the run and many sympathizers were unwilling to provide safe houses. There were 100 internees in the Republic and over 200 in Northern Ireland. In 1959 de Valera made way for a new Taoiseach, Sean Lemass, who believed the IRA was by then a beaten force. Internment in the Republic was phased out, but the Unionists continued the policy, claiming the IRA still posed a threat. In fact some of those released from the Curragh joined depleted units in the North. The shootings and bombings continued until 26 February 1962, when the IRA announced an end to the campaign.

Internment not only demoralized the IRA but led to dissent within the ranks of those in custody. Traditional splits occurred between those who argued that the politics of the gun were futile, and those who insisted that the only way to pursue the republican ideal was to plan a better military campaign. The cynicism in the movement was best illustrated by the comment of one IRA leader that the 1950s border campaign began at midnight on 11 December 1956 and ended on 12 December of the same year.

One of those who emerged from the Curragh with a new philosophy was Cahal Goulding. He was transformed from the archetypal gunman into a man with a new vision of a political way forward. He claims the metamorphosis took place in prison, where he read books on socialism and where there was time for dialogue. The IRA had always been an organization which demanded strict adherence to both discipline and doctrine. In prison, debate and dialogue allowed for an expression of dissenting views that would have been dismissed outside. Younger IRA officers were in a position to assess the intellectual ability of their leaders, often men they had known only by name and whom they had revered. Many of these leaders proved incapable of articulating their views and were rooted in the past.

Goulding, and others who believed the gun was redundant, told the veterans that the IRA had emerged as losers from every campaign. The only means of changing that was to reshape their political philosophy. Although the gun would not disappear altogether, it would be preceded by a political dynamic designed to win the hearts and minds of the people. The one obvious lesson of the campaign was that Catholics, North and South, had turned away from the IRA. Its political wing, Sinn Fein, was in serious decline because people no longer supported traditional IRA policies.

Many of those who emerged from the camps, throughout the island, returned to the fireside to marvel at past glories; others felt humiliated in their own communities, where they were forgotten figures. For others, it was a changed world. People were fighting to survive economically and saw republicanism as a political anachronism. Catholics in Northern Ireland had no appetite for armed struggle, and viewed the failure of the IRA as the death-knell of romantic nationalism. Many of the Northern republicans blamed the Dublin leadership; there was no love lost between Belfast IRA men and their Southern counterparts. After all, the IRA in the Republic at least lived in a liberated part of the island, whereas IRA men in the North had to suffer Unionist repression.

An IRA veteran who helped found the Provisionals eight years later explained it to me in this way: 'Some of us felt that the Dublin leadership had got it wrong once again. There was too much infighting down there and they lost sight of the objective. Like Goulding they could walk away and get involved in armchair politics and pub rhetoric in Dublin. They could talk a lot of bullshit about socialist principles. They were free to do that while those of us in the North were left to suffer. The Dubliners never properly understood our plight.'

In 1962 Goulding became Chief of Staff, and admits he took over the job because no-one else wanted it. He began to advocate a socialist programme but did not have the intellectual ability to formulate a political strategy for the IRA. He looked further afield for people who could help him achieve that objective, and found fellow travellers among the Irish in Britain, particularly within the Connolly Association in London. This organization espoused the socialist philosophy of James Connolly, founder of the Irish Citizen Army and one of those executed by the British after the 1916 Rising in Dublin. Goulding was drawn to Dr Roy Johnston, a Marxist theoretician who was appointed to the republican leadership and quickly became the IRA's political guru. Goulding and Johnston organized discussions and debates in Dublin, often in pubs, and attracted other intellectuals who regarded it as fashionable to be on the fringes of the IRA.

Johnston produced a Marxist analysis which called for a realignment of the working class on the basis of

Catholic and Protestant class unity throughout Ireland. The guru's views were shaped into what the new IRA leadership called the 'Stages Theory'. Stage one was the breaking down of sectarian barriers in Northern Ireland; this was to be followed by a campaign to detach workers in the Republic from the conservatism of the Catholic State, leading, finally, to a transformation of communal interests into class interests. It is easy to see how this philosophy with its Marxist language was far above the heads of traditional IRA men who believed in a simple objective of ridding Ireland of the British. Republican supporters in the United States who shared an orthodox view of the IRA voiced their disapproval of the Goulding leadership. To them, and their fellow travellers within the IRA in Ireland and in Britain, socialism was synonymous with communism. It was godless, and a deviation from the purity of republicanism. The new brand of republicanism did not please the Catholic Church in Ireland or the Irish political establishment, who saw themselves as constitutionally republican.

Goulding's new-look IRA advocated confronting the Republic's policy of inward foreign investment. It complained about absentee British landlords who owned fishing rights to the detriment of the native Irish. Such tactics were far removed from the recent history of physical-force republicanism with its insistence on preparing for another campaign against the British and the Unionists. Goulding ordered the removal of all IRA weapons to a central dump and placed them under the control of GHQ. Not all IRA units responded to the order – some of them claiming they did not have guns, others sending only half the quantity they possessed.

Again to the dismay of the traditionalists, the Chief of Staff restricted arms training, and sold part of the IRA armoury to Welsh Nationalists. None the less, he did not entirely divest the IRA of the prospect of a military future, and he demanded a military restructuring to make the organization a better fighting force.

Meanwhile, he pursued his political objectives by asking GHQ to devise ways of infiltrating trade unions in Northern Ireland. He had identified the unions as a vehicle for realizing 'stage one', namely the breaking down of sectarian barriers in Northern Ireland. The Goulding leadership also sought to establish a better network of contacts in Britain. On the surface it was a hearts-and-minds exercise in which the IRA conveyed a new and modern political message through Sinn Fein, the Connolly Association and the Trotskyist organization known as the Young Socialists (*not* the Labour Party group with that name). That helped the IRA recruit within the Irish community, particularly in London, but not on a scale which would provide a cell structure. It did ensure, however, that the IRA had members on the ground who were not merely sympathizers but under the control of IRA General Orders.

The only people who continued to regard Goulding's IRA as a security threat were Unionists. The Irish government, though disturbed by the Marxist doctrine, perceived the IRA as a spent military force. The British Labour government of Harold Wilson was unconcerned about them, though Special Branch, particularly in London, maintained agents within Irish political groupings in the capital. Ireland and the IRA were not on the political agenda at Westminster. Northern Ireland was peaceful and in 1963 had a new Prime Minister who advocated liberal policies towards Catholics. He was an Old Etonian and Guards officer, Captain Terence O'Neill, who was from the county set. He shocked fellow Unionists when he shook hands with Catholic nuns and visited Catholic schools. Nevertheless, he was leader of a State which lived off repressive legislation. Unionists still regarded all Catholics as republicans, closet IRA supporters who would overthrow the State given the right opportunity. Catholics were still discriminated against in jobs, housing and schooling; electoral boundaries were still rigged to deny Catholics fair political representation at local and national level.

British governments were content to ignore the plight of Catholics as long as the Unionists maintained order. No-one at Westminster or in 10 Downing Street had any wish to rule Northern Ireland directly or to interfere with the subordinate parliament at Stormont. In fact, British mainland MPs were not permitted to debate or even ask questions about Northern Ireland in the House of Commons, whereas Unionist MPs could discuss the politics of Great Britain. The House of Commons ruling on this absurd arrangement dated back to 1922, when several hundred people died in sectarian rioting in Northern Ireland. The Speaker of the House ruled that the matter could not be discussed. That was one of several precedents which effectively muzzled those British MPs who believed that Unionist misrule should be laid bare by open debate at Westminster. The convention deprived people in Britain of knowledge of the peculiar politics of part of the United Kingdom, and led to apathy in the Commons.

The early to mid-1960s was a period when both the IRA traditionalists and the Catholics in Northern Ireland were in a political wilderness. While Goulding had control of the IRA the traditionalists were forced to take a back seat. Catholics could not change the State, and appeared resigned to the status quo. Captain Terence O'Neill made liberal promises, but he could not deliver because his cabinet, his party and a sizeable section of his own community feared and resented change. His failure to introduce reforms generated a growing disenchantment within the Catholic community. Similarly, the Labour government of Harold Wilson which came to power in 1964 made promises to the Catholics that change would arrive, but economic issues in Britain took priority.

Unionist extremism, in the form of the firebrand preacher Ian Paisley, represented the spectre of things to come. He warned against liberalism, denounced Catholicism and claimed the IRA was waiting in the wings to overthrow the state of Northern Ireland. Many political observers made the mistake of depicting him as part of a lunatic fringe, whereas, in reality, he was articulating a purist doctrine supported by Unionist cabinet ministers. Paisley was the ideal figure for whipping up fear, suspicion and opposition to reform. He was centre stage while others within the Unionist Party and government shaped squalid little backroom conspiracies to unseat their Prime Minister. In 1966 the Ulster Volunteer Force (UVF), named after the private army set up by Sir Edward Carson in 1912 to resist Irish Home Rule, was re-established and began to orchestrate bombings which would be attributed to the IRA. Obviously these bombings served to heighten Unionist fears.

It was inevitable in the 1960s that young Catholic radicals would seek to emulate their counterparts in the United States and Europe. Throughout the world people were involved in civil rights demonstrations, and in Northern Ireland there was every motivation for protest: part of the United Kingdom was being denied the rights of other British citizens. The IRA leaders, forever watchful for an opportunity to exploit events, decided they could channel Catholic agitation through a vehicle which they could control. In 1966 three members of the IRA leadership, Cahal Goulding, Roy Johnston and Thomas MacGiolla, attended a meeting at the home of Kevin Agnew, a republican solicitor who lived at Maghera in Northern Ireland. They proposed that the IRA should instigate a civil liberties campaign modelled on the civil rights movement in the United States. That meeting led to a gathering at the International Hotel in Belfast in January 1967. Those present included members of the Communist Party of Ireland, radical lawyers, several liberal Unionists, socialists, constitutional nationalists, and republicans from the Goulding faction of the IRA. They unanimously agreed to form the Northern Ireland Civil Rights Association, which would be a fact-finding body and would lobby Westminster MPs. In its first year NICRA achieved little and had a low profile, but many Unionists believed it to be an IRA front organization. It might well have become redundant but for the decision of the nationalist MP Austin Currie to stage a protest march in the Northern Ireland town of Dungannon on

22 June 1968. He asked NICRA for permission to use its name for the march, which was aimed at highlighting discrimination in housing allocation. Goulding provided seventy republican stewards to control the event, and the IRA was back in business in a prominent fashion.

The Army Council ordered its men to play a low-key role to deflect Unionist criticism that the civil rights movement was being controlled by the IRA. None the less, Special Branch officers who monitored the march reported the presence of many known IRA personnel and the singing of traditional republican songs when the march ended. Catholic leaders did not regard the presence of republicans as a malign ingredient in the civil rights process. They saw them as showing solidarity along with the majority of the Catholic community in its quest for democratic change. In 1968 the shape of the civil rights movement was being dictated not by the IRA but by disparate groupings led by young Catholic politicians such as John Hume and Austin Currie. There was a distinct naïvety among many civil righters who could not foresee that mass protest in Northern Ireland could lead to violence. Goulding has said that the IRA was apprehensive about putting large numbers of people on the streets and advised against mass membership of the civil rights movement. Despite this retrospective claim, at the time the IRA made no attempt to restrict marches and, if anything, was highly prominent in many of the protests. The IRA was fully conscious of the historical dangers of marching in a divided society. The only organization allowed to march wherever it wished was the Orange Order, which claimed the right to the territory of the province of

Ulster. The concept of Catholics marching, even in towns where they were in the majority, was anathema to the State and to the Protestant Unionist population. The awakening of a subjugated community frightened the Unionist hierarchy, angered Protestant extremists and placed Catholics in a potential confrontation with the security apparatus of the State. Paisley was among the first to decide that a response was needed and he initiated the process of the counter-demonstration. The prospect of elements of the two communities meeting in protest presented a serious security problem because of the probability of sectarian clashes.

Some of the wiser heads in the Catholic community advised against a civil rights march planned for Derry on 5 October 1968. Derry was the blatant symbol of injustice. It was a city with a majority Catholic population where the Unionists employed every aspect of discrimination to ensure Catholics remained second-class citizens. The outcome was that the RUC batoned the protesters and displayed a brutality which shocked the outside world and focused attention on the province. The British government was obliged to scrutinize this festering problem which demanded prompt action. At a cabinet meeting in Downing Street, Harold Wilson discussed sending troops to contain disturbances and keep Captain O'Neill in power. Wilson still believed, five years after O'Neill's inauguration, that he was the man to deliver reforms and to see Northern Ireland out of its difficulties. Wilson's cabinet did not understand the complexities of Ulster politics or the inflammable material which was being assembled for a conflagration.

The IRA ingredient within the civil rights movement induced a radicalism which transferred politics to the streets, generated demands among some Catholics for a campaign to smash the State, and transformed a quest for democratic reform into an effort to end Unionist rule. Within left-wing student politics at Queen's University there were many, some of them republicans, who contended that the Northern Irish State was irreformable and there should be direct British intervention. The students regarded Hume and Currie as 'soft on the issues'. They described them as reformists and ignored pleas from Catholic politicians and Church leaders to suspend marching to allow tensions to ease. No-one was in control of the civil rights movement and therein lay the seeds of its destruction. Many radicals were beginning to look to the IRA for guidance because they were the only people with a history of conflict. The student movement known as People's Democracy was led by young men and women from Catholic nationalist or republican backgrounds who inherited a detestation of Unionist rule and a desire to end it. Many PD members argued that the civil rights leaders were irredeemably reformist and that the IRA constituted the main strategists within NICRA. Other PD leaders argued that, irrespective of NICRA and the IRA, the situation should be pushed to the limit to make Northern Ireland ungovernable.

On 1 January 1969, to the dismay of NICRA and Goulding, the students took to the streets in a march that mirrored the black civil rights march from Selma to Montgomery. Goulding was angry that People's Democracy was stepping outside IRA control, but he was powerless to intervene. The students' objective was to march from Belfast to Derry, a route which would take them through hardline Protestant territory. Provocation was a deliberate part of the PD thesis. They knew they would be harassed by Paisleyites, possibly the RUC and the B Specials. Taking into account the impact on British and international public opinion when the Derry protestors were attacked on 5 October, they hoped to cause a similar reaction. The demonstration achieved its objective: B Specials, out of uniform, colluded with loyalist extremists and ambushed the march. At Burntollet Bridge, close to Derry, the students were savagely beaten and many were injured. The stragglers who reached Derry were attacked by another mob on their way into the city. Those who had condemned the march quickly changed sides and applauded the students. Catholics were angered by the presence of B Specials among the crowds and by the blatant failure of the RUC to protect the march or arrest the culprits. That evening RUC personnel and members of the police reserve rampaged through Catholic areas of Derry. It was the most reckless display of police ill-discipline since the 1930s. The PD protest, which became known as the Burntollet March, was the most important single factor in polarizing the two communities. It drew many civil righters to the PD argument that the Unionist government at Stormont was irreformable. The attacks on the marchers, and the subsequent behaviour of the police in Derry, created a tribal bonding in both communities.

Street protests continued, as did Paisley's counter-demonstrations, and sectarian clashes increased. The

RUC was overworked, overstretched and incapable of dealing with the situation. The Ulster Volunteer Force, by this time the equivalent of the IRA in the Protestant community, again caused explosions which were attributed to the IRA. The RUC and its Special Branch could only find fault with one community and ignored the threat from loyalism. These bombings further fuelled Unionist agitation and coincided with more plots against Captain O'Neill. Members of his cabinet, and a large number within the parliamentary party, conspired to force him out of office. Others encouraged the UVF to increase tension to expose O'Neill's reluctance to abandon his reform programme and admit defeat. His last visit to the despatch box at Stormont was to announce the introduction of one man one vote. He left office on 25 April 1969 and was succeeded by his brother-in-law, Major James Chichester-Clark.

The Wilson government watched the collapse of the man they thought could introduce reform and avert the need for British intervention. Between January and April the British Cabinet discussed 'active intervention' with the use of troops. The Home Secretary, James Callaghan, was asked to draw up contingency plans for the deployment of soldiers but the plans were consigned to files in the Home Office. The Crossman Diaries of that period conclude that no-one in the Cabinet appeared to know very much about Ulster. It had been emphasized to Wilson and Callaghan by the Unionists that if troops were deployed they would have to be placed under Stormont control. That was unthinkable to the Cabinet, which unanimously disapproved of the hardline elements within the Unionist government. The matter was sidelined and Downing Street resorted to the hope that the new Stormont Prime Minister would bring matters under control. No-one in the British Cabinet relished the prospect of military involvement or direct political intervention.

6

The Arrival of the Troops

In April 1969 the *Sunday Times* Insight team made the stark observation that the 'monster of sectarian violence was well out of its cage'. They prophetically warned of the danger of wild men on both sides settling the issue with blood. The Home Secretary sent 500 soldiers to bolster the small British Army garrison of just over 2,000 men led by Lieutenant-General Sir Ian Freeland and based at Thiepval Barracks in the town of Lisburn, fifteen miles from Belfast. Their task was to assist in the guarding of vital installations. Stormont, on the advice of the Inspector-General of the RUC, Anthony Peacocke, told Downing Street the RUC was well able to cope with the civil unrest, and troops would not be required for that task; in any case the B Specials were mobilized in an emergency. However, Stormont did not object to British soldiers assisting the B Specials in guarding major electricity stations and reservoirs. The Stormont Cabinet had no wish to see troops used in support of the civil power because that would call into question the authority, and possibly the very existence, of the Northern Ireland State which had been permitted to act with unlimited independence from its inception. The Government of Ireland Act required that Stormont use all means of the civil power before the British Army could be deployed.

The 'sectarian monster' was indeed out of the bag, and protest marches and counter-demonstrations constantly ended in sectarian clashes. Northern Ireland society was moving inexorably towards a major conflict, and *Sunday Times* journalists appeared to recognize the portents of catastrophe. Nevertheless, the British Army garrison was not preoccupied with making preparations for conflict. Historically, the Northern Ireland posting, particularly for the officer corps, was a pleasant exercise. Senior staff were wined and dined by the Unionist establishment, and there was always time for a game of golf or a spot of fishing. The garrison knew little of the complexities of political life beyond the obvious sectarian divide, and the fact that Northern Ireland had a troubled past. No attempt was made to train soldiers in urban unrest, to acquaint them with the sectarian geography of Belfast and Derry, or to inform them about the complexities of political life in the province. From January to August 1969 there were no briefings about the possibility of troops being deployed on the streets or exercises in map-reading to determine the exact dividing lines between the communities in those areas historically renowned for conflict.

The leaders and the hard men in both communities knew the society was on a collision course. IRA traditionalists in Belfast discussed the organization's potential for dealing with violence and how they could protect the Catholic districts. An IRA delegation from Belfast, led by veteran Joe Cahill, travelled to Dublin and asked Goulding to release guns for the defence of nationalist enclaves in Belfast and Derry. They told him that if there were incursions by loyalist extremists they would be unable to respond. Goulding rejected their request, though he had immediate access to a Dublin arms dump which held fifteen sub-machine-guns, two machine-guns, twenty .303 rifles and two Mark 1 carbines. He told Cahill that a continued campaign of civil disobedience would not attract the violence he envisaged. Cahill and his deputation left Dublin embittered, and confirmed in their view that Goulding was out of touch with events in the North and preoccupied with his Stages Theory. The meeting exemplified the difference in strategy and perception between the traditionalists and the Goulding-led faction. A veteran of that period said:

It was the same old story. Dublin never understood the problems we faced in the North. That asshole Goulding was content to sit in his ivory tower in Dublin and pontificate about a situation we were experiencing. He was out of touch with reality. He talked all this Marxist bullshit . . . He was still convinced about uniting the working class in the North. We knew the place was about to go up in flames. People talk about the split in the IRA which led to the creation of the Provisionals. It began then. Goulding and his mob were not prepared to protect their own people. All they wanted to do was theorize.

Goulding now says he knew that, once guns were released to Belfast and used there, they would create a Protestant backlash which would lead to a massacre of Catholics. I am not convinced that was his sole reason for denying the weapons, since there is no doubt he did not approve of the traditionalist veterans in Belfast; they represented the kind of IRA he sought to change. However, later that year he began to obtain guns and started handing them to men prepared to use them against British soldiers.

The situation on the streets reached boiling point in May and June with the beginning of the Protestant Orange marching season. The Orange Order, and offshoots such as the Apprentice Boys, traditionally marched through or on the fringes of Catholic areas during the summer. Every year there was a special march to celebrate the Protestant artisans, or apprentice boys, who had defended the city of Derry against the Catholic forces of the former king, James II, in 1689. Astute observers identified Derry and not Belfast as the potential flashpoint, suggesting that the planned Apprentice Boys' march in Derry on 12 August would be a catalyst for violence. After the events of 5 October 1968, Catholic agitation moved to the streets and young men in Derry were involved in continual clashes with the police. The city, with its Catholic majority, was seething with anger at the failure of Unionism to bring in reforms or take action over police ill-discipline after the Burntollet March. The

British Prime Minister, Harold Wilson, considered banning the Derry Apprentice Boys' march, but was persuaded to let it proceed. In his memoirs Wilson stated that his decision was influenced by 'unwiser counsels'. Wilson does not make it clear whether it was the advice of the Home Secretary, James Callaghan, who was the cabinet minister responsible for Northern Ireland, that he was accepting. The Home Secretary, for his part, was briefed by the Stormont government, who told him it was confident the march would not lead to violence. Stormont could not have advised otherwise, since the hardliners in Unionism would not have countenanced banning an Orange parade. The Catholics of Derry saw the decision to permit the march as yet another example of injustice; Stormont had no such qualms about banning civil rights events.

The level of debate in Downing Street was not of a high quality. The Cabinet met occasionally within a committee known as 12B which dealt with Northern Ireland affairs. The Crossman Diaries reveal that in May 1969 ministers were poorly informed about the developing situation. Crossman quoted Denis Healey as saying that it was 'like the blind leading the blind'. James Callaghan complained that he was working with a small staff. It is fair to say, however, that Callaghan made every effort to acquaint himself with the situation as it worsened. He made it clear to his cabinet colleagues that they could not hand over control of British troops to Stormont, because, he argued, it would be comparable with the British government giving control of the army to Durham County Council.

In the days before the Apprentice Boys' parade, the Catholics of Derry's Bogside district began making preparations for confrontation and defence. There were many republicans within the city's citizens' defence committee who argued that the march would lead to violence. A young man who was on the streets at that time and is now a respectable accountant gave me this account of the atmosphere in Derry:

Everybody in the Bogside was expecting violence, and in retrospect there were some who relished the prospect. There were genuine fears that the RUC and loyalist mobs would invade the Bogside and a bitter resentment that, after all that had happened, the Unionists were going to parade their sectarian sloganizing in our city. There was a street culture and many of the young men on the streets were out of control . . . They were part of a new culture of confrontation and some of them went on to join the Provisionals. There was a feeling that, whatever had happened in the past, it was not going to happen to us again. The younger element who later joined the Provos were dismissive of their elders as though they felt they had failed and now it was the turn of a new generation to confront the State. That meant confronting the RUC and the Protestants, and that was a recipe for disaster. At that time, the State was corrupt and the RUC and B Specials were the apparatus for enforcing injustice. That was the problem and it was also the fear which combined to create a near-siege mentality in the Bogside.

Petrol bomb installations were set up on the rooftops of flats, and makeshift barricades were erected at potential incursion points. Men, women and children tore up paving stones and shattered them to provide manageable projectiles. On the afternoon of 12 August over 15,000 Apprentice Boys from all over the province descended on the city accompanied by bands, banners and flags. No-one is sure how the violence began, but in the late afternoon marchers and Bogsiders exchanged missiles and the RUC tried to force their way into the Bogside. The RUC repeatedly charged the Catholics and tore at their barricades. The newly elected Westminster MP, Bernadette Devlin (Independent Unity MP for Mid-Ulster), urged the Bogsiders not to weaken and personally fought the police. By nightfall the battle was still in progress. RUC officers summoned reserves and armoured vehicles. Burning buildings created an unearthly atmosphere as the early hours of 13 August saw no let-up in the violence. The police chief at the scene was given permission to use CS gas, but that failed to deter the rioters and often irritated the police when the wind took it in their direction.

At Thiepval Barracks, General Freeland despatched the Commanding Officer of the Prince of Wales' Own Regiment to survey events in Derry. He also released the military supplies of CS gas that were used by the RUC in the Bogside battle. The RUC's Deputy Inspector-General, Graham Shillington, travelled from Belfast to assess the situation personally. He was dismayed to find rows of tired and injured policemen and many others demoralized by their failure to control the situation. The RUC's problem was aggravated by the demands on its resources elsewhere in the province, and the force was poorly equipped for a major street conflict. General Freeland took the precautionary measure of placing troops on standby, and quietly moved a small section of his garrison to the British naval base on the outskirts of Derry. The violence continued throughout 13 August but the Stormont Cabinet refused to request the use of troops. Then the Unionist Prime Minister, Major Chichester-Clark, publicly announced the mobilization of 8,500 B Specials. This was like a red rag to a bull, and word quickly spread through Catholic districts to prepare for an onslaught. Republicans in Belfast discussed diversionary attacks to take the heat off the Bogside. Barricades were erected in West Belfast and other centres, and the RUC came under attack from petrol bombs and missiles. The RUC were losing the battle of the Bogside, and at midday on 14 August the RUC Inspector-General, Peacocke, conceded defeat. He told the Stormont Cabinet that his men could not hold the line and they were in danger of being overrun in Derry.

The overall situation was so serious that the Dublin and London governments were in constant communication. London turned down a suggestion from Dublin that United Nations troops be called in, but listened to the pleas of Catholic leaders in Northern Ireland who demanded the use of British soldiers. The Taoiseach, Jack Lynch, appeared on television and warned that the government of Ireland could 'no longer stand by'. His comments worried an already edgy British Cabinet. James Callaghan was on his farm when Lynch made the speech, and the Home Office telephoned him and asked him to return to London. Callaghan has since confided that 'everybody was jumpy', and that he thought the Taoiseach made the speech because he 'had a rush of blood to the head'. Harold Wilson was on holiday, as were most cabinet ministers, and the Home Secretary was left to deal with a worsening crisis. Callaghan was unsure about how the Irish Cabinet, in particular the Taoiseach, would act. The British government believed that members of Lynch's cabinet such as Charles Haughey, Neil Blaney and Kevin Boland were sympathetic to republicanism. Blaney, the Minister of Agriculture, maintained close links with the IRA. The British Home Secretary was concerned that the emotionalism being exhibited in the Republic could lead to an escalation of events in Ireland. Rumours were already circulating that the Irish Army was on its way to the border with orders to move into Northern Ireland and take the city of Derry. The British Cabinet had no means of judging exactly how the Protestants or the B Specials would react if Irish troops moved to the border or if British soldiers were deployed in Derry or Belfast.

Late in the afternoon of 14 August the RUC Inspector-General put his signature to an official document requesting the use of British soldiers. James Callaghan informed the British public that General Freeland had been authorized to take all necessary steps to restore law and order. He stressed that it was only a limited operation and that the troops would be exclusively under the control of the General Officer Commanding in the province, who was responsible to the UK government. Unionists were told that the arrival of the troops would not compromise pledges that there would be no change in the constitutional position of Northern Ireland without the consent of Stormont. The British Army was ready, and eighty men of the Prince of Wales' Own Regiment moved into Derry. From that moment there have been contradictory explanations of the British government's decision to concede the use of its soldiers. Some people have argued that the troops were deployed to support the civil power – which undoubtedly was a role they were required to fulfil. However, according to Lieutenant-General Sir Anthony Farrar-Hockley, a former army commander in Northern Ireland, the real reason was the need to protect Catholics from the B Specials.

The first batch of troops in Derry arrived to find clouds of tear gas hanging in the air and the Catholics facing B Specials and RUC policemen. The soldiers were ordered to form a protective cordon round the periphery of the Bogside, while the B Specials and the RUC were told to leave the vicinity – much to the delight of the Bogsiders. The general reaction of Derry Catholics was relief followed by celebration. Although some people within the area, mainly republicans, warned against a welcome for the soldiers, that did not deter the battle-weary Catholics from regarding the soldiers as their protectors, and Catholic housewives offered them tea and sandwiches.

Elsewhere in Northern Ireland the situation was grim, especially in Belfast. West Belfast was historically a powder keg with the two communities living in ghettos in close proximity to each other. Throughout the nineteenth and twentieth centuries the Catholic Falls and

Protestant Shankill districts were symbols of the two warring factions, though there was no exact dividing line to separate them. Many Catholics lived in streets leading into the Shankill which were infamous for sectarian skirmishes. Both communities watched events in Derry and expected incursions into their districts. It was simply a question of who would make the first strike. The Protestants of the Shankill, with the B Specials and RUC in their midst, felt confident they could make forays into the Falls. But they were motivated as much by bigotry as by fear, because republicans in the Falls were attacking the RUC in order to overstretch the security forces and draw them away from the Bogside in Derry. The British Army and the British government, closely monitoring events, took the precaution of ordering the 3rd Battalion of the Light Infantry stationed in Plymouth to be ready to move to Northern Ireland at short notice. The army had a ready supply of intelligence from two of its officers who were in Hastings Street police station in the Falls area which was besieged by mobs; and the situation grew uglier by the hour.

On the night of 14 August, while the eighty men of the Prince of Wales' Own Regiment contributed to a de-escalation in Derry, shots rang out in West Belfast. There is no evidence to determine which side fired but the action was sufficient to set alight the smouldering resentment in the Shankill area. Protestant mobs, with the aid of B Specials, rampaged through the streets between the Shankill and the Falls. They ransacked homes and set them alight; groups of people fought each other in hand-to-hand combat. The IRA unit in the Lower Falls assembled a small quantity of weapons including a Thompson sub-machine-gun, a Sten gun, a .303 Lee Enfield rifle and several revolvers. As midnight fell, the rioting was replaced by gunfire as the RUC and B Specials confronted the Catholic rioters, and allowed Protestant mobs to continue their policy of ethnic cleansing. Families forced from their homes risked being shot as they fled with the few possessions they could salvage from their burning houses.

The RUC overreacted by deploying Shoreland armoured vehicles against the Catholics. The Shorelands were armed with heavy-calibre .303 Browning machine-guns and were unsuitable for use in a densely populated area. One bullet from a Browning entered the walls of Divis Flats in the Lower Falls and killed nine-year-old Patrick Rooney in his bed. The IRA unit with its small armoury was no match for the opposition and could not operate at all the incursion points along the Falls. The enormous firepower of the Shorelands cleared the streets of Catholic mobs and enabled the Protestants to continue their arson and looting. Many of the high-velocity bullets from the Browning machine-guns travelled into the sky, and some struck a police station on the edge of the city centre. The men in the building believed they were under attack from the IRA. A similar occurrence in the Crumlin area led to RUC personnel and B Specials firing wildly into the Catholic Ardoyne district.

At first light, the Falls was a scene of devastation, with whole streets of burning homes. Hundreds of Catholic families, their belongings piled on handcarts, made their way to safety. Their attempt at living close to their Protestant neighbours had failed. Five hundred homes, most of them belonging to Catholics, were damaged, at least one hundred of them beyond repair. Six people were dead and scores of others injured by gunfire. Twelve factories were on fire, sending a huge pall of smoke rising above the city. Sporadic firing continued as the Catholic exodus took on the character of the days of the Blitz. At midday on 15 August the RUC and the Stormont government conceded that the British Army would have to deploy soldiers in Belfast. It was not an easy decision for Chichester-Clark and his cabinet, knowing that the troops would not be under their control. Three hours later, men from the Royal Regiment of Wales and the 2nd Battalion of the Queen's Regiment were ordered to move from their barracks into Belfast. Their brief was to place themselves between the Catholics and Protestants, but they still did not know the sectarian geography and had still not been given the opportunity to study maps of West Belfast. Men from the Queen's Regiment were the first to witness the devastation as they walked in combat gear, bayonets fixed, into the Lower Falls. The RUC and B Specials remained within the Shankill as the British soldiers did their best to establish a line along the roads linking the two communities. All the soldiers discovered the Catholics were at first bemused by their presence and then grateful they were deployed to protect them. To the dismay of republicans, the soldiers, and not the IRA, were hailed as their saviours by the population at large. Housewives followed the example of their Derry counterparts and welcomed them as heroes, providing tea, sandwiches and cakes.

The British Army did not have the manpower to cover every potential flashpoint. That evening Protestant gunmen opened fire on Clonard Monastery in the Falls area, and set alight all the homes in nearby Bombay Street. Two IRA men armed with a .22 rifle and a shotgun positioned themselves at a corner of Bombay Street and returned fire into the adjacent Protestant district. Army orders were to use minimum force, yet this was a situation that required more drastic action. When Lieutenant-Colonel Napier of the Prince of Wales' Own Regiment arrived on the scene and saw the houses ablaze, he was unable to intervene because there were insufficient troops at his command. Republicans tried to convince the Catholic community that the British Army was prepared to stand by and allow streets to be razed to the ground. In reality, the army was overstretched and ignorant of the politico-religious complexities. In both communities, mobs began erecting barricades which effectively sealed off whole districts. The army made no attempt to remove the barricades; it merely remained in readiness, more as a deterrent than a threat.

Within forty-eight hours, men of the 3rd Light Infantry arrived from Plymouth, increasing troop strength on the streets to three battalions. Yet the communal violence continued, with mobs from the Shankill invading two Catholic streets in the Lower Falls and setting alight all the houses. Troops were being moved from one crisis to another, often arriving too late to prevent the fighting and damage to property. Within six days of the arrival of the army, ten people were dead, over a hundred were wounded by gunfire, and several hundred homes and ten factories were destroyed. The cost of the damage by today's standards ran into hundreds of millions of pounds. The soldiers erected barbed-wire barriers, and often tried to reason with the local hooligans and community leaders. Their orders to use minimum force were illustrated by their reluctance to return fire when a soldier was shot by a Protestant gunman who was giving cover to a mob burning homes in Conway Street. The RUC and B Specials remained in Protestant areas but it was apparent that the British Army was constantly acting without the approval or the support of the police. It was therefore acting independently of the civil power, and not in support of it.

In Catholic areas, Goulding's IRA was condemned for its inability to defend its community. That was music to the ears of the republican traditionalists in Belfast and Derry, who now began to oppose the Goulding leadership and became prominent in the creation of barricaded 'no-go' areas. Representing themselves as the true defenders of the Catholics, they established citizens' defence committees, and told people that the British Army was not there to defend them and that soon soldiers would be pointing their guns at Catholic enclaves. The defence committees made it clear they did not want the army inside the barricaded zones. However, the majority of Catholics ignored the advice about the army and continued to exchange pleasantries with the troops and give them refreshments. Meanwhile, Goulding, who had consistently and publicly voiced his opposition to violence, was engaged in procuring guns from members of the Irish government and from units throughout the

Republic. To resurrect the declining fortunes of his leadership, the Chief of Staff abandoned his socialist rhetoric and started to adopt a violent approach.

General Freeland, the British GOC, tried to calm the situation. He was televised visiting his troops and talking to local people along the sectarian dividing lines in Belfast. He made it clear that his men were subject to military and not police authority. It was apparent from his demeanour, and his freedom to speak publicly, that he believed the British Army was the organization in charge of security. He was also in no doubt that the honeymoon period for the army would be short-lived. The army's problems were considerable from both a political and a military point of view. The British government did not know how long the troops would be required to remain in place, and the Stormont government was unhappy about their continued presence as peacekeepers. Stormont would have preferred the British Army to be under the control of the RUC, and deployed in an aggressive role against the Catholics. Senior army staff were obliged to attend meetings of the Stormont government's security committee and face impossible demands that they use their troops against the Catholics. For the ordinary soldier, the daily duty was a tiring and thankless task. Soldiers were on duty often for twelve and sixteen hours without a break and were living in makeshift barracks where facilities were inadequate. Most of the troops were untrained in riot tactics and, with their orders to use only minimum force, felt constrained in dealing with mob violence. They were in the middle, not knowing which community might suddenly make them the target of their anger. Furthermore, the presence of barricades made it difficult to maintain law and secure a peaceful future, but the prospect of removing them did not appeal to the army or their political masters in London. There was a real danger that an assault on the barricades, particularly in Catholic neighbourhoods, would lead to bloodshed.

Behind the barricades there was a world far removed from the Belfast the troops first encountered. In Catholic areas the IRA carried out armed patrols, the defence committees planned the procurement of guns and the IRA began to split between the Goulding faction and those who detested his Marxist rhetoric. The barricades prevented the army from building a profile of the membership of the IRA and the new recruits flocking to it. In particular, they stopped military intelligence from assessing the rise of the defence committees and discovering they were being controlled by orthodox physical-force republicans who would soon shape the committees into a new IRA which would be known as the Provisionals. Because of Catholic resentment at the Goulding-led IRA's lack of preparedness in the violent days of August, the defence committees run by Goulding's opponents were more successful in the recruiting drive.

Despite the presence of the British troops as peacekeepers, members of the Irish government conspired with the IRA and the defence committees to provide money and guns for Catholic districts in Northern Ireland. Many members of the ruling Fianna Fail party in the Republic favoured support for the defence committees because they were controlled by traditionalist republicans. The Minister of Agriculture, Neil Blaney, had a meeting with a senior IRA officer in Donegal in early September 1969. Blaney suggested that Northern units of the IRA should detach themselves from Goulding and form their own command. That would enable them to attract financial investors from the Republic.

For its part, the British Army Command was at the mercy of the Home Office and the Ministry of Defence, which in turn dealt with Stormont. An army requires a clear line of authority and a defined policy but there appeared to be none. In September the Defence Secretary, Denis Healey, predicted that the troops would be there for two years but he did not rule out the possibility of ten. The Derry writer and political activist Eamon McCann has argued that the benign attitude to the soldiers has been much exaggerated and sentimentalized. In some respects he makes a valid point because the Catholic welcome was so short-lived. Many Catholic politicians began to believe Stormont was in control of the troops; this was untrue, but the continued presence of the Stormont government made it appear to be in control. From an army standpoint, it would have been wiser for the British government to suspend Stormont, and in retrospect that would have been a sensible strategy. It would have allowed the army a direct chain of command, it would have placated the Catholics, and it would have given time for both communities to begin a process of political reconstruction.

In October, a British government decision to disband the B Specials led to the army's first major confrontation, not with the Catholics but with the Protestants of the

Shankill. Angered by the demise of a paramilitary force which they regarded as their own, mobs descended from the Shankill on Unity Flats, a small Catholic enclave at the edge of the city centre. The army held the line to protect the Catholics and forced the mobs into the Shankill, where soldiers of the Light Infantry came under fire from automatic weapons. The first police victim of the conflict, Constable Arbuckle, was killed, and the army shot dead two rioters. The honeymoon period was over, and the Protestant loyalist hard men walked away defeated, determined not to encourage any further confrontation with the army. By December, plans for a new IRA were well under way, the army was tired of its neutrality and there was a growing awareness in political and military circles that the Protestants posed no threat. The army began to identify an enemy – namely all republicans who wanted to end the state of Northern Ireland. Members of the Army Command maintained it was their duty to defend the civil power, in particular Stormont.

In the opening months of the conflict, Callaghan constantly scrutinized the army's role, but as the new year approached his mind was focused on the forth-coming general election. December proved to be a quiet time for the troops and Christmas appeared to herald a thawing in relations between them and the Catholics. But in January 1970 the Provisional IRA came into existence. Its members established their own Army Council and command structures, and a political wing, Provisional Sinn Fein. They declared that the use of the term 'Provisional' would be dropped after twelve months. The new organization, whose first Chief of

Staff was Sean MacStiofain, contained veterans of the 1940s and 1950s who were determined to return to a purist republican doctrine with origins in the War of Independence and the 1916 Rising against British rule in Ireland. The Provisionals primarily defined their role as the defence of the Catholic population, but anyone with knowledge of the history of republicanism knew they were part of a tradition that held that armed rebellion was the only way to unite Ireland. Privately the Provos identified the British Army as 'the forces of occupation', but knew they were not militarily capable of waging a campaign.

They saw the development of their strategy in three phases: first, the building of an arsenal for the defence of Catholic areas; then a retaliatory role; and finally an all-out campaign against the British Army. The Provisional Army Council warned its members to avoid direct confrontation with the troops until the organization had reached the second, retaliatory phase of its planned growth. This decision to avoid skirmishes with the army for a given period shielded the Provisionals' rise to power. They would begin by using rioting and constant street confrontation with the military to generate a hatred of the troops. The army now faced both the Provisionals and Goulding's IRA, which became known as the Officials.

The new year saw the British Army truly in the front line because it was the only armed force available to counter subversion and civil unrest. The RUC was disarmed; the B Specials were consigned to history. The Army Command began to get tough with rioters. Petrol-bombers were warned they would be shot and rioters were often treated with brutality. In many instances the soldiers behaved with extreme force when faced with extreme provocation. The army was beginning to identify the enemy as the Catholic population with the IRA in its midst. Harold Wilson and his cabinet were preoccupied with the impending general election, and the army was free to develop its own strategy. It was apparent the politicians had failed, and that convinced senior army officers that a military solution was a viable option. The soldier on the street would no longer be worried about petrol bombs or paving stones but the sound of bullets and bombs.

7

Government and the Generals

When the Conservatives won the General Election in June 1970, the Army Command believed the new government would allow them greater freedom to introduce their own solutions. One of those was internment; another was the right of troops to adopt tougher tactics to deal with rioters.

The British Army Command, from the GOC in Northern Ireland, General Freeland, to the Chief of the General Staff, George Baker, had already drawn up plans to put to the politicians in London. Baker had been Director of Operations and Chief of Staff to the Governor in Cyprus in the 1950s, and Cyprus was the model he wished to apply to Northern Ireland. He appointed staff who shared his view and who had colonial experience. Anthony Farrar-Hockley, the army's Director of Public Relations, and an articulate officer who had served with Baker in Cyprus, was made Commander of Land Forces in Northern Ireland. This appointment was evidence that the army knew it was facing a propaganda war and that the soldiers would have to move from policing to a tougher combat role.

The new British Prime Minister, Edward Heath, appointed Reginald Maudling to the post of Home Secretary, but Maudling cared little for Irish politics and paid no more than three visits to Northern Ireland during his time in office. His first brief visit, two weeks after taking office, was a public relations disaster. He told the army it was up to them to deal with 'these bloody people', and on the flight home he turned to one of his aides and said, 'For God's sake bring me a large Scotch. What a bloody awful country!' By effectively placing control of the province in the hands of the army, the British government gave a clear indication that they believed the problem was purely a military one. Whether the army was happy about that arrangement is irrelevant; it was simply obliged to get on with the job without political direction. The responsibility for that development lies squarely with the Heath administration, and the cynical way in which Maudling abdicated responsibility.

Within weeks of the general election, and two days after Maudling's first visit to Northern Ireland, the army had the opportunity to display its get-tough policy in line with its general thesis that the Catholic population and the IRA were the sole enemy to be confronted. After the shooting of six Protestants by the Provisionals, the army decided to act on a tip-off by an RUC informer who had told them they would find a supply of guns in the Lower Falls, the heartland of the Official IRA. The information proved accurate. On 3 July soldiers moved in, and nineteen guns were seized. Local people reacted to the search by attacking troops, despite Official IRA pleas to them to stop. The Official IRA leadership reckoned the nineteen guns were lost but were concerned that rioting would lead to a full-scale search and the capture of their arsenal. The Provisionals were not burdened with such considerations, since it was not their territory, and they threw nail bombs at the troops.

In response, the army poured 3,000 soldiers into the area and fired 1,600 CS gas canisters into the rows of tiny streets. The size of the military presence far outweighed the forces ranged against them. At 10 p.m. a military helicopter broadcast an announcement that everyone was to go indoors or be arrested because the army was moving in. The atmosphere was frightening, with clouds of CS gas hanging in the air and elderly people and children crying and choking as the gas irritated their eyes and throats. As the army assault began, it was met with gunfire, and throughout the night soldiers fought IRA snipers to gain the area street by street. General Freeland denied there was a curfew but that is in effect what he imposed on the area. Four civilians were shot dead, another was killed by an armoured vehicle and there were 67 injured. When the shooting stopped the army ransacked the houses. Members of a Scots regiment showed their politico-religious bigotry by destroying religious items in homes and shouting sectarian slogans. The damage to property by the army was considerable, and much of it resulted from recklessness, if not a deliberate policy to intimidate the population.

The army judged the operation a success because they seized over a hundred weapons, ranging from shotguns to pistols, rifles and machine-guns – in addition to the nineteen guns found the previous day. The discovery of this arsenal proved the army's theory that many guns were being amassed in Catholic areas. They also captured thousands of rounds of ammunition and several hundred pounds of gelignite.

The Lower Falls curfew was a turning point militarily and politically. It contributed to the rise of the Provos, and should never be underestimated. It poisoned the army's relations not just with the Catholics but with their Church and political leaders. In the absence of any political direction from Downing Street or the Home Office, the army had simply acted as it thought fit. The political fallout within the Catholic community was immense; and it was the Provisionals who benefited because they were able to convince people that their assessment of the situation – that the army was in the pocket of Stormont and that the Tories were, after all, Unionists – was correct. This Provo thesis was shared by moderate Catholic leaders; it was the basis of republican politics.

The British Army's concern with politics was limited to a hope that the politicians would agree to impose a state of emergency and establish a clear line of command. It would then be up to the Government, as in other colonial situations, to find the political mechanisms to resolve the problem. Although the army may have believed it had a military solution, in fact it merely had a strategy to deal with subversion. That is why the Chief of the General Staff, George Baker, added

Brigadier Frank Kitson to his Northern Ireland team in September 1970. Kitson was a military intellectual with considerable experience of counter-insurgency techniques in colonial outposts; prior to his arrival he had completed his book *Low Intensity Operations*. He became the *bête noire* of both wings of the IRA and was attributed with every counter-insurgency operation, yet many of the military options he developed were already on the drawing-board before he arrived. But Kitson was certainly well versed in methods of intelligence gathering, interrogation, the use of propaganda and urban warfare. From the beginning of his term, he recognized that the army was operating with one hand tied behind its back: it could arrest rioters caught in the act of violence but it could not get at those who were orchestrating the violence. He described the Stormont government's security committee as a hindrance, and he agreed with Farrar-Hockley that public relations and propaganda were essential for convincing the population in Northern Ireland and, particularly, in Great Britain that the British Army was doing a good job.

Since the IRA operated within a population which was strongly nationalist, Brigadier Kitson believed there was a need for a process of de-escalation and attrition. 'De-escalation' involved the use of propaganda and community projects to damage the IRA's image and detach the organization from its base within Catholic areas. 'Attrition' consisted of a programme to arrest the 'extremists', but Kitson knew the normal processes of law were inadequate to achieve that.

The Provisionals exploded over a hundred devices during 1970, but resisted demands from their rank and file to go on the offensive against the British Army, because the leadership believed the time was not right for such a campaign. There was still a degree of Catholic support for the army among Catholic moderates, who condemned military searches yet also railed against attacks on the soldiers. But things were about to change. A new General Officer Commanding had replaced General Ian Freeland. General Harry Tuzo, who had commanded an infantry brigade in Borneo, was a tough, uncompromising soldier, recommended to George Baker by the incoming Chief of the General Staff, Sir Michael Carver, now Field Marshal Lord Carver. Carver was undoubtedly one of the outstanding intellectuals within the military, singleminded and outspoken when politics compromised the army's autonomy.

At the beginning of April 1971 Carver and Tuzo attended a meeting of GEN 42, the cabinet committee set up by the Heath government to deal with Northern Ireland. GEN 42 comprised the Prime Minister, Home Secretary, Foreign Secretary and Chancellor, and, when necessary, the Chief of the General Staff or the General Officer Commanding in Northern Ireland. The generals entered 10 Downing Street through the back door to avoid being seen by the press.

Brian Faulkner, the new Unionist Prime Minister at Stormont, also attended the meeting. He stressed the need for tougher security; his suggestions included internment and cross-border incursions to seize members of the IRA, and he recommended sealing off the Irish border – a move which would have antagonized Dublin. Some of his more bizarre proposals were supported by members of the committee but not by the generals.

Carver was opposed to internment not in principle but on the grounds that the army could contain the IRA and give politicians time to find a political settlement.

In his autobiography, *Out of Step*, Lord Carver reveals that after that meeting General Tuzo told him that his own objectives were to arrest and prosecute the IRA, impose law and order in Catholic areas and embark on large-scale searches for weapons. Tuzo had hoped to involve the RUC in the role of guarding police stations and doing duty on the border, but they had refused. They had replied that the army was in control and it was their job to provide security. There was no love lost between the RUC and the army, and British intelligence relied little on the advice of RUC Special Branch. In April 1970 the B Specials had been replaced by the Ulster Defence Regiment – simply the Specials in different uniforms. There was no screening to determine the political affiliations of recruits to the UDR. Within one year, it was thought acceptable for the UDR to recruit loyalist paramilitaries, train them, arm them and put them on the streets in uniform. At that stage the UDR was a part-time regiment, but Brian Faulkner demanded that it be transformed into full-time units working with the British Army.

In 1970 the nationalist Social Democratic and Labour Party had been formed, and was the official opposition in Stormont. Heath hoped that the pragmatic Faulkner might be capable of striking a political deal with the SDLP that would marginalize the IRA. As the Provisionals' recruiting drive gathered momentum, the Official IRA knew it was losing support to its competitors and responded by publicly declaring a policy of defence and retaliation. That was demonstrated when Officials in the Markets area of Belfast shot dead a corporal of the Royal Green Jackets. Although Paddy Devlin of the SDLP talked about deals with Faulkner, and Faulkner spoke of involving the SDLP in committees at Stormont, the language of compromise was washed away when two youths, Desmond Beattie and Seamus Cusack, not members of the IRA, were shot by the army during a riot in Derry. The SDLP demanded an inquiry into the deaths but Faulkner refused, and the SDLP left Stormont.

The killings transformed Derry into another Belfast. The city had been quiet, and had not realized much support for the Provisionals. After the deaths, the Provisionals shot a soldier in the head and there were concerted bomb and bullet attacks on army posts. The army defended the killings, claiming Cusack had been about to fire a rifle and Beattie had been preparing to throw a nail bomb. Catholics did not believe that version of events.

The mounting violence led to a meeting of GEN 42 on 19 July. Derry was again alight with conflict and the Orange marching season was in progress, bringing memories of what happened in August 1969 when Wilson allowed 'unwiser counsels' to deter him from imposing a ban on the Apprentice Boys' march. Faulkner told the members of the cabinet committee that if tougher security measures, including internment, were not introduced he would be forced to resign, and the British government might be dealing with Ian Paisley as Prime Minister, or might have to take direct control of the province.

As the scale of IRA activity increased during the summer of 1971 and the Unionists demanded tougher action from the army, Generals Tuzo and Carver reached agreement that the marches should go ahead but be re-routed to avoid the flashpoints which had led to the battle of the Bogside in 1969. They still agreed to avoid introducing internment, but decided that 'disruptive actions' against the IRA would be a way of placating the Unionists. 'Disruptive actions', part of Tuzo's strategy, would include mass arrests, large-scale searches of Catholic areas, and increased stop-and-search measures on the streets. Carver told Lord Carrington, the Defence Secretary, that the fact that the Orange parades in the first two weeks of July had passed off peacefully illustrated the army's ability to deal with the situation. He persuaded Carrington to allow the Derry march to go ahead and to accept the plan for 'disruptive actions'.

GEN 42 met again at 10 Downing Street on 3 August 1971. General Carver advised the Prime Minister that he should not allow himself to be blackmailed on two fronts – namely Faulkner's argument that his resignation would force British intervention and secondly that he would not consider the re-routeing of Orange marches unless internment was the quid pro quo. Carver repeated that the army could handle the situation and 'ride it out'. GEN 42 unanimously accepted his assessment.

After further discussions with General Tuzo, Faulkner rejected the army's advice and demanded a meeting with Heath, who again summoned the members of GEN 42, on 5 August. Faulkner went to Downing Street accompanied by his Private Secretary, Kenneth

Bloomfield, and Howard Smith, the Foreign Office adviser at Stormont. Smith was part of the intelligence connection in Northern Ireland, and was later knighted and appointed Director-General of MI5. He and Bloomfield were present to support the Faulkner thesis. Generals Carver and Tuzo were asked to wait in a downstairs hallway in Number 10 while Faulkner spoke to the other members of the cabinet committee. Faulkner repeated his warnings and his request for internment. Heath listened to Faulkner's views and then summoned the generals to join the discussion.

Harry Tuzo played the leading role because he was the senior officer in Northern Ireland. According to Carver's autobiography, his colleague 'skilfully walked a tightrope'. Tuzo explained the problems facing the army and, in particular, Kitson's view that the judicial process prevented the military from reaching the IRA leaders; they were reduced to arresting rioters and foot soldiers. Unless they were able to round up the middle-ranking IRA officers and brigade staff in cities like Belfast, the conflict could not be contained. I am reliably informed that Tuzo, by explaining the army's difficulties, was unknowingly providing an argument for Faulkner about the need for internment without trial. Tuzo supported Carver's opposition to internment but his explanation of the inadequacy of the powers available to the army suited Faulkner's thesis that more extreme measures such as internment were required to deal with the IRA.

Heath and Carrington decided to extract a compromise from Faulkner to satisfy the Catholics if internment was introduced. Under Faulkner's leadership the number of legally held weapons in Protestant hands had increased by 30 per cent to 110,000. Carrington asked Faulkner to agree to a ban on rifle clubs but he refused. Heath asked him to agree to an indefinite ban on marches but he would only accept a six-month ban. Faulkner was getting more concessions from the meeting than Heath would ever extract from him. He knew the British government would capitulate to keep him in power. Carver and Tuzo were asked to leave the meeting, and in their absence it was agreed that internment without trial would be imposed in August. Heath and Maudling believed that internment would ensure the continued existence of Stormont and wreck the IRA. I believe that decision ensured the continued rise of the Provisionals, a long war and a bombing campaign on mainland Britain.

When Edward Heath agreed to the implementation of internment without trial, plans were already in place at the Home Office, where there were dossiers with the names of 450 suspects. RUC Special Branch provided a list and assured the army that it contained the 'real activists' in the IRA. In fact it included names dating back to the period of internment in the 1950s, as well as many people who were not IRA personnel at all. Two sites, a disused airfield outside Lisburn and an ageing prison ship, HMS *Maidstone* in Belfast Lough, were chosen for housing the internees.

At 4 a.m. on 9 August the army launched Operation Demetrius. Thousands of troops assisted by RUC Special Branch raided Catholic districts throughout Northern Ireland and arrested 342 men. The Provisionals received a tip-off from a highly placed source at Stormont and most of their leaders went into hiding to evade the swoop. Within forty-eight hours, 116 of those arrested were released. Not one loyalist terrorist was included in the swoop, even though the Ulster Volunteer Force was the first organization to introduce bombing and killing to the situation in 1966; the UVF was still causing violence and yet was not considered a threat. Many of those arrested were merely political activists from the trade-union movement and from People's Democracy.

The reaction to the news of internment was bloody, and twenty people were killed during rioting in Catholic areas. Nationalists throughout Ireland were united in condemning the army and Stormont. The scale of the reaction illustrated the failure of the policy. Within days, reports began to emerge that the internees were being brutally treated by the army, and those accounts further inflamed nationalist passions. PD and civil rights leaders such as Michael Farrell were dragged from their homes, beaten with batons and forced to run barefoot over ground littered with glass. Military guard dogs were used to intimidate the internees. A selected number of men were hooded and dropped from helicopters which hovered several feet from the ground. There was a recklessness and ill-discipline within the ranks of the soldiers who shepherded internees to Crumlin Road prison and military barracks. Michael Farrell described to me in an interview how he was kicked and beaten, as he and others were forced to run between two rows of soldiers wielding batons. The internees were in their bare feet and when they stumbled and fell they were kicked until they stood up again. Some were also made to stand on a tea-chest and sing 'God Save the Queen', and beaten if they refused. Farrell was attacked by dogs and dragged to the ground as they tore at his clothes.

After three days, internees at Crumlin Road became aware that some of those arrested were unaccounted for. Eventually it was discovered that seven men had been chosen for selected interrogation techniques which the British Army had developed in colonial outposts such as Kenya and Aden. The authority on what was known as sensory deprivation methods was Brigadier Frank Kitson. The Chief of the General Staff, Michael Carver, denied in his autobiography that he had been consulted about the use of 'special treatment' in the internment process. In fact, senior staff from the interrogation wing of the Joint Service Intelligence School had closely studied the effects of interrogation on British and American servicemen captured by the North Koreans in the 1950s, and similar tactics had been used by the British Army in Cyprus. As the RUC and its Special Branch had no expertise in that field, the authority for the operation would have come from the upper echelons of the Ministry of Defence. The Director-General of Intelligence, who was responsible to the Defence Secretary, Lord Carrington, authorized the setting up of a small team of experts to instruct RUC Special Branch in the relevant techniques. This was not conveyed to General Carver because some people at Whitehall felt he would disapprove. It is not clear whether Tuzo, Farrar-Hockley or Kitson were consulted, though since they were responsible for the day-to-day activities of the army, they could not have been unaware of a specialist interrogation team working within one of their centres. The techniques involved hooding, white noise, standing for hours with fingertips against walls, a diet of bread and water, constant harassment and sleep deprivation.

Preparation for a special interrogation centre had been made long before internment was agreed by Heath. It had its origins in the period when George Baker was Chief of the General Staff and when the army was beginning to draw on its colonial experiences. The Director-General of Intelligence and the Deputy Chief of Defence Staff Intelligence formed a liaison group at Stormont which co-ordinated the preparation of a special unit and the selection of members of RUC Special Branch. Carrington, Maudling and Heath were told of the strategy but not furnished with the details of techniques that were to be used. The Chief Co-ordinator of Intelligence within GEN 42 was Sir Dick White, who was formerly with MI5 and MI6. He was tasked to keep the members of the secret committee informed of intelligence matters. He failed to provide them with exact details of the special interrogation techniques and Lord Carver accepts that he, Heath, Maudling and Carrington, were 'misled'. Lord Carver regrets that he did not pursue the matter with vigour when it was intimated that such an operation was being planned. He agrees it was a crude operation and led to unnecessary criticism and embarrassment for the political and military authorities. Lord Carrington should have known what was going on; it was his area of responsibility, yet it is clear he was not told the true nature of the plans for the use of special interrogation techniques.

Contrary to government intentions, internment suc-ceeded in uniting the nationalist population in the island of Ireland and provided the biggest recruitment boost the IRA had ever experienced. Neither the Officials nor the Provisionals could cope with the number of young men seeking to join their ranks. The Catholic Church, the SDLP, the republican movement and the government of the Irish Republic represented a broad alliance of opposition to the army and Stormont. The one-sided character of internment and the arrest of people who were simply political radicals provided a propaganda platform which the Provisionals exploited more than their rivals within the Official IRA. Both groupings launched a campaign of violence which within four months claimed the lives of thirty soldiers, eleven policemen and over sixty civilians. Damage to property was widespread, and rioting and bombings became a daily occurrence. The internment policy continued unabated, and men young and old from within the Catholic community were arrested and held without trial at the disused airfield at Long Kesh, at Magilligan army base and on HMS *Maidstone*. The conditions in the camps were deplorable. Long Kesh was an assembly of Nissen huts ringed with barbed wire, surrounded by lookout posts and arc-lights.

Ironically, the initial swoops removed the older republicans who could have exercised control over the younger elements. A new leadership emerged in many areas, particularly Derry, where young Provisionals such as Martin McGuinness, more extreme than their predecessors, were more willing to answer all calls for action from new recruits. The loyalist reaction to the introduction of internment was that it was insufficient to deal with the republican threat. Ian Paisley responded predictably by setting up yet another loyalist body, 'The Third Force' – a vigilante organization claiming a membership of 15,000–20,000. The continued political uncertainty emanating from Faulkner and Heath led to the creation of an even larger loyalist paramilitary body, the Ulster Defence Association. Both groupings appeared within a month of the implementation of internment but their members did not attract the attention of the security forces. They were not judged to be the enemy within the United Kingdom. UDA men paraded in masked groups, and their obvious immunity from prosecution angered nationalist politicians. Internment continued to be directed at republicans; and 1971 ended with no hopes of peace.

In January 1972 General Tuzo attended a meeting of the Joint Security Committee. He informed Faulkner and the other members of the group that a civil rights march was planned for 30 January and said the military would adopt a low-key strategy to avoid confrontation with Derry Catholics. Tuzo received a frosty response, and was told it was the duty of the army to take a hard line with troublemakers. Faulkner forecast that the march would lead to violence. The outcome was that the army shot dead thirteen innocent people in what became known as Bloody Sunday. Seven of the dead were under nineteen years of age. I believe the tragic events of that day owe much to the failure of the army to resist the demands of the Joint Security Committee. The 1st Parachute Regiment in Derry acted recklessly and, according to the former Bishop of Derry, Edward Daly, they were guilty of 'mass murder'. Irrespective of the provocation from hooligan elements within the parade and the fact that several revolver shots were fired by a member of the Official IRA, there was no justification for the actions of the soldiers who discharged their weapons. Forensic evidence proved that none of the dead had fired a gun or been in possession of explosives.

In the inner sanctum of 10 Downing Street, the argument between the politicians and the generals did not end. In the summer of 1972 Lord Carver found himself faced with a proposition which he regarded as 'unlawful'.

It was being suggested that it was perfectly legal for the army to shoot somebody whether or not they thought that they were being shot at because anybody who obstructed or got in the way of the armed forces of the Queen was, by that very act, the Queen's enemy, and this was being put forward by a legal luminary in the Cabinet. I said to the Prime Minister that I could not, under any circumstances, order or allow a British soldier to be ordered to do such a thing because it would not be lawful. He did say his legal advisers suggested it was all right but I said, 'You are not bound by what they say. What I am bound by is my own judgement of whether or not the act of the soldier concerned would be legal because in the end it is the courts that decide.'

Sir Edward Heath could not recollect the GEN 42 meeting at which this conversation took place. He told me that it was a long time ago and he would need to 'check up' on such matters. He added that he would never have considered anything unlawful. I also discovered that in 1972 Lord Carver sought permission from ministers in GEN 42 for undercover operations by Brigadier Frank Kitson. That procedure implied that Lord Carver was always concerned that the Government should accept responsibility for military policies which might, at a future date, generate controversy. The conflict between the generals and the Government was to continue until the mid-1970s.

Reactions in Ireland and throughout the world to Bloody Sunday focused condemnation on both the army and the British government. In Dublin feelings of outrage led to a protest by 30,000 people and the burning of the British Embassy. Members of the SDLP declared publicly and privately that the only way forward was a united Ireland.

Edward Heath, faced with mounting international criticism of his government and army, decided that Stormont should be the sacrificial lamb. Its removal would be welcomed by the Dublin government and Catholics in Northern Ireland. The army would be free from the constraints of Stormont, which interrupted its chain of command, and would be able to deal directly with London. Heath played his final card and summoned Faulkner to a meeting of GEN 42 at which he declared that Stormont could remain in place but it would not have any responsibility for security. A Stormont without security would resemble a county council with very highly paid executives with private cars but little power. Heath knew Faulkner could not deliver that package to his cabinet colleagues, his parliamentary party or the loyalist population. Faulkner and his cabinet had no option but to resign. Stormont was suspended, direct rule was introduced, and William Whitelaw became the first Secretary of State for Northern Ireland. Fifty years of Unionist rule were at an end, and the conflict was about to begin in earnest.

8

Echoes of the Coventry Tragedy

The British people watched events in Northern Ireland with a mixture of horror and disbelief. They were happy that 'it was over there', and no-one predicted that both wings of the IRA would turn their attentions to mainland Britain. For the older generation there was the lurking fear that the IRA might repeat its pre-war campaign, but for most people the violence of the late 1930s was only a vague memory. Bloody Sunday changed all that: the deaths of thirteen people at the hands of members of the Parachute Regiment in Derry on 30 January 1972 was the catalyst for the beginning of a bombing campaign in mainland Britain.

Both wings of the IRA were concerned only with revenge. The Official IRA had an advantage over the newly formed Provisionals because it had a small core of sympathizers and the basis of a small unit in London. Even before Bloody Sunday both wings of the IRA had separately discussed revenge attacks in Britain. For older members of both organizations the recollection of the 1939–40 campaign and the inability of the IRA to mount a campaign in the 1950s had been a deterrent. Now Cahal Goulding and the rest of the Army Council of the Official IRA listened to suggestions from the rank and file that a revenge attack on the Parachute Regiment at its home base at Aldershot in England would be met with approval because of the international outrage flowing from Bloody Sunday. Within a week the Army Council had sanctioned an operation at Aldershot. There was an urgency within the Official IRA to upstage the Provisionals, since both were seriously committed to winning the hearts and minds of the many young men who were clamouring to play a part in the conflict. The Officials moved swiftly, and scheduled the bombing for 22 February. Without their England connections, they would have been unable to meet such a close deadline, but they intended to act quickly and kill a large number of soldiers. Throughout the 1960s the Officials had nurtured their small network in England, and within it was the basis of a tiny unit which could be activated to assist hard-core operatives from Ireland who might be required for their expertise in bomb-making or operational tactics.

Seamus Costello, the Officials' Director of Operations, felt confident that he could move explosives into Great Britain using a ferry route from Ireland. He knew that the English police were not vigilant because they were not expecting an extension of the IRA campaign to the mainland. A London unit was to store explosives, hire cars and make available any other items required for the attack. Costello and four volunteers from Ireland travelled to London in two cars and met at the home of forty-two-year-old Noel Jenkinson, who lived at St James's Lane in Muswell Hill, North London. Over several days they discussed their objective, and Jenkinson was asked to buy military combat gear which Costello then used to gain access to the parachute base at Aldershot. He walked around it and made a mental picture of the layout and the most suitable place for planting a bomb to take the most lives. When he returned to Muswell Hill he sketched a plan of the barracks. He later told Goulding that he had marked the regimental sleeping quarters as the target. I was told by a former associate of Costello that in fact he had targeted the building which contained the restaurant.

Eventually Costello decided against bringing explosives into Britain, after the London unit told him it would be easy to steal a quantity of explosives from a firm in Somerset. Two of the Irish volunteers were sent to check out security at the company, and two days later they removed 222 lb of gelignite, as well as detonators. The loss was not immediately detected, and the terrorists proceeded with their plans, storing the gelignite in a rented garage 300 yards from Jenkinson's home. Costello told his team that they would drive a car containing a bomb into the base. He said security was lax and no-one there expected a car bomb. He calculated that it would be advisable to put the bomb in place at least five hours before it was due to explode, so as to give the bombers time to make their escape. He wanted his team out of the country when the bomb exploded. A similar tactic had been employed by the IRA in Coventry over thirty years earlier. Several of those on the Army Council in Dublin were in the IRA during that period and they knew it was important to get the active service team out of England before police sealed airports and ferry routes. The team could fly out of London well before the bomb went off, or leave on a ferry the day before. Costello decided that two cars would be driven to Aldershot in the early morning of 22 February when civilian workers were entering the base. The car containing the explosives would be put in place, and another car would follow with a small detonating device which would be attached to the car bomb as the final stage in the operation.

Jenkinson hired a blue Ford Cortina from a firm in Holloway, using the fictitious name 'Michael Carey'. A large quantity of explosives were placed in the boot of the Cortina. Three small bombs were made using clothes'-peg timers, and stored in plastic lunchboxes. Costello reckoned that only one of these smaller devices would be needed to detonate the main charge; the others would be retained in the rented garage for future use in mainland Britain. Jenkinson was detailed to drive the car bomb to the base at 7 a.m. and park it. The second car would not attract attention because the smaller detonating bomb would be in a plastic lunchbox; the driver would activate it, put it in the hired Cortina and then drive Jenkinson from the scene. Costello planned to have all but one member of his Irish team out of the country the evening before the explosion. He would leave one explosives expert to accompany Jenkinson and remain in London for a week to ten days.

The plan went ahead without a hitch on 22 February, except that the car bomb was placed not near sleeping

149

accommodation but outside the officers' mess. Costello later lied to the Army Council and said his men 'fucked up' and left the bomb in the wrong place. The timer was set for midday, when officers were gathered in the mess for lunch. The car bomb was parked at the side of the three-storey building which contained the dining area on the first floor and the kitchens directly below. Seconds before the bomb exploded, fifty-eight-year-old John Hasler was working on the lawn outside the mess and Captain Gerry Weston, the Roman Catholic padre, was making his way to the mess. They were killed instantly. Five women died when they caught the impact of the blast as it ripped through the ground-floor kitchens, reducing the area to rubble. The force of the explosion wrecked windows 200 yards from the scene and left many injured. Soldiers used their bare hands to pull away the debris to find the dead and rescue the injured. Before the full horror of the crime was known, the Irish Republican Publicity Bureau in Dublin, a front for the Army Council, stated that the explosion was in retaliation for Bloody Sunday and had claimed the lives of high-ranking officers of the Parachute Regiment.

The public reaction in both islands was swift and uncompromising. Brendan Corish, leader of the Labour Party in the Republic, said the killing dishonoured the dead of Bloody Sunday and put back any notion of Irish unity.

Police officers investigating the atrocity had a breakthrough when two constables on the beat arrested twenty-eight-year-old Michael Duignan, who lived in Raynes Park in London. It was the day after the explosion, and the constables found Duignan carrying a polythene bag: inside were a .410 gun with a shortened barrel, 200 rounds of ammunition for use in a variety of weapons and twelve copies of the Sinn Fein newspaper the *United Irishman*. Duignan admitted he was on his way to dump the bag because he did not want to be in possession of incriminating materials. Under interrogation, he said he had been given the bag by Noel Jenkinson. Within twenty-four hours police arrested the leader of the London unit and found the two small explosive devices in his garage. Explosives experts reckoned that, if they had not arrived that day, the small bombs would have exploded within 85 and 72 minutes respectively. Police believe they were intended for targets in London. Other items found in Jenkinson's garage were a combat jacket, two camouflage suits, a pistol holder and a webbing belt; this confirmed that the IRA had used military fatigues to gain access to Aldershot. Jenkinson's prints were found on the inside of tape used to hold the sticks of gelignite to the timer of one of the smaller devices. At his trial he was found guilty and sentenced to life in prison with a recommendation that he serve at least thirty years. Duignan was given three and a half years for possessing a firearm without a certificate and conspiracy to pervert the course of justice. The ringleaders, including Costello, were never found. The court was told that Duignan admitted to having been a member of the IRA before he arrived in London in 1965 and that he had visited Dublin earlier in 1972. He had told Detective Sergeant Thompson that he had gone to the Sinn Fein office of the Official IRA at Gardiner Place and while there met Sean Garland, the IRA's Assistant Chief of Staff, and Mick Ryan, the Quartermaster, whom he knew before he lived in London. The purpose of his trip to Dublin, he said, was to buy quantities of the *United Irishman* because the paper was not available in London.

Cahal Goulding was never sought for the crime, yet he was the Chief of Staff and had sanctioned the operation along with other members of the Army Council. Several years ago I interviewed Goulding, and he used the word 'we' to indicate his part in the bombing. He talked about Seamus Costello being a good Director of Operations and how 'we' decided to 'put a bomb in the billet and blow them to bits'. 'Seamus had one of his specialists in charge of it and he wasn't such a great man,' he told me. 'When he went in with the bomb in the car he got cold feet. He decided he would set the time for one o'clock or something like that, and put it against the restaurant. But the bomb went off one or two minutes sooner and there was no officers in the thing . . . the operation wasn't carried out as it should have been.'

The mastermind of the Aldershot murders, Seamus Costello, later met a violent death at the hands of those who sanctioned the killings of innocent people in February 1972. He split from the Official IRA in 1974 to form the Irish Republican Socialist Party and its military wing, the Irish National Liberation Army, of which he appointed himself Chief of Staff. The breakaway from his former colleagues led to a feud which caused the death of the Official IRA Commander in Belfast and a failed assassination attempt on Sean Garland. Goulding and other members of the Army Council knew Costello was the mastermind of those actions, and they ordered his assassination. In 1977 Costello was blasted with a double-barrelled shotgun as he sat in his car in a Dublin street.

The bombing at Aldershot was compounded within weeks by the brutal killing of a young British soldier returning on leave to his native Derry. Ranger William Best, aged nineteen, had escaped the misery of unemployment by joining the army. In 1968 he was one of the youths on the barricades. The Official IRA in Derry seized him, interrogated him and shot him dead. The next day 500 women marched through the Bogside to Official IRA headquarters and vented their wrath for the killing of a local youth. The murder lost the Officials support in Derry, and the Provisionals became the dominant force there. As a result of the condemnation following Aldershot and the death of Ranger Best, the Officials called a ceasefire, and from that time they abandoned their campaign in Britain and watched while the Provos controlled the conflict.

The Provisional IRA also considered a revenge attack in Britain after Bloody Sunday, but did not have the London connections which the Officials had nurtured for so many years. Sean MacStiofain, the Chief of Staff, pointed to some of the successes of the 1930s campaign, and suggested that a long-term strategy was desirable. He advocated putting volunteers into England to become integrated into the community, so that they would be there to be activated when a plan was finalized. Daithi (David) O'Connell, an IRA veteran and member of the Provisional Army Council, argued that bombing England would be counter-productive. He thought there was a possibility that, with Stormont abolished, the British might seek a deal with the Provisionals; bombs in mainland Britain would destroy such a prospect. The disagreement at Army Council level resulted in a stand-off between MacStiofain and O'Connell and discussion of the matter was suspended. O'Connell could be compared to the Gerry Adams of today because he believed there was room for a negotiated settlement. He felt that a long campaign would lead to further bloodshed, and the eventual disintegration of the IRA through splits and war-weariness. Having watched the failure of the 1930s and 1950s campaigns, he believed the disappearance of Stormont offered a window of opportunity for the IRA provided they could maintain pressure on the British soldiers on the streets of Northern Ireland.

O'Connell was not far wrong in his assessment of British political attitudes. In 1972 the cabinet committee GEN 42, without the presence of the Chief of the General Staff or General Tuzo, contemplated a negotiated settlement and the eventual withdrawal of troops. I was told that those discussions were kept secret from the army because it was felt that some of the military leaders would disapprove of negotiations with the IRA.

The IRA leadership had begun to feel the pressure for peace within its own community, and from the Catholic Church in Ireland. Much of the community pressure originated in Derry, where the killing of Ranger Best, and other acts of violence, encouraged calls for an end to IRA violence. Martin McGuinness, the young Provisional Commander in Derry, conveyed the feelings of his area to the Army Council in Dublin in a statement suggesting that a temporary ceasefire would cool public anger towards the IRA. O'Connell saw an opportunity to use a plea for peace as a means of suspending violence and demanding talks with the British. William Whitelaw, the Secretary of State for Northern Ireland, rejected the offer, and replied that he could not talk to people who were pointing a gun at his head.

John Hume and Paddy Devlin of the SDLP were impressed with the IRA decision to seek a constitutional way out of the crisis, and met O'Connell and MacStiofain. They were assured of the IRA's sincerity and called on Whitelaw to respond positively. They suggested that the Secretary of State should begin the process by conducting a dialogue with the Provo leadership. Events moved quickly, perhaps too quickly for the British government, and Whitelaw was given the backing of GEN 42 to talk to the IRA. Two big mistakes he made in convening talks with them were to allow them to dictate the size of the IRA delegation and to agree to London being the venue for formal talks. He also agreed to the release of a young Provisional, Gerry Adams, whom the leadership chose for their delegation. Whitelaw ordered his release from Long Kesh internment camp and placed him in the custody of the SDLP Chief Whip, Paddy Devlin. Adams was provided with a special pass to allow him to negotiate a safe passage at military roadblocks. The Provisionals demanded that talks be preceded by the guarantee of political status to IRA prisoners. The IRA leadership was elated when that was agreed without argument. It conferred on internees a prisoner-of-war status which enabled them to behave as a military force within the camps and prisons, and to portray the holding centres as concentration camps. The release of Adams was significant, because he was one of the young hardline Provisional leaders who saw compromise as dangerous. Many senior IRA officers regarded the inclusion of the articulate Adams as a foil to the Dublin element in the delegation, particularly O'Connell.

A meeting was organized for 20 June 1972 between two Whitelaw aides and Adams and O'Connell. Its purpose was to hammer out the details of an IRA ceasefire to accompany formal talks between the two sides. Whitelaw's aides reported back that O'Connell was a man with whom they could do business. He was articulate, intellectually sophisticated, and he knew how to conduct himself without being threatening. Adams, on the other hand, was a tough, uncompromising person who demanded that a truce would only be agreed if the British Army stopped its arms raids and arrests.

Whitelaw was too far down the road to retreat. He had already conceded a great deal, and was forced to declare publicly that the army in Northern Ireland would reciprocate. The British Army was dismayed and angry that decisions were being made without proper consultation with the Army Command in Northern Ireland and the Chief of the General Staff in London. It appeared that a new political approach was being employed to reverse the process that had existed from August 1969 whereby the army shaped the political and military policy for the province. The army was presented with a *fait accompli*: within a fortnight of the IRA truce, which came into force on 26 June, a secret meeting would take place between representatives of the British government and the IRA. Two military intelligence officers would be handed over to the IRA in Derry, and held there to guarantee the safe return of Martin McGuinness from talks in London.

The Provo delegation comprised two of the founders of the Provisionals, MacStiofain and O'Connell; McGuinness, the Derry Commander; Adams, representing those in the internment camps; Seamus Twoomey and Ivor Bell, leaders of the Belfast Brigade. On 7 July the IRA men were flown by helicopter to the military base at Aldergrove Airport outside Belfast, transferred to a Royal Air Force flight and taken to London, to a house at Cheyne Walk in Chelsea which was the venue for the Whitelaw conference. The Provisionals were in uncharted waters, and they lacked the experience and finesse to conduct fruitful negotiations. O'Connell saw the occasion as the beginning of an important dialogue with the British; he appreciated that his opponents had already conceded a great deal and knew they could not move too quickly because of the risk of alienating the army and provoking a loyalist uprising. But Adams, Twoomey and MacStiofain made impossible demands on Whitelaw. They called for a public declaration of British intent to withdraw from Northern Ireland; the removal of the troops by 1 January 1975; and an immediate amnesty for all political prisoners. Whitelaw, unable to yield to these demands, proposed a gradualist approach, with continued dialogue and a second meeting a week later, when he would spell out the British government's position on partition and on British military withdrawal. Adams, Twoomey and MacStiofain were not convinced of Whitelaw's sincerity. Nevertheless, they agreed to meet him again, and planned to use the intervening period to pressure the British with the aid of the clergy and nationalist politicians.

Two days later the peace process was in ruins, and with it an end to direct negotiations with the IRA. No-one will ever be sure whether the events that wrecked the negotiations were engineered by the British Army or by members of the 1st Battalion of the Provisionals in West Belfast, but they took place in the Lenadoon area. For two days there had been tremendous intimidation of Catholic families in Belfast, and the army had appeared to do little to halt this loyalist violence, which had caused 300 Catholic families to leave the Rathcoole district on the outskirts of the city. It seemed at the time that the army was under instructions not to confront the UDA. Some of the displaced families were allocated Northern Ireland Housing Executive properties vacated by Protestant families in the vicinity of Lenadoon. The UDA was angry that more Catholics were moving into that district and threatened to destroy the houses if the government-controlled Housing Executive proceeded with its plan. Housing Executive officials asked the army to provide protection for the re-housing programme, and the Provisionals said they would defend the families if the army declined to help. Talks were held between Twoomey and British Army officers in West Belfast. The IRA's truce and the prospect of a second meeting with Whitelaw were probably on Twoomey's mind when he contacted the Provisional Army Council and told them what was happening. MacStiofain advised him to discuss the matter with the army and if he received no satisfaction he was to give them a deadline for agreeing to provide protection for the displaced families. MacStiofain and O'Connell observed that if Whitelaw was serious about finding a settlement his resolve would be tested by the army's response.

Five hours after Twoomey met the army a van loaded with furniture for a Catholic family arrived on the fringe of Lenadoon and was turned away by soldiers. Near by, a UDA mob formed behind the army lines, and a Catholic crowd gathered to witness the outcome. A riot developed, the Provisionals appeared with guns and a major gun-fight followed. The truce was over and, with it, hopes for peace. One can speculate on who scuppered the negotiations and the truce, but my own suspicion is that the army was not prepared to go down the road with Whitelaw, and seized an opportunity to draw the Provisionals into a situation where they would have to deliver on their primary role of defending their own people.

I spoke to former members of the IRA who were in the Lenadoon area the weekend the truce ended. They said the army was unwilling to confront the loyalists and was unhappy with Whitelaw's dialogue with their enemy; there was a deliberate military policy to ignore loyalist paramilitaries, and that would have influenced the events at Lenadoon. It is doubtful, however, if Whitelaw could ever have successfully negotiated with the IRA. Adams and MacStiofain distrusted the British and were not able negotiators. Whitelaw's capitulation early on in the discussions encouraged the Provisionals to believe they had the upper hand, and that violence easily achieved its goals.

From that moment onwards, the Provisionals were confident that they could bomb their way to a conference table even if it meant a long war. Later that month, on what became known as 'Bloody Friday', they bombed the heart out of Belfast, killing nine people and injuring scores of others – men, women and children. The slow-burning fuse of resentment in the loyalist community, intensified by the anger at secret deals between Whitelaw and the Provisionals, set light to one of the worst periods of violence in the last twenty-five years. While the IRA continued its violence, the UDA and the UVF killed hundreds of Catholics before the year ended. Some of the victims were tortured in the most horrific way, yet little military action was taken to stamp out the loyalist murder squads. The end of the political dialogue, brief though it was, also placed the British Army once again in a primary role.

Covert military squads, using both loyalist and republican agents, carried out killings which were blamed on the IRA. They employed the type of counter-terrorist tactics used in Kenya, Palestine and Aden. At British Army HQ a psychological-warfare unit, known as the Information Policy Unit, indulged in a propaganda war which eventually proved an embarrassment for Whitelaw and his successors. It appeared that once again there was no effective political control of the army on the ground. Its leaders believed they had ways, some of them bizarre, of winning the war. On 1 December 1972 bombs exploded in Dublin while the Dail was sitting to discuss anti-terrorist legislation. Blame for the blasts, which killed two and injured eighty, was attributed to the IRA. The Dail learned of the carnage and passed the legislation; but the perpetrators were not the IRA. Irish Special Branch told the Taoiseach that British intelligence colluded with loyalists to plant the devices. That assertion was not made public until two years later when a similar operation was carried out, killing twenty-two people in Dublin and four in the town of Monaghan in the Irish Republic.

MI6 controlled intelligence until the end of 1972, and many of their methods, contacts and use of dubious agents were blamed on the British Army and loyalist paramilitaries. The army had its own covert groupings such as the MRF, the Military Reconnaissance Force (or Military Reaction Force). It recruited military personnel from different regiments and terrorist organizations, then put them in units which carried out unattributable shootings of a sectarian nature. Their activities were not always sanctioned by the Army Command, but their brief was to draw the Provisionals into a shooting war with the loyalists in order to distract the IRA from its objective of attacking the army. It was part of the counter-insurgency tactic of trying to criminalize the enemy: by committing acts of violence which could be blamed on the IRA, or by shooting inno-cent Catholics to make it appear as if loyalist murder squads were responsible, the army intended to drag the Provos into a campaign of revenge killings. This can only be described as 'State-sponsored murder': the State did not sanction such operations, but the army left it vulnerable to that charge.

At British Army HQ in Lisburn, the shadowy figures in the corridor which housed the Information Policy Unit mounted a campaign of lies. In blackening the reputation of Northern Irish and British politicians, and in their often successful attempts at manipulating the media, they demonstrated the extent to which parts of the military structure controlled the dissemination of information. This poses the familiar question: whether an army in control is by definition an army out of control. At some levels it was undoubtedly acting against the interests of both its own command and the Government of the United Kingdom. Perhaps this was a symptom of the confusion within the Government itself, and the absence of a clear political objective. The year 1972 was the beginning of the long war. It epitomized the failures of all those involved: politicians, churchmen, paramilitaries, governments and the British Army.

9

Close England

At the end of 1972 the Provisional IRA Army Council met in Dublin to discuss the failure of their talks with Whitelaw and how to continue their campaign. There was general agreement that the Heath government was prepared to accept a certain level of violence in Northern Ireland. Sean MacStiofain returned to his theory that 'the British people needed a short, sharp shock'. He was supported by Daithi O'Connell, who had opposed bombing mainland Britain when it was proposed in the wake of Bloody Sunday. Within Long Kesh, where there were constant debates about the way forward, there was a demand for action on the mainland. A representative of the Belfast Brigade told the Army Council that they were prepared to undertake a mission in Great Britain and had the people to do it. The brigade had developed an intelligence cell which handled a grouping of well-educated young men and women who were not known to the security forces. The cell was run by the

1st Battalion, which covered the Andersonstown and Upper Falls districts. There were two teacher training colleges, St Mary's and St Joseph's, sited within the 1st Battalion precincts. Several women students in the former and a number of young men in the latter were recruited, and they stored guns in the colleges.

The three most promising recruits were Hugh Feeney and two sisters, Dolours and Marion Price. They were controlled by an intelligence officer attached to the Brigade Staff who later disappeared in mysterious circumstances. His departure led to Feeney and the sisters coming under the direct control of the Brigade Staff. There have been many stories written about the Price. sisters which included outrageous claims that they were 'deadly snipers with Armalite rifles', that they made bombing runs in Belfast, that they were on the Brigade Staff and that they hid weapons after ambushes. Dolours and Marion Price joined the Provisionals in 1970 through the female wing of the IRA, Cumann na mBann. A short time later, they were recruited for intelligence gathering and met members of left-wing organizations from Europe, which resulted in Dolours making a trip to Milan in March 1972 in order to establish contacts with people in the Lotte Continua, who had lines of communication to the Middle East and the arms route. The Italian government expelled her after a week, but British intelligence simply regarded her as just another student flirting with the European Left. The sad state of the intelligence community in Northern Ireland was illustrated by the fact that on her return to Belfast she was not interviewed by the army or placed under surveillance.

The Price sisters and Hugh Feeney were not asked to undertake operations which would place them at too great a risk, and expose their cover. However, unlike Feeney, the sisters expressed support for the Provos in their area and occasionally spoke to visiting journalists. None of those journalists suspected they were active IRA volunteers. Much of what was written in later years was pure fantasy. It was alleged they organized the bombings on Bloody Friday in July 1972. One report claimed Dolours was involved in the assassination of the Milan police chief, Luigi Calabresi. An outsider reading many of the newspaper stories would have concluded that these two young women were the most deadly operatives in Belfast. According to another report, Dolours travelled 1,400 miles in five cars to collect money for the IRA. Unless a journalist or member of the intelligence community had clocked the cars, how could anyone have known the mileage was 1,400? What is true is that the Price sisters were dedicated republicans, from a family with a history in the movement, and they made no secret of their allegiances but were careful to conceal their IRA membership. Their family history made it almost inevitable that they would join the IRA at a time when feelings were running high, particularly among young people.

When the Belfast Brigade told the Army Council it could provide the staff and expertise for a successful bombing in mainland Britain, the sisters were already on the register for such a job. The Provisionals did not trust IRA sympathizers in England, and the experience of the 1930s campaign and the Aldershot bombing convinced them that they should rely on their own people. The Army Council ordered that bombing be restricted to targets in the centre of London but also ruled that there should be no loss of life to civilians (though they did not say how that would be achieved!). MacStiofain recommended striking at the heart of the English judicial system with an attack on the Old Bailey. O'Connell added New Scotland Yard to the target list. The planning for the operation began in January 1973, and it was intricate in its detail. The objective was to place car bombs in central London, timed to explode while the IRA team were on flights out of London. Dolours Price, who was a methodical individual, was placed in overall control of the operation. She was told that only she would be in possession of all the information about the people involved, the targets, the hotels where the team would stay in London, and the routes to and from the capital. It would be her role to delegate jobs to the others.

The Brigade Staff chose the following volunteers: the Price sisters, Roisin McNearney, Hugh Feeney, Martin Brady, Gerard Kelly, William Armstrong, Liam McLarnon, Roy Walsh, Paul Holmes and a young man whom I can only refer to as 'Dave'. Roisin McNearney was a recent recruit to Cumann na mBann when she was selected for the mission. She had been recruited by older and more experienced women and, by IRA standards, was a novice who had yet to finish her probationary training; she was also nervous about the operation. Aside from Feeney, the male members of the group were volunteers with experience of active service. The oldest was William Armstrong, who was aged twenty-nine and married with five children. Paul

Holmes joined the team in January on his release from the Long Kesh internment camp.

In addition to the bombing team, the Belfast Brigade and members of GHQ staff in Dublin picked a larger group of IRA staff to provide logistical support in Belfast and Dublin. The Army Council selected 8 March 1973 for the attack on London, and preparations began in earnest in the middle of February. Between 16 and 21 February four cars were hijacked in Catholic districts of Belfast. Their owners were held at gunpoint, detained for a short period and warned that they would be shot if they announced the disappearance of their vehicles. A garage in West Belfast was 'encouraged' to undertake the respraying of the vehicles: a Vauxhall Viva was sprayed blue; a Hillman Hunter, bronze; a Ford Corsair, green; and a Ford Cortina, green. The cars were driven to Dublin, where they were fitted with false number-plates of English origin and converted into travelling bombs. They were then kept in lock-up garages awaiting a signal that the team would be arriving in Dublin. GHQ also kept two stolen back-up cars in a Dublin garage and armed them with explosives.

In February, Dolours Price and Martin Brady visited London on several occasions and selected hotels where the team would stay, and places where their cars could be parked the night before the bombings. Brady went on the trip because he was the only one with a good knowledge of the capital; he had worked for a short time as a waiter in a restaurant in Jermyn Street, near Piccadilly.

On 4 March the team was shown the four resprayed cars, and two members of the group were instructed in the techniques of arming the bombs. They were given a detailed briefing by a senior member of GHQ staff, and discussed their project with the Chief of Staff, MacStiofain. The following day, the Vauxhall Viva and Ford Cortina were driven onto the *Munster*, the ferry to Liverpool. In that first group were Feeney, Armstrong, Walsh, Kelly and McLarnon. One would have thought that, after the bombing of Aldershot only the year before, two cars from Dublin with five young men might have attracted attention. The ferry docked at 6 p.m. and the two cars were driven to London. They arrived after midnight and parked the cars, as prearranged by Dolours, in a car park at Clipstone Street close to the Post Office Tower. Feeney took his companions to Bloomsbury Street where they booked into the Gresham Hotel. Feeney had £800 in cash and paid for two rooms. Each of the men signed the register with a false name.

On 6 March the Hillman Hunter and the Ford Corsair boarded the same ship accompanied by Holmes, Brady, Marion Price, Roisin McNearney and 'Dave'. Their arrival in England became fraught with difficulty when a Customs and Excise officer noticed that the Hillman Hunter did not have a tax disc. He asked to see the car's log-book but was told that it had been left in Dublin. Under further questioning the driver said the car was registered in Dublin but he was from Belfast. The officer asked why the driver was travelling from Dublin when he could have taken a ferry from Belfast. The driver replied that he had been on holiday in Dublin. The conversation became even more bizarre when the Customs officer asked why the car had English registration plates. The driver replied that his brother had bought the car in England, taken it home to Dublin and lent it to him for a few days. The log-book, he said, was with his brother in Dublin. The Customs officer would not know until later that he was standing beside a car loaded with explosives. He told the driver to remain in the car while he went to his office to make further enquiries. Marion Price left the car to go to the lavatory, while the other passengers remained in the vehicle. After ten minutes the Customs officer returned to the car and told the driver he was free to leave.

During a two-night stay, the IRA team stayed in different hotels in order not to attract suspicion. Feeney spent part of his time booking airline tickets for the return trip to Dublin, and taking his companions on a tour of the target sites. Dolours Price flew to London on 7 March and joined Feeney and her sister in the Belvic Hotel, where they went through the final details of the plan. Dolours Price had a notebook containing all the necessary information, much of it in a code which only she understood. Under the initials of various members of the team were her assessments of their performance with the letters 'OK', and alongside Feeney the phrase 'connections connections', referring to the bombs which Feeney had been instructed to wire up. Dolours also had a detailed diagram of a bomb-timer circuit on one of the pages, since the wiring-up of the bombs in the four cars was complex. Each timing mechanism consisted of an interceptor, a clothes' peg, a warning bulb, wiring, an electrode, a battery and wires which would only be connected at the last possible moment.

Each car was wired in the following fashion. Under the front passenger seat was a small wooden box with two compartments: one contained a modified alarm clock for setting the detonation time, the other a switch and warning bulb. A double length of white plastic detonating cord ran from the box, under the floor carpet, to a detonating charge under the rear seat. That charge was made up of twenty 8-ounce cartridges of gelignite known as Quarrex. This was the initiation charge to set off twenty-nine plastic bags containing a home-made explosive comprising potassium chlorate and nitrobenzene.

The notebook also contained the times when the car bombs were scheduled to be placed at their targets, and details of the gang's return flights. The name of each car was written against the name of the respective target and the initials of those responsible for the task. Later that day the sisters went to the Royal Court Theatre to watch *Freedom of the City*, a play about Bloody Sunday. Feeney asked to accompany them but was told to talk to the others and ensure they knew exactly what they had to do.

The following morning most of the gang received alarm calls at 6 a.m. and had breakfast before setting out on their mission. They picked up the cars from a garage in Dolphin Square where they had left them overnight. At 7.15, Holmes, accompanied by 'Dave', drove the Corsair to New Scotland Yard and parked it in a spot vacated by a detective who had just finished night duty. The Hillman Hunter was parked at the Army Central Recruiting Depot in Whitehall; the driver was Brady and McNearney was in the front passenger seat.

The Vauxhall Viva was taken by Kelly and Walsh to the building housing the British Forces Broadcasting network in Dean Stanley Street in Westminster. The fourth car, a Cortina estate, was driven to the Old Bailey by Armstrong, with McLarnon seated beside him. Armstrong waited in a queue of cars to find a parking space. A policeman saw the car being parked and two men walking from it. At New Scotland Yard a secretary saw one of the men kneeling in the rear of the Corsair (in fact he was wiring a bomb). She was intrigued when he left the car and placed money in a parking meter because there was a rail strike that day and it was public knowledge that parking in London was free. Her curiosity did not encourage her to question what she saw and the car driver made his way from the scene. By 8.30 a.m. all the bombs were at their targets, and the alarm on each of them was set for 3 p.m. By 10.15 a.m. all the members of the team were at Heathrow Airport.

In the meantime two observant police officers at New Scotland Yard had become intrigued by the registration plates on the Corsair. Constables Stanley Conley and George Burrows were on duty when their attention was drawn to the fact that the number-plates showed a J registration which was a 1970 issue, whereas the car itself was a 1968 model. Believing it to be a stolen vehicle, they contacted Inspector Ronald Edwards, who noticed that the entry holes used to secure the plates were duplicated by others, confirming the constables' suspicion that someone had changed the number-plates. Then the inspector peered inside the car and saw detonating wires under the front passenger seat. Immediately he radioed for assistance, and when explosives experts arrived they found the passenger door open and were instantly struck by the pungent smell of gelignite. They defused the bomb; half a cleaning cloth was wrapped round the timing device. The other half of that cloth was later found in Marion Price's coat pocket.

The bomb contained 170 lb of explosives and would have caused massive damage to life and property. The discovery of the device led Commander Robert Huntley of the Anti-Terrorist Squad at the Yard to issue the order: 'Close England'. Airports and ferries were warned that IRA bombers might be about to leave the mainland, and police officers throughout the country were put on alert as the other bombs ticked away.

At Heathrow, the IRA team members were discussing their good fortune as they waited with other passengers for their flight. They were unaware that one of their bombs had been defused, and that every police officer at the airport was watchful. The Price sisters and Hugh Feeney were booked on a later flight but were waiting in the departure lounge with their companions. At 10.45 it was announced that passengers travelling to Dublin should embark. PC Brian Moberley and a colleague were watching several of the group when they sensed that one of the men was nervous about their presence. Moberley radioed his suspicions as they moved out of his sight. At Scotland Yard orders went out to Special Branch and other staff to make for the airport and arrest the group.

McNearney, Brady and Kelly were seated in the plane when seven of their companions were held in the airport precincts. An order was given to detain the flight and the three were escorted back into the terminal. All passengers for that flight were questioned, but suspicion centred on ten people who could not provide satisfactory answers for documents found in their possession. Dolours Price, travelling under the alias 'Una Devlin', was found in possession of a second airline ticket in the name of a Miss S. Sinclair, the alias used by her sister. The others also had aliases which they gave to the officers detaining them. McNearney was 'Susan Brady'; Kelly, 'James Lyons'; Brady, 'James Baker'; Holmes, 'James Sinclair'; Walsh, 'Brian Clark'. Armstrong used the surname 'Hunter', and McLarnon said his surname was 'Jones'. Some of the gang pretended not to know each other, but their answers to particular questions and their general demeanour convinced the officers that they had the bombers. By midday all the team members were in custody apart from 'Dave', who had escaped the net at the airport. He had gone to the men's lavatory and returned to see his companions being questioned. He left Heathrow and returned to Ireland several days later on a ferry.

Time was running out for Scotland Yard. Two bombs had been defused but if the IRA had used such a large team it was likely that other bombs had been planted in the capital. Detectives pleaded with the gang to tell them if there were other devices but were met with a wall of silence. Anti-Terrorist Squad officers were at a loss to identify the individuals in the gang, but some of them felt that the two older women (the Price sisters) and Feeney demonstrated an intelligence and superiority which pinpointed them as the ringleaders. At 1.56 p.m. the IRA telephoned

The Times, using a recognized code. The caller named four targets and claimed the IRA team had returned to Ireland. Meanwhile, a detective asked Marion Price if he could infer that the timing on other bombs was about to expire. Marion Price smiled, looked at her watch but did not reply.

Despite the warning, there was confusion, and police on the streets were not properly informed of the exact location of the targets. Only the bomb at the British Forces Broadcasting centre was discovered and defused. When the remaining two bombs exploded shortly before 3 p.m. scores of people were injured, some of them seriously; cars were flung across roads, and the damage to property was extensive.

In subsequent interrogation sessions, detectives found eighteen-year-old Roisin McNearney and nineteen-year-old Liam McLarnon were the only ones willing to make statements and to express regret. After the trial, which began on 10 September 1973, McLarnon and McNearney were both sent to prisons where they were separated from the others. On the day they were all sentenced, many of them convicted largely on the strength of these statements that had incriminated them, the male members of the gang hummed the death march when McNearney entered the dock. They believed that she, more than McLarnon, had divulged many of their secrets, and the IRA penalty for that offence was execution.

The lesson from that period was that, with committed members of the IRA such as the Price sisters and Hugh Feeney, the Provisionals were proving they could target Britain with greater 'success' than those who mounted previous campaigns. Scotland Yard later told the media that in the weeks before the bombings they had received intelligence that an atrocity was being planned by the IRA. That was damage limitation after the event, and was to be a feature of Scotland Yard tactics over the next twenty years. It was patently obvious, even in 1973, that luck had played a greater part than hard intelligence in the detection of the IRA team. The IRA squad had been able to move explosives freely across the Irish Sea and into London. Security at the ports was lax, and it was not much tighter at Heathrow. The operation had been carefully planned, but its failings were what mattered to the IRA. It was an organization that learned from its mistakes. The same could not be said of the security forces. Nevertheless, it was difficult to maintain tight security on sea traffic because 50,000 heavy vehicles, and as many cars, used the ferries each month. There were also continental routes out of the Irish Republic which were sometimes used by the Provisionals to put their activists into Europe and then into Great Britain.

After the capture of the Price sisters' team, at least two separate units of the Provisionals were operating in England, travelling over to carry out attacks and returning to Ireland immediately afterwards. These groups were organized from Dublin and there were usually four in a team, including couriers. They were responsible for a spate of bombings in England in 1973–4.

On 29 August 1973 two bombs exploded in Solihull and an incendiary device went off at Harrods in London. Attacks were made on transport, including explosions at two London railway stations on 10 September 1973. Ten days later a bomb exploded at Chelsea Barracks, and on

23 September a soldier in Birmingham was killed when he tried to defuse a bomb. There were further explosions in London in December that year.

On 4 February 1974 a bomb was planted on a coach carrying servicemen and their families. It exploded when the coach was on the M62 near Bradford. Eleven people died, and the size of the bomb was such that some of the bodies were found over 200 yards from the scene of the blast. Judith Ward, a young woman who confessed to being involved, was convicted of causing the explosion and sentenced to thirty years in prison. She later retracted her confession, and after a long campaign eventually her conviction was quashed on 4 June 1992. The real culprits were never found.

From June 1974 London began to be hit very hard by the Provisionals. On 17 June a 20-lb bomb exploded at Westminster Hall, injuring eleven people. There were explosions in Manchester and Birmingham on 14 July, and three days later a bomb went off at the Tower of London, killing one person and injuring forty-one. Despite the severity of the bombings, the IRA personnel involved were still based in Ireland and obliged to travel to and from England to carry out these attacks, and operatives therefore still ran the risk of being trapped, like the Price sisters, as they hurried back to Ireland within hours of planting the bombs. It was not possible for the Provisionals to organize a sustained campaign in Great Britain in this way.

The procurement of Semtex made it easier to move explosives into England because it does not give off a smell and can be moulded into many shapes for easy concealment. At the same time the Provisionals learned that they needed people living inside English communities if they were to develop a major campaign in England; such people could be activated when the materials were in place and the targets identified. Therefore they returned, in part, to the methods of the IRA in the campaign of 1939. O'Connell and MacStiofain were associates of many of the veterans of earlier campaigns, and drew on that history when they planned their actions and tactics.

The Price sisters, Gerard Kelly and Hugh Feeney illustrated the Provos' reliance on past history when they employed the traditional tactic of the hunger strike to force the British government to allow them to serve their sentences in Ireland. The sisters went on hunger strike for 205 days and were force-fed for much of that time. Their resilience should have been a warning of the type of terrorist being recruited into the ranks of the Provisionals. They won their battle with the support of leading figures in Britain, Catholic churchmen in both islands and senior members of the SDLP. In 1974 Harold Wilson's government relented and removed them to the women's prison in Armagh in Northern Ireland. By 1981 the ringleaders such as the Price sisters, Feeney and Kelly had been released. Ironically, several of those who had played subordinate roles remained in prison. The hunger strike proved a successful form of political blackmail, and the Provisionals used it again in 1980 and 1981. By that time there was a more ruthless Prime Minister in power: the tactic failed, and ten IRA men starved to death, one of them the Westminster MP, Bobby Sands.

10

The Most Dangerous Men

By 1974 there were heightened fears that the British Army in Northern Ireland was no longer under the control of the elected government of the United Kingdom. On 6 December 1973 the Heath government had arranged for representatives of the British and Irish governments to meet members of the Unionist Party, the SDLP and the Alliance Party at the Civil Service College at Sunningdale in Berkshire. The outcome of this conference, the Sunningdale Pact, consisted of a plan for power-sharing in government and the establishment of a Council of Ireland for cross-border co-operation in trade, industry, transport, roads, health and so on. In January 1974 a Northern Ireland Executive was established at Stormont Castle with Brian Faulkner as Chief Executive and Gerry Fitt of the SDLP as his deputy. Executive ministers were drawn from all three main Northern Ireland parties.

Not unexpectedly, hardline Unionists denounced the

Sunningdale Pact and set up an organization they named the Ulster Workers' Council (UWC) to oppose the Northern Ireland Executive. With the collapse of the Heath government in February 1974 after the miners' strike and the three-day week, the lack of continuity in the British government as usual led to political confusion and on 14 May the UWC began a 'strike' which paralysed industry throughout the province. The loyalist paramilitaries barricaded streets and highways and by means of intimidation prevented people from going to work. Harold Wilson, once again British Prime Minister, asked the Chief of the General Staff, Sir Peter Hunt, if troops could be used to bring the strike to an end. However, the GOC in Northern Ireland, General Frank King, was not prepared to use his soldiers against the loyalists, and a message was eventually relayed to Harold Wilson through the Ministry of Defence asserting the established British Army policy of concentrating on the IRA and avoiding confrontation with the loyalist paramilitaries.

There was a serious conflict of interest between the army and the Labour government in May 1974. In many respects, it was reminiscent of the disagreements between Lord Carver and the members of GEN 42 in 1971–2. In May 1974 Sir Peter Hunt spoke to General Carver, who was then Chief of the Defence Staff, and conveyed his concern that the Secretary of State for Northern Ireland, Merlyn Rees, and General Frank King disagreed about the role of the army. General King and his superiors felt that the army could not deal with two enemies. He told Merlyn Rees that there was a danger that the army would have the IRA at its back if it faced the loyalists. King also contended that the army did not have the technical expertise necessary to run power stations should a decision be made to wrest them from loyalist control. Army policy was consistent in that it assumed the IRA posed the major threat to the State and the whole of the British Army of the Rhine would be required if the army moved against the Protestants. There were many soldiers in the army with Ulster connections and there was no guarantee that elements of the RUC and the Ulster Defence Regiment would not support the UWC.

Wilson's capitulation to the UWC led to the collapse of the Northern Ireland Executive on 28 May 1974. This reinforced the Unionist claim to hold a veto on any future settlement, further lowered the Catholic community's opinion of the army, and convinced Unionist hardliners that the army would never do the bidding of Downing Street if that would conflict with the will of the Protestant population. Relations between the British Army and the Government deteriorated, and the army was judged to be out of control.

Already the army in Northern Ireland seemed to have the freedom to do as it wished, although ministerial approval had certainly been given for most of the covert operations and exercises in black propaganda that occurred during the 1970s. Military intelligence officers were recruited by the security service, MI6, for cross-border operations and told not to reveal this to their army superiors. When the intelligence service, MI5, took over security in 1973, MI6 instructed its agents from the military not to divulge their MI6 activities to members of MI5 and not to assist MI5 in field intelligence work. The British Army itself used blackmail techniques to coerce young men to join the IRA and act as agents (I have given detailed accounts of all these tactics in my book *The Dirty War*).

After five years of dirty tricks and political mis-management, the Ministry of Defence, Home Office and Foreign Office provided a joint report that led to the setting up of a committee at Stormont to 'clean up the mess' and remove control of information from the army. The solution, however, was merely a propaganda drive to improve the image of Northern Ireland, organized from Stormont Castle with guidance from Foreign and Home Office controllers. To prevent the army from manipulating the media, the new committee supervised the handling of most of the press enquiries about political and security matters.

While the British mess was being cleared up in Northern Ireland, the Provisional IRA was putting into practice lessons learned from the capture of the Price sisters and their accomplices. The Provos were preparing to send their most dangerous men to England.

In 1970 Harry Duggan was a fresh-faced eighteen-year-old from a respectable family in the beautiful countryside of County Clare on the west coast of Ireland. His school records suggest he was a bright and quiet lad who excelled at sport and whose talent lay in practical pursuits. He left school at sixteen, trained as a carpenter, and showed little interest in politics until the violence in Northern Ireland led to the formation of the Provisional IRA. In the spring of 1970 he was frequently observed attending Sinn Fein meetings – the prelude to his entry into the IRA. From that moment his lifestyle became erratic, and his training sessions with the Provisionals resulted in frequent absences from his family home which he explained to his mother by telling her he was looking for work. One of his IRA colleagues told me that Duggan quickly became committed to the IRA and demonstrated considerable skill in the use of weapons. He was regarded as fearless, and cool under pressure. Within three years he was operating outside the jurisdiction of his native county. This enabled him to evade the scrutiny of local police and Special Branch. His father, who lived apart from his wife, saw his son for the last time at Christmas 1972. Harry Duggan had gone underground with IRA units.

In 1970 Duggan's friend, nineteen-year-old Martin Joseph O'Connell, joined the Provisionals, and brought to them his experience as a radio operator with Marconi in Cork. His knowledge of electronics and signals helped him transfer his skills to the techniques of bomb-making. Like Duggan, O'Connell lived in the rural environment of County Clare. His parents were law-abiding and his mother was a teacher in a local primary school. They were unaware of their son's commitment to republicanism. O'Connell's school records showed he was an intelligent and academically gifted pupil. By 1973 he was a skilled bomb-maker whose activities were unknown to Irish Special Branch or the security forces in Northern Ireland. Like Duggan, he operated with active service units on the Irish border.

Edward Butler was twenty when he decided to express his inner republican feelings by painting 'Brits Out' slogans on walls in his home town of Castleconnell in

County Limerick. The Irish police arrested him and he was charged and fined for defacing public property. He did not pay the fine and disappeared from the area into the hands of the Provisional IRA in Dublin. It was 1971 and he was twenty-one years old.

Duggan, O'Connell and Butler were three young men living far away from the violence in Belfast and Derry. A burdensome history, cultural memory and the fashionable and accepted nature of republicanism at that time drew them towards expressions of conflict. They were living in a Republic where cabinet ministers believed it was acceptable to support the IRA and to furnish them with weapons. Their State was born out of conflict and yearly celebrated the blood-sacrifice tradition of the 1916 Rising. Many people in the Republic, not just in the IRA, believed that partition represented unfinished business. The three young men were motivated to help their co-religionists who claimed to be under attack in the North. Butler's 'Brits Out' slogans highlighted the growing disillusionment with the role of the British Army by 1970. The three only had to look at the constitutional claims of the Irish Republic to justify the ongoing march of republicanism.

In 1970 Hugh Doherty lived with his family in Glasgow and worked as a labourer. That summer, when he was twenty-one, he made the annual pilgrimage with his family to the ancestral home at Carrigart in County Donegal. Ireland was where he preferred to be. The wild and rocky hillsides of Donegal offered a beauty and tranquillity not to be found in the hard streets of Glasgow. Donegal was also ideal terrain for IRA training camps, and provided a rest and recreation centre for IRA

Provisionals from Derry, the closest Northern city. It was the territory of the Irish cabinet minister Neil Blaney, who advocated support for the republicans. Doherty was imbued with romantic nationalism, much like the American tourists who visited Ireland every year. The opportunity to join the IRA detached him from his humdrum life in Glasgow.

These four young men were brought together to form a self-contained IRA unit because their exploits, their dedication and their ability to evade scrutiny and capture set them above many other volunteers. Duggan was the only one who was registered as a republican activist, but his whereabouts were unknown to the security forces and he was not on any wanted list. Towards the end of 1973 the IRA Army Council planned a fresh campaign of bombing in England and asked GHQ to find ideal recruits, young people who could live in England for a long period. It was not long before Duggan and the others were identified, summoned to Dublin and interviewed by staff from GHQ. They were told they would be required to live in London and should 'acclimatize themselves with the city' before they were made active. It was pointed out that the Price sisters' experience was an important lesson to the IRA. The sisters and their team were caught because they had to leave the country a few hours after an operation. Their usefulness had been limited to one job, since police and Special Branch in England had been able to seal off the ports and airports within minutes of the discovery of one of the car bombs. The method of avoiding that trap was to put a small unit into England where its members could become part of the society.

As O'Connell seemed more intelligent than his companions he was given the superior rank within the unit. He was the bomb-maker – a role vital to the whole operation. Each of them was told that on no account were they to frequent Irish pubs, be seen in Irish communities or talk to anyone with Irish connections. They would be given enough money to rent accommodation away from Irish neighbourhoods. The Provisionals did not trust the Irish community, believing it to be penetrated by Special Branch and MI5. O'Connell was instructed that the unit would operate at all times in teams of two, and it was his task to decide which of his companions went on operations. They would have two flats so that, in the event of capture or detection, two members of the unit could continue to bomb London. If captured, they were not to make statements and their duty was to refuse to recognize a British court.

GHQ explained that a separate IRA team comprising two women would find them suitable flats. There were two regular women couriers who were living in England; they were not known to the intelligence community. They would give the unit £1,000 a week in cash to pay for their accommodation and other living expenses. GHQ suggested they dress respectably, though such advice was not necessary in the case of Duggan or O'Connell, who liked wearing suits. None of the four resembled any tabloid portrayals of terrorists as shabbily dressed and wild-eyed. GHQ chose them because they were capable of blending into London society. They were warned against having English girlfriends, but were allowed normal leisure activities such as going to the cinema or restaurants. The money was intended to finance a social life that would enable them to become familiar with London. The story of the four is critical to an understanding of the manner in which the IRA developed its England operations over twenty years. It was the beginning of the use of long-term activists on the mainland, similar in some respects to the IRA campaign of the 1930s. The age, demeanour and commitment of the group of four made them a ruthless and formidable team. They shared the same interests and regarded their work as more interesting than chasing girlfriends. If there was a failing in the unit, it was their arrogant belief that they were superior to the forces ranged against them. O'Connell and Duggan were cocky, and often expressed the view that they would never be taken alive.

IRA planning had been more meticulous and extensive than the preparations for the Price sisters' operation. Explosives had been stolen from English and Welsh quarries and small quantities of detonators and gelignite were transported from Dublin in cars driven onto ferries. An additional supply route had been set up between England, Amsterdam and Brussels. A small European cell stored supplies of guns, explosives and detonators which were provided by ETA, the Basque separatist organization. They in turn arranged for a link between the Provisionals, the Libyans and the Palestine Liberation Organization (PLO); the go-between was based in Italy and was part of the left-wing Lotte Continua. Dolours Price had been photographed with members of that group before she was deported from Italy. Since British intelligence was unaware of the supply routes to European capitals, the new team of terrorists was guaranteed a constant and unlimited supply of guns. The IRA knew that, once a campaign began in England, Scotland Yard Anti-Terrorist Squad officers would increase security on all the British—Irish ferries and airport routes between Britain and Ireland but not between Britain and continental Europe.

In the spring of 1974 Duggan and his companions travelled separately to London and stayed in hotels and boarding houses until two flats were acquired. Another team of four was installed in the Midlands with a similar brief. By September the London team were living in two flats and were in regular contact with their couriers. The four met to discuss targets, and went to cinemas, pubs and restaurants. O'Connell had some scope in selecting targets, and there was a list from GHQ of people and places they wished the team to 'hit'. O'Connell drew maps of target areas, pubs and homes of politicians. He also had maps of Amsterdam and Brussels, cities he visited to discuss and examine the quality and quantity of the explosives held by IRA people in both places. Duggan was O'Connell's right-hand operative and always carried a Magnum pistol. Doherty was given the job of maintaining surveillance on target areas and reported to O'Connell any potential security problems. Butler, like Duggan, was a gunman and his job was to protect O'Connell or Duggan when they planted explosive devices.

In Ireland, the IRA informed many of its members that Duggan was dead. They said he had been killed in an explosion in Ulster and been buried secretly. The news was conveyed to his father and others close to him. The IRA knew that the information would filter into the public arena, and eventually be heard by British security forces. It had been discovered that the British Army and Special Branch in the North had asked questions about Duggan during the interrogation of an IRA volunteer who had operated with him. GHQ reacted quickly to plug what they saw as the only dent in the security of the London unit.

The four young men began their work on 5 October 1974. They planted bombs in two public houses in Guildford, Surrey, killing five people, two of them soldiers, and injuring fifty-four. No warnings were given because the bombs were intended to cause the maximum loss of life. Both bars were often frequented by soldiers. One month later, they struck again at a pub in Woolwich which was the 'local' for soldiers stationed at a nearby barracks. The no-warning device killed two people, one of them a soldier, and injured twenty. Three weeks later, on 21 November, the team in the Midlands exploded bombs in two pubs in Birmingham, killing twenty-one people and injuring 162, many of them seriously. One bomb was placed under a bench in the Tavern in the Town, the other beside a telephone in the Mulberry Bush. Bomb warnings were later telephoned to the *Evening Mail* and the *Birmingham Post*, but the caller gave only general locations and not the names of the pubs. The Midlands team was withdrawn within weeks, after police arrested the wrong men, and they later returned to the Irish Republic, where the squad's leader, a twenty-six-year-old Dubliner, was eventually gaoled on arms charges.

Unfortunately, the six innocent men were convicted

and sentenced to life imprisonment until a miscarriage of justice was admitted and they were released in March 1991. A similar fate befell four young Irish people who were wrongly convicted for the bombings at Guildford and Woolwich. The Guildford Four were not released until October 1989. Although the scandal of the wrongful convictions has tended to overshadow the tragedy of the deaths from the bombs, in 1974 the sheer scale of the carnage in England created an overwhelming sense of outrage and generated a degree of anti-Irish feeling.

The Army Council sent a message to the London team to suspend operations for several weeks in December, but to prepare a plan to bomb the London Underground system during the Christmas 'rush'. O'Connell and his fellow terrorists were elated at the prospect of further action, and felt no remorse about the loss of human life in the pub bombings at Guildford and Woolwich. A former member of GHQ staff informed me that O'Connell and his team told a courier they were 'at war' and 'casualties were inevitable'.

Provisional IRA violence in London had the effect of renewing contacts between the organization and intermediaries representing the Wilson government. Those contacts were constantly in place from 1972, but at times there was little dialogue. The England bombings generated frantic exchanges between two Foreign Office officials and the Provos; the conduit for that contact was a number of churchmen who were trying to convince the IRA that its campaign in both islands was counter-productive and lacked popular support. In circumstances similar to those of 1993–4, it was suggested that there could be a role for the IRA in the political process, a recognition of its political wing, Sinn Fein, and concessions in relation to internment. Sinn Fein was not an effective body, and was run by men with limited experience of politics and few ideas. It was no match in the political battle with the SDLP, which was run by men like Austin Currie and John Hume who were well educated and politically astute.

The Northern leadership of the IRA was in the hands of Joe Cahill and Seamus Twomey, part of the older generation of activists who were politically inflexible. To them, political talks and Sinn Fein's electioneering were merely interruptions in the campaign of violence. They told their followers that the British would be only too happy to drag the IRA towards a political role so as to distract them from their objective of overthrowing British rule. Cahill said there was no room for a constitutional deal with the British. The Provisionals had been happy to watch the loyalists destroy the power-sharing Northern Ireland Executive because it intended to draw Catholics into a political framework which would have negated the existence of the IRA.

At the beginning of December 1974, while the London team was planning its campaign to bomb the London Underground, a Protestant clergyman, William Arlow, made contact with the IRA. He was surprised to find that they did not fit the tabloid image of mindless thugs and he had drinks and a chat with them. He went away, assembled a group of leading Protestant churchmen from throughout Ireland, and organized a conference attended by seven members of the IRA Army Council. The outcome was that the IRA leaders stated they were prepared to declare a ceasefire. Their conditions for an end to violence make interesting reading twenty years later, and deviated little from the impossible demands of the Provisionals who met Whitelaw in 1972. They called for the creation of a constitutional assembly, to be elected by people throughout the island; a replacement of the Republic's constitution with one for the whole of Ireland that provided for a Northern Ireland parliament; a commitment from the British to withdraw from Northern Ireland within a year of the new constitution being introduced; and an amnesty for political prisoners.

Those demands were more extensive than anything the Provisionals were seeking from a political deal in 1993–4. Twenty years later, rather than calling for British withdrawal within a year, they were agreeing to the existence of a Northern Ireland administration until Catholics became a majority. The IRA 'initiatives' of 1972 and 1974 were contextualized within an 'Ireland solution' imposed on the Unionists; twenty years on there was a degree of moderation in the IRA position, and recognition of the Unionist position and of the need for British involvement without a determined time-span.

In December 1974 the Army Council voted to call a temporary ceasefire to demonstrate their good faith. The decision was reached with a 5-to-2 vote; Twoomey and Billy McKee, the Northern complement on the Council, opposed the gesture. GHQ was then told to issue orders to the London unit to cease operations until further notice. O'Connell was instructed to keep his team in place, and to continue to compile intelligence on future targets, particularly politicians, including the former Prime Minister, Edward Heath. While the IRA was doing 'business' with churchmen and the British government, it simultaneously planned for future mayhem and death. The temporary ceasefire was scheduled to come into effect at midnight on 22 December and to last until 2 January 1975.

Five days earlier, the London unit had communicated its desire to mark the beginning of the ceasefire with two bombings. They also told Dublin that they were in a position to assassinate Edward Heath. The Army Council replied that the killing of Heath should take place on the 22nd. I was told that the decision to murder the former Prime Minister was the IRA's means of showing how lethal it could be and therefore of reinforcing the need for a ceasefire. It was echoed with the killing of a young soldier on 3 December 1993 on the eve of John Major's visit to Dublin: the objective in 1993 was the same.

On 20 December 1974 O'Connell planted a bomb which exploded at Aldershot Station. On the evening of 22 December they threw a bomb through the window of Edward Heath's home in Belgravia. It landed on a balcony and failed to explode.

At midnight the same day the ceasefire began. The Northern Ireland Secretary of State, Merlyn Rees, responded privately to the IRA, since he did not wish it to be publicly known that he was talking to them or that he was even interested in their proposals for an end to violence. He knew he could not meet the IRA demands, but felt that by involving the Provos in a political process he could weaken their resolve to fight on. The British military assessment was that a long ceasefire would erode much of the IRA's support within its own ranks and make reactivating the campaign more difficult.

The new Northern Ireland GOC, Frank King, believed the future of military activity lay in the use of technology. He was keen to exploit new surveillance equipment and use covert organizations such as the SAS. MI5 agreed with General King and advised the Government to phase out internment as part of a deal with a twofold objective. First, internment had not just outlived its usefulness: it offered the IRA propaganda and the means to portray themselves as political prisoners; and it reduced the camps to military training centres and parade grounds. The normal process of law would allow the authorities to treat the IRA as common criminals. Second, a deal on internment might suck the IRA into a prolonged ceasefire, which would give the intelligence community more time to build up dossiers rather than simply act in a reflex manner to defeat terrorism.

Merlyn Rees used two Foreign Office officials to communicate his thoughts to the IRA. He began with a gesture, by reducing the military presence in Catholic areas and releasing some internees. His officials told the IRA that there could be a further and much more generous response if the IRA extended its ceasefire. I think there is little doubt that the IRA bombings in England weighed heavily in the British decision to expand its contacts with the IRA. My belief has been backed up by a member of GHQ from that period, who told me:

If there was one thing which fixed the minds of the Brits in dealing with us, it was the bombing campaign in England. We knew they could continue to have an acceptance level of violence in the North, but when it was killing people on their soil it concentrated the mind wonderfully on seeking a deal with us. We were politically naïve at that time. We demanded too much, but we learned from that, just as much as we learned from '72. There were always contacts with the Brits. Sometimes they passed messages to us through what they called 'emissaries'. They used conduits such as churchmen or journalists. We also had a line of communication with the Brits which was activated regularly for conveying codes for bombs etc. Now the campaign in England taught us that we would never get to the conference table, get them into talks, until we made it clear we could extend the campaign to England. We learned from that.

Rees conceded the phasing out of internment; the eventual withdrawal of the army to barracks, to be replaced by the RUC; a gradual end to all military screening and identity checks; the creation of 'incident centres' for Sinn Fein, with links to an operations room at Stormont Castle, to monitor the ceasefire; and the issue of firearms permits to those in the incident centres who felt vulnerable to assassination. That guaranteed a declaration of an indefinite ceasefire from 2 February 1975. The IRA agreed not to target the army or police, while it reserved the right to protect Catholics against loyalist gunmen. One of the Rees concessions, the incident centres, allowed the terrorists in both communities to parade openly and to have legally held firearms. It was a dangerous precedent, and gave Sinn Fein the opportunity to develop politically. There was a feeling that Merlyn Rees was much too malleable, and the SDLP was angry that the Government was funding an incident centre for Sinn Fein. The Unionist Party was equally unhappy that the UDA and UVF were being granted a status as political groups. The IRA stood down the majority of its units, except those in London.

The GHQ staff member whom I quoted earlier explained to me the effect of the ceasefire on the Provisionals:

> It was the worst period in our history. Volunteers were confused. The British government won in the short term. The phasing out of internment we handed to them on a plate. That led to the policy of criminalization in which we were portrayed as thugs, as criminals. Political status we had to fight for and it cost the lives of ten of our best, six years later in the hunger strike. The Prods took the opportunity of stepping up sectarian attacks and dragged us into it. That helped the Brits depict us as sectarian murderers and no better than the loyalists. The Brits detached us from our main objective. We were suckers. The blame lay with the older leadership in Belfast and Dublin. The younger people in prison like Gerry Adams and Danny Morrison knew that we were being destroyed.

The British government turned on and off the release of internees like a light bulb. Any sign of IRA activity such as sectarian killings, and the flow of releases was switched off. It was euphemistically the technique of giving the dog the bone when he was good and removing it from him when he misbehaved. The GHQ staff member told me: 'We were engaged in so many rounds of talks with British officials that our heads were filled full of nonsense and useless information. We were even dragged into a feud with the Official IRA which further damaged us. The sectarian thing we suspected – but now know – was being orchestrated by elements of British military intelligence. They ran the loyalists, pulled their strings.' By the end of June 1975 there had been 159 sectarian killings, and the majority of the victims were Catholics. It is clear from much of what I have written in other books that there was an orchestration of killings by members of the security forces, including the Ulster Defence Regiment and covert units of military intelligence.

The 1974–5 ceasefire not only damaged the IRA but led to the gradual take-over of the movement by the younger element. The young IRA officers blamed the older leadership for leading them into a period of despair. Among those who denounced the older leaders were Gerry Adams, Martin McGuinness, Brendan Hughes, Danny Morrison, Brendan McFarlane and Seamus Loughran. Within a year the Provisional IRA as a whole was controlled by the organization in Northern Ireland, and by men with a long-term strategy of the ballot box and Armalite. It could be argued that the British government underestimated the ability of young men in the organization to resurrect the IRA. In 1994, when the British government was calling on the IRA to declare a permanent ceasefire, the 1975 experience was uppermost in the minds of

Adams and McGuinness. The benefits to security from the 1975 episode were also a factor in British government thinking in 1993–4. One government official remarked that if they could 'sucker' the Provos into a long ceasefire it would create space to attack them on political and military fronts. That was a short-sighted view and did not take account of the powerful control of the organization by men who had learned from the 1974–5 ceasefire.

In the spring and summer of 1975 the IRA lost its prisoner-of-war status. Non-jury courts had been inaugurated and the British government felt it had won. It was decided by Downing Street to close the incident centres by the end of the year. British military and political advisers believed the IRA was in decline and there was no need for any further concessions. On the orders of Downing Street, communications between IRA leaders and Foreign Office contacts were scaled down. From within Long Kesh, men who shared the younger men's views about the ceasefire demanded the overthrow of the Dublin leadership of Daithi O'Connell and Rory O'Bradaigh. Adams believed the 'struggle' could only be effective if it was in the hands of people in the war zone and not armchair generals in Dublin. The discussions in Long Kesh were the genesis of the Provisionals we know today.

The general IRA reaction to the erosion of dialogue with the British was to resume the bombings in England. An Army Council meeting in Dublin in August 1975 was told of the growing disenchantment within units in Northern Ireland. The British had conceded nothing and gained considerable advantage. Daithi O'Connell, knowing his position was vulnerable, proposed the re-activation of the London unit as a means of placating the dissenting elements of the Provisionals in the North. Harry Duggan, Martin O'Connell, Edward Butler and Hugh Doherty were happy with the news. They had used the ceasefire to draw up a comprehensive list of potential targets. They had changed their accommodation and were renting another two flats in North London. O'Connell, posing as 'Joseph Powell', rented a flat at Milton Grove, Stoke Newington, for himself and Duggan, whom he described as his friend 'John'. The other two members of the team were based at Crouch Hill.

They began bombing London on 27 August and in ten days exploded five devices, causing extensive damage to property, injuring many civilians and killing Captain Roger Goad, a bomb-disposal expert, on 29 August. His death was part of a deliberate ploy by O'Connell to demonstrate his skill with explosives. The bomb that killed the captain was constructed with a built-in anti-handling device. It was left in Kensington Church Street and resembled the other bombs planted by the team. It was made with an 'inertia' device which activated the explosives the moment there was the slightest movement of the bomb. Bomb-makers tend to construct devices in a fashion which is unique to that individual, leaving what is known as a 'finger-print'. When forensic teams examine bomb debris, they search for one piece of evidence which will tell them that a bomb has been made by a particular terror-ist because of the similarities in its design. Terrorist bomb-makers take a bizarre pride in their work and deliberately leave a 'fingerprint', much in the manner of US covert units in Vietnam who left calling cards to let the enemy know it was a particular unit which had assassinated their colleagues. It is important for forensic scientists to gather 'fingerprints' for the prosecution of bomb-makers and for bomb-disposal experts it is vital to know the adversary when defusing a bomb. If you know his techniques, it can save your life. On 29 August the anti-handling device was used by the gang for the first time; this established O'Connell's 'fingerprint' and warned bomb-disposal experts to be wary of trying to defuse his devices.

The IRA unit's targets included hotels and banks in Central London. On 5 September a bomb at the Hilton Hotel killed two people and injured sixty-nine. On 22 September they bombed the Portman Hotel. Three days later they changed their area of operations and struck at the Hare and Hounds pub in Maidstone.

As the bombings continued, the gang received orders from the Army Council, through GHQ and its female couriers, to carry out political assassinations. The first target was Sir Hugh Fraser, the Conservative MP. O'Connell planted a 10-lb bomb, of the type which killed Captain Goad, under Fraser's car, which was parked outside his home in Holland Park. As the bomb package was visible from the pavement, it was seen by the MP's servant when he went to the front door to collect the papers on the morning of 23 October, but he did not realize what it was. A short time later, Professor Hamilton Fairley, one of the world's leading cancer specialists, was walking his dog when he spotted the package. He was seen bending down to examine it. As he began to walk away, the device exploded, killing him instantly.

Five days later, in what was the most sustained bombing campaign since 1939, the gang bombed Lockett's restaurant at Marsham Street in Westminster. Another bomb followed, and the unit switched its attention again to political targets. They were determined to make another attempt on the life of Sir Edward Heath. O'Connell constructed a device which was similar to the one which killed Professor Fairley, but more sophisticated. Butler and Doherty, who carried out surveillance, reported that Heath's Rover car was parked outside his Wilton Street home overnight and driven off each morning. As the former Prime Minister did not leave home at a regular time, there was no way of determining the time-delay that should be built into the bomb. O'Connell said he could circumvent that problem by arming the bomb with a 55-minute delay; after that a micro-switch would be activated which would detonate when pressure was put on the device. The bomb would be placed under the Rover and would explode when the car was driven away. On the morning of 9 November Edward Heath got into his car and drove away. A minicab was driven into the empty parking space, but luckily it did not touch the device, which was later discovered by a passer-by and defused by a Scotland Yard bomb-disposal expert. The bomb-disposal expert was a very brave man, yet he had the advantage of knowing the 'fingerprint' of the device because of the murder of Captain Goad.

In November the gang bombed Scott's restaurant in Mayfair, killing a customer and injuring many others.

Their choice of restaurants said a great deal about their lifestyle in London as well as their objective of bringing terror to the capital. When O'Connell was later asked why he bombed Lockett's restaurant, he replied that 'it was a class restaurant', reflecting a working-class resentment of expensive eating-places.

Shortly before this event, Ross McWhirter, co-editor of *The Guinness Book of Records*, had denounced the IRA bombers and offered £50,000 for information leading to their arrest. The Army Council regarded the money as a 'bounty' and ordered the gang to kill him. Duggan later remarked: 'McWhirter thought he lived in Texas. He placed a bounty on our heads. He asked to be killed.' Duggan, the gang member who carried a Magnum with him at all times, was more suited to Texas than was his victim. He asked O'Connell for permission to 'do the hit', and selected Doherty as his back-up because he had conducted surveillance on the North Enfield home of the McWhirter family.

At 6 p.m. on 27 November, Duggan and Doherty travelled across London by taxi and Underground. They were about to ring the doorbell of the McWhirter home when they heard a car entering the driveway. The driver of the vehicle was Mrs McWhirter, who was confronted by the two terrorists. They demanded the keys to the house and she handed them over. One of them was the front-door key. Doherty got into the driver's seat of the car while Duggan went to the front door and opened it. Ross McWhirter must have thought it was his wife because he came into the hallway. Duggan shot him several times at close range in the stomach and head, killing him almost instantly. Then the two terrorists drove off in the car while Mrs McWhirter was left to cradle the blood-spattered body of her husband.

By December 1975 the gang had become cocky and forgotten the orders laid down by GHQ staff to operate only in teams of two, and to leave no incriminating material at their flats. At Crouch Hill and Milton Grove there were maps, bomb-making materials, lists of potential targets, including scores of politicians, cartridges from the Magnum which killed Ross McWhirter, and the names of IRA contacts in London and Southampton. On 6 December their arrogance encouraged them to mount another attack on Scott's restaurant in Mayfair. They were annoyed that the restaurant was back in business despite their earlier bombing. The London *Evening Standard* had announced increased police patrols and the use of covert teams to combat the unit, yet they insisted on returning to the scene of a crime. They went armed with a formidable array of weapons including a Sten gun, two .357 Magnums, a .30 carbine, a semi-automatic pistol and 100 rounds of ammunition. Their weaponry was evidence of their intent to carry out several attacks that evening.

Fortunately, two policemen near Scott's restaurant saw a man lean out of the rear window of a Ford Cortina and fire two shots from a carbine. As the Cortina sped off, two other policemen heard a radio alert about the shooting and commandeered a taxi. They gave chase and the Cortina was forced into a cul-de-sac. One of the gang tried to fire the Sten gun at the taxi but it jammed. Duggan later said that if the Sten gun had worked they would never have been caught. The Cortina had turned into Rossmore Road, where the IRA team leapt from the car and ran off, with the police officers pursuing them on foot. When members of the gang turned and fired their handguns and the carbine, police officers from a Special Patrol Group returned fire. Other policemen who arrived on the scene gave chase. One of them was Detective Inspector Dowdeswell, who was unarmed. He was within five yards of Duggan when the terrorist turned and fired his Magnum. Fortunately, the bullets were not on target. Radio messages about the chase led dozens of other policemen to the area as the gunmen ran into Balcombe Street. The sound of police sirens and the screeching of brakes panicked the gang into seeking refuge. They fled into a block of flats at 22b Balcombe Street and forced their way at gunpoint into an apartment on the first floor. The occupants were a middle-aged couple, John and Sheila Matthew.

It was 9.45 p.m., the gang was trapped, and the Balcombe Street siege began. The Metropolitan Police Commissioner resisted the advice of MI5 and the British Army to storm the building using the SAS. Instead he put into operation the contingency plan which had long been in preparation. Police marksmen were rushed to the scene to ensure that the gunmen did not escape, and to be ready to storm the building if there was a threat to the residents of the flat. Home Office advisers on siege tactics joined Scotland Yard experts to decide the next moves. The Police Commissioner was prepared for a long operation, and wanted the gang to be caught alive: not only would this be better for the image of the London police but it might provide detectives with leads to IRA operations in Britain. At that stage no-one knew the identity of the gunmen. MI5 bugging experts were detailed to provide a sound image of the siege flat and the conversation of the terrorists and their hostages. Miniature bugging devices were placed in the walls adjoining the flat; radio waves were bounced off the front window and relayed to a machine to unscramble the sounds into taped conversation. Land lines were installed to establish contact between the gang and the police.

The electronic operation was vital to the police, psychiatrists and terrorist experts whose job was to determine the mind-set of the terrorists. Conversations between the gang and their captives exposed weaknesses in the psychology of the four gunmen and enabled police to judge whether the terrorists posed a threat to their hostages. I was told that O'Connell and Duggan were convinced the SAS would be employed to make an assault on the building. The longer the siege went on, the more the fear of waiting for the SAS to burst into the flat and kill the gang played havoc with the relationships within the IRA team and increased their stress. They discussed trying to shoot their way out of the building, using their hostages as cover, and wondered if they could do a deal with the police. On the first night of the siege, they used an armchair to block the front door of the flat and turned off all the lights. Then they tied John Matthew's hands and feet, but left his wife free. The four gunmen smoked incessantly, and during the night two of them slept while their companions remained awake and armed. They adopted that procedure over the following days. The captives were not subjected to any physical assault, yet their fear was at times overwhelming. Eventually the police persuaded the gang to accept the offer of a field telephone, which was lowered onto the balcony of the flat. From that moment, siege experts knew that the IRA men were mentally vulnerable. O'Connell asked police for cigarettes and food, and these were provided.

It was six days before O'Connell and his companions surrendered. The police operation was a classic of its kind. It secured the arrest of the most dangerous men in Britain, the safety of the hostages and no further loss of life. During the siege, part of the police ploy was to discover the men's identity. Experts listening to the bugged conversations knew Duggan only as 'Z' and were pleased when he told them he was Michael Wilson, which was his London alias. Under subsequent interrogation, the four revealed little about their activities but police were able to discover where they lived. Their flats held the real clues to their handiwork. Not only were there explosives, rifles and lists of targets but, significantly, the nicknames and Christian names of fellow IRA operatives in Britain. Scotland Yard Anti-Terrorist Squad analysts were able to piece together the Christian names with surnames of wanted IRA personnel. There were also addresses and an important letter from a courier known as Grainne, which was an alias. It contained suggestions from Dublin that the four should examine ducts above the ceiling of Goodge Street Underground station. An explosive device would have shattered those ducts, sending a torrent of water onto the electric lines and cables of the railway. The letter also referred to Walthamstow Reservoir and lakes which fed into

Hackney Downs pumping station: 'A new station was built two years ago. Do intelligence on it with a view to poisoning the lakes and blowing up the pumping station.' There was also a mention of 'two Belfast fellows' and other people who provided a back-up service for the Balcombe Street gang:

Get those two Belfast fellows home and clean them up. Send them through Glasgow singularly . . . These are the addresses for collecting from Mick Gill's man whatever weapons etc. . . . At . . . in West Hampstead ask for Ernie Johnston and say 'Damage' sent you. Ask him to get the Army list from Spotter Murphy and send it back to us through Liverpool. Everything this end under Brendan's control, so everything should be O.K. When you write, make it 'Dear Annie etc.', in case it gets opened in error.

The letter identified a place in London for international phone calls, a telex exchange used by dealers in the City, and a club frequented by senior military figures. It listed large stores such as Fortnum's as recommended targets; names were marked in civil service year books, and there was a photograph of the funeral of a former London Police Commissioner, with some of the mourners ringed for assassination.

The Balcombe Street Four, as they came to be known, operated alone but had considerable back-up. The whole IRA operation was to be the framework, in a scaled-down version, of the IRA's England Department from 1989. Most of the back-up personnel were never apprehended. O'Connell and his companions treated their ensuing trial as a charade, and revelled in their crimes. They were charged with ten murders and over twenty bombings. The scale of their terror was much greater. An IRA source told me they were responsible for planting as many as forty devices, and killing seventeen people.

At their trial early in 1976 they made a statement from the dock admitting the Guildford and Woolwich atrocities, but their admission of guilt was ignored. That was a dreadful indictment of the judicial system. The four could easily have convinced police of their guilt, except that no-one within the judiciary or the police wanted to listen. It was a time in Britain when the need for the police to show a full score-card in the war against the terrorists and for the Government to satisfy the clamouring of the public for results militated against justice and fair police work. While the Birmingham Six and the Guildford Four languished in English prisons, the Provisionals benefited years later from the outcry about the obvious miscarriages of justice. It was difficult for those in the higher echelons of the judiciary and police to see beyond the apparent success of the arrest of the Balcombe Street gang. Who was going to believe the testimony of four young men who were prepared to kill at will?

Many people in the world of journalism praised Scotland Yard for their work in catching the gang, whereas in my view it was the arrogance of the gang and police luck which led to their capture, not hard intelligence. So often in the war, the police operated in a reflex fashion and hoped their quarry would make a mistake. Whatever indignation one may wish to express about the crimes, the gang was a formidable unit. They were far removed from the tabloid portrayal of 'mindless killers' or 'psychopaths'. They saw themselves as soldiers in a war, and were prepared to kill, maim and destroy to satisfy the objectives of the organization to which they were committed. None of them was insane, nor mentally disturbed. They were a group of cold, clinical and ruthless young men of a type which the IRA recruited in the 1970s. I believe it is dangerous to underestimate the IRA by branding them as either common criminals or madmen. The Israelis did that to the PLO, and it proved counter-productive. In 1989 I talked to a group of Parachute Regiment officers. Each of them said they would rather the IRA was depicted as a serious enemy, because it was a war. One of them observed: 'We do a fine job in combating the IRA. We are facing one of the most sophisticated terrorist organizations in the world, and people should recognize that. When people say they are mindless thugs, that downgrades our role. It is the job of the police to deal with mindless thugs and it is our job to deal with subversion.' That comment showed that at least some people in the army had a more realistic view of the IRA than many of the journalists in Britain.

The judge at their trial had been on their hit-list, but that did not deter him from handling the case. He gave them multiple life sentences with a recommendation that each of them serve at least thirty years. Duggan was the most talkative of the four during the trial, and all of them treated the sentences with disdain. One or two writers have since argued that the gang never intended to kill innocent people, but their actions do not support that claim. They were tasked to bring terror to London, and they told investigating detectives that casualties were inevitable in war. The IRA figure named as 'Brendan' in the courier's letter found in O'Connell's flat was the GHQ mastermind of England operations. He was also the person who set up the 'England Department' cell system in the late 1980s. The IRA maintained a continuity of personnel in charge of England operations, and thereby constantly learned from mistakes and developed new ways of operating.

The Balcombe Street episode convinced the new IRA leadership that, with careful planning, they could mount a sustained campaign. O'Connell and his companions were not true 'sleeper' agents. 'Brendan' told the Army Council the IRA should plan years ahead, like the Israeli intelligence agency, Mossad. People should be put into England for years, but not necessarily in London. The capital attracted too much 'heat'.

11

The IRA's England Department

The arrest of the Balcombe Street Four was not a
serious setback for the IRA. The organization had
plenty of young men and women who were willing to
undertake operations in Britain. The prospects of long
prison sentences or being shot dead in an ambush were
no deterrent. Within the psyche of many republican
idealists in the late twentieth century was a belief that
there would eventually be an amnesty. (In 1993 the
Provisional leadership demanded an amnesty as part
of any future political settlement which would require
them to lay down their arms.) The take-over of the
IRA by the Northern Command in 1976 was a vital
factor in the organization's ability to select many of its
younger recruits from within Northern Ireland. Those
responsible for that selection process were from the
North and had an intimate knowledge of the level of
competence and the commitment of those it chose for
the mainland campaign. In the late 1970s the bombings

Box-cycle bomb kills five, injures 70, in main street

CENTRE OF A CITY IS WRECKED

BRIDE-TO-BE WAS LOOKING AT WEDDING RINGS

Daily Express Staff Reporter

COVENTRY, Friday.

A N I.R.A. time-bomb placed in a tradesman's box-cycle, it was established tonight, caused the explosion which killed five and injured more than seventy in Broadgate, centre of Coventry, this afternoon.

Twenty shop frontages were wrecked; a small car and at least three bicycles were blown sky-high; trams and buses were damaged.

Two men who were wheeling a tradesman's bicycle propped it on the kerbside beside a shop and hurried away.

The explosion came a minute or two later. A piece of the bicycle frame crashed through two or three windows of shops sixty yards away.

Cascades of splintered glass rained on people in the street. Some were killed, some injured, others, Nearly one hundred.

Fragments of the bicycle and motor car were found embedded in the ground.

Ambulances rushed to the scene. They picked up the dead and injured where they lay, and placed them in hospital.

More than twelve people were killed, they said tonight, among them were five men, a woman and a girl of thirteen.

The five dead were:—
Mr. James Clay, aged ...

The scene of the explosion.

Daughter and son-in-law to bankrupt father

MR. JOHN KELLY WHITE, eighty-one-year-old solicitor who recently brought an action for trespass against certain members of his family, is to be made bankrupt by one of his daughters and a son-in-law ...

Yesterday at the offices of the Official Receiver for South ...

"Captain Fury" weds actress

British film star Brian Aherne married Mr. Joan O'Brien, Capthers ...

RAIL TALK ENDS IN DEADLOCK

Daily Express Industrial Reporter

Efforts to reach a settle...

Daily Express, 26 August 1939. Coventry. (*John Frost*)

Birmingham shop after an IRA bomb attack, 1940. (*Popperfoto*)

Eamon De Valera and Clement Attlee at 10 Downing Street, September 1947. (*Hulton Deutsch*)

Manus Canning, Sean MacStiofain (Sean Stephenson) and Cahal Goulding leaving Bishops Stortford police station, October 1953. (*Hulton Deutsch*)

Scotland Yard detectives at Caledonian Road, Islington, recovering the arms stolen from Arborfield army camp in Berkshire, 1955. (*Popperfoto*)

Ian Paisley.
(*Camera Press /
Don McCullin*)

Catholic Nationalist Leader John Hume pleading with members of the
Royal Ulster Constabulary to stay out of the centre of Derry, April 1969.
(*Syndication International*)

Two conflicting traditions: Catholic women protestors and members of a
Scots regiment, Belfast 1970. (*Camera Press / Brian Aris*)

Evening News

London
Tuesday
February 22, 1972
No. 28,013   3p

Night Special

Women die in revenge blast at Paras' HQ

IRA KILL SEVEN
IN ALDERSHOT

POLICE CHASE MEN IN CAR AFTER THE BLAST
By BARRY WIGMORE

After you, Mrs. Mao

Yard order round-up of fanatics
By JAMES REID

Evening News Reporter

AT LEAST seven people—five of them women—were killed this afternoon when IRA terrorists brought "Bloody Tuesday" to Aldershot—by blowing up the officers' mess of the 2nd Bn. Parachute Regiment.

Six of the dead were civilians, working in the officers' mess of the 16th Parachute Brigade. The seventh was a Para officer. Two dead women are believed to be cleaners and a nun.

Early reports said that two others were missing.

Fleet of ambulances

Aldershot,
February 1972.
(*Popperfoto*)

The wife of an internee pleading with Secretary of State for Northern Ireland, William Whitelaw on a walkabout in the Bogside of Londonderry, April 1972. (*Syndication International*)

Belfast Provisional IRA leader Joe Cahill who escaped the internment swoop of 1971. (*Rex Features*)

Four members of the Provisional IRA leadership (*left to right*): Martin McGuinness, Daithi O'Connail (David O'Connell), Sean MacStiofain (Sean Stephenson) and Seamus Toomey. (*Syndication International*)

Gerry Adams in 1972. He was released from internment under a special government licence to attend talks with the British government in Cheyne Walk, Chelsea, in July of that year. (*Syndication International*)

Left and middle: Old Bailey bomb, March 1973.

Below: Men in black berets, dark clothes and sunglasses – the traditional dress of the IRA – march through Kilburn in London, 1974. (*Syndication International*)

Marion Price (*left*), and her sister Dolors outside 10 Downing Street, on a sightseeing trip, a year before they returned to London with an IRA bombing team. (*Camera Press / Colman Doyle*)

Explosion at Whitehall, 1973. (*Hulton Deutsch*)

Westminster Hall ablaze, June 1974. (*Hulton Deutsch*)

BIRMINGHAM
Evening Mail

SPECIAL EDITION

AR OF THE WEEK
£1,595
Trust Thomas Startin.

By far the largest evening sale in the Midlands   FRIDAY, NOVEMBER 22, 1974   3p

WORSE THAN ULSTER:
19 DEAD, 202 HURT

Rescuers remove barefoot body from wreckage of Birmingham pub bomb. (*Press Association*)

Interior of Mulberry Bush pub, Birmingham, November 1974.
(*Syndication International*)

The Balcombe Street Four (*left to right*): Martin O'Connell, Harry Duggan, Hugh Doherty, and Edward Butler. (*Hulton Deutsch*)

One of the gang surrendering. (*Hulton Deutsch*)

Police marksmen surround the Balcombe Street flat where a couple are held hostage, December 1975. (*Hulton Deutsch*)

John Frost

Mrs Thatcher's dramatic plea

'HANG THESE ASSASSINS'

Now it's terror by the bullet

By MAURICE ROMILLY

ROSS McWHIRTER'S assassins "have forfeited their right to live," Opposition leader Margaret Thatcher told the Commons today.

EVENING NEWS REPORTER

FEARS that an IRA assassination campaign has now started in London were being expressed by police

Top and above: Ross McWhirter, murdered by the IRA after he had offered a £50,000 reward for information on the London bombers. (*Syndication International*)

The INLA kill Airey Neave, Tory spokesman for Northern Ireland, as he drives from the underground car park at Westminster. (*Hulton Deutsch*)

Right: Regent's Park
bandstand after the explosion
that killed six people,
20 July 1982.
(*Hulton Deutsch*)

Hyde Park on the same day,
when an IRA bomb killed
two soldiers and seven
cavalry horses.
(*Syndication International*)

Damaged canopies at Harrods after a car bomb killed five people and
injured ninety-one, Christmas 1983. (*Associated Press*)

Grand Hotel, Brighton, on the
night of the bomb blast during
the Tory Party Conference in
October 1984.
(*Press Association*)

Bathroom of Margaret
Thatcher's suite. She was there
when the bomb exploded.
(*Press Association*)

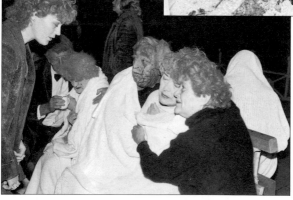

Some of the people who escaped death in the
Grand Hotel explosion. (*Camera Press*)

Left: Margaret Thatcher and Dr Garret FitzGerald put their signatures to the Anglo-Irish Agreement in 1985. (*Press Association*)

Middle: Rescue workers recover the body of one of the ten Royal Marine musicians killed at Deal Barracks, October 1989. (*Camera Press*)

Funeral of Royal Marine Band Corporal, David McMillan. (*Press Association*)

10 Downing Street: John Major lays down the law to Northern Ireland political leaders, February 1992. (*Press Association*)

Van burns near Whitehall after mortar attack on 10 Downing Street, February 1991. (*Press Association*)

Provisional leaders Gerry Adams and Martin McGuinness who were at the centre of secret talks with the British government. (*Press Association*)

After the Bishopsgate bomb, April 1993. (*John Frost*)

A man carries a small child away after a bomb exploded without warning in Camden Town, London, 1993. (*Hulton Deutsch*)

Warrington, March 1993: Colin Parry, father of young bomb victim Tim Parry, breaks down at his son's funeral. (*Press Association*)

London, the IRA's major target. (*John Frost*)

in London continued with extensive damage and loss of life. The IRA leadership needed attacks in England to demonstrate its effectiveness, because the security forces in Ireland were making life difficult for the Provo planners through increased electronic surveillance, and a tightening of the police and military presence on the periphery of all republican neighbourhoods.

GHQ continued to recruit small cells of activists, and smuggled quantities of explosives and guns into Britain. Small cells were told to store their equipment in specially constructed hides in the English country-side. Lock-up garages in London were not regarded as ideal because they had to be rented, and police warnings alerted the public to report any suspicious persons seen using garages. One of the major IRA considerations was the manufacture of bombs requiring the transport and storage of large quantities of fertilizer. GHQ recommended the development of underground dumps in forested areas in the Midlands. 'Brendan', who masterminded operations in Britain with a small group of planners, suggested that England activists be 'rotated': one cell should be sent in and after a short time replaced by another. The same couriers would remain in place, as well as the quartermaster responsible for ensuring that the cells were always supplied with the right amount of equipment. A team from the IRA's internal policing organization, Internal Security, was given the task of constantly examining the security and the personalities of each cell. Their role was to look for faults in the cell structure and devise ways of preventing it from being penetrated by British intelligence; they were also instructed to examine the lifestyle of members of each

England cell and report to GHQ if any of the activists showed too much stress or over-confidence.

IRA experience showed that the major anti-terrorist operations were in London where the police and public were vigilant. Accommodation, and meetings of cells and their couriers, should be extended to quieter parts of Britain. That would offer greater freedom of movement and attract less suspicion. Female couriers would be the only links between the cells. In the event that Scotland Yard identified one cell, their inquiries would not lead them to another team. In the late 1970s and 1980s, Cumann na mBann provided at least ten young women who were trained as couriers and who conveyed messages from GHQ to the cells' leaders and from one cell to another. They selected meeting-places where money was provided for the costs of running a particular cell. Because of increased security in Britain, some of the bombers went to Holland, France and Belgium for short periods, and used those countries as entry points for Britain. The European continent continued to be a storage place for guns and electronic parts for bombs. It was also ideal for laundering the cash which flowed from the coffers of Libya's President, Colonel Qadhafi.

The most dangerous IRA operators after the Balcombe Street Four were Gerard Tuite, Patrick Magee, Paul Kavanagh and Thomas Quigley. Their activities outstripped those of their predecessors because they were provided with more back-up, and were moved in and out of Britain during time-lapses between operations. They were ruthless and dedicated, and learned from the mistakes of their predecessors. Rather than enumerate all the activities in which these individuals were involved, I shall attempt to convey something of the character of the terrorists and of the overall conduct of the operation of cells in England.

All the cells at that time were supplied with sophisticated bombing devices which included memo-park switches like those used in European parking meters, but modified to provide long-term delay periods between the planting of a device and its detonation. Kavanagh and Quigley belonged to a unit of six young men who operated in pairs and had storage points at Salcey Forest in Northamptonshire and Annersley Forest in Nottinghamshire. At Annersley Forest, under several feet of soil, were bins of fertilizer, while the other dump contained a bin holding a terrorist arsenal: high-powered rifles, pistols, memo-park switches, mercury tilt switches, detonators and tiny batteries. A third weapons cache, near Pangbourne in Oxfordshire, held fourteen automatic and semi-automatic guns. Kavanagh, Quigley and the unknown members of their unit carried out the bombing of Chelsea Barracks on 10 October 1981 when two died, including a bomb-disposal expert; and bombing the home of Sir Michael Havers, the Attorney-General, on 30 November. They were responsible for more terrorist acts than those on the charge sheet and were caught through a mixture of luck and an IRA error. Workmen discovered the arms cache at Pangbourne in January 1984, and GHQ panicked. 'Brendan' sent a quartermaster to Britain to examine the dumps in Annersley and Salcey forests. He was also worried that Kavanagh's team had too much freedom in their choice of targets. The quartermaster was told to pull the team out of Britain and to examine the dumps to determine whether they were secure. When he arrived by plane at Heathrow Airport accompanied by his wife, he was tailed by undercover police and was seen meeting Kavanagh and travelling to Salcey and Annersley forests.

A member of the second IRA cell was Gerard Tuite, one of the most devious and cunning of the IRA operatives in the late 1970s and early 1980s. His youthfulness and inoffensive manner made him seem an untypical recruit to those who met him in London in 1978. He courted Helen Griffiths, a nurse whom he met at a party. He moved into her apartment at Trafalgar Road in Greenwich and used that as his base. She thought he was an upwardly mobile young businessman. Her nursing shifts allowed Tuite plenty of opportunities to hold meetings in her flat. On several occasions she returned home to find him examining documents and maps. He always locked them away in a briefcase, explaining the papers related to his job. In January 1979, IRA Internal Security ordered him to end the relationship because they wanted him back in Ireland for a short period. One month after his sudden departure, for various reasons Helen Griffiths became suspicious following an explosion in London. She went to the police, who searched her flat for two days but told her they had found nothing to incriminate her boyfriend. Tuite was a major operator in the bombings of that period, yet, when he was finally captured, the security at Brixton prison was not tight enough to prevent him escaping to Ireland. He persuaded two criminals to assist him for two months in digging a tunnel, and his ability to do this using only basic materials demonstrated his ingenuity.

An IRA volunteer with similar characteristics was Patrick Magee. His family had moved to Norwich in 1953 when he was two years old, and after he left school at the age of fifteen he took to petty crime. For two years he committed burglaries, and was given a two-year suspended sentence in October 1969. In the spring of 1970 his family took the unusual step of moving back to Belfast, where Patrick became attached to the IRA in the north of the city. His parents returned to England several years later, but their son remained in Belfast to develop a career in violence. He rarely contacted his parents and only informed them, by postcard, of his marriage in 1977. By the summer of 1980 he was working in Holland, at a factory near the German border. This stay in Europe was due to the IRA's policy of taking operatives out of circulation for long periods so that the security authorities would not know their whereabouts. Operatives who remained in Ireland were always in danger of being spotted in a street or pub and placed under 24-hour man-to-man surveillance. When someone like Magee had been out of Ireland for a time, it was easier to spirit him to Britain.

The IRA reckoned there was a limit to the number of suspected activists the intelligence agencies could track at any given time. They would get tired of searching for a known bomber and move on to their next target. It was a game of cat and mouse between the security forces and the terrorists. The British surveillance teams worked on the principle that, if someone disappeared from circulation, all effort should be made to find that person, since often a terrorist disappeared from his usual haunts because he was being summoned to commit an act of violence. The discovery of that terrorist would lead to others, possibly an IRA cell. The IRA countered that technique by using well-known volunteers as bait to draw their adversaries away from the real activists. They also sent people out of the British Isles to where it was more difficult to trace them.

Magee's name was on file as a suspected terrorist but he was not wanted for a particular crime. In September 1980 he was arrested by Dutch police after MI6 asked the Dutch government to crack down on republicans living in the country. Magee came to their attention because he was a new arrival. It was a question of 'anyone will do', and Magee, with a known history of republican activity, would be a useful catch. There was no evidence to connect him directly with any bombings, but the British government decided it was worth demanding his extradition, which, if successful, would enable them to interrogate him and perhaps acquire information on IRA cells in Britain and Europe. It was increasingly obvious that the IRA was using Europe as a storage place, a training ground and a hiding place for 'sleeper' agents. However, the Dutch refused the British request, setting in motion a tragic series of events.

Magee was released from custody in Holland in January 1981 and returned to Belfast. Later that year, the deaths of ten hunger strikers in the Maze prison, including the Westminster Sinn Fein MP Bobby Sands, placed Margaret Thatcher at the top of the IRA's assassination list, and in 1982 plans were made to kill her on one of her many trips from Downing Street. IRA surveillance teams reported that it was impossible to guarantee a time at which she would leave Number

10, and security would make it difficult to place a car bomb in the vicinity without it being detected. They said the assassination would have to be carried out at short notice, using a car bomb to be detonated by remote control. The Army Council vetoed the idea because the quantity of explosives needed to shatter her bullet-proof car would make the civilian death toll massive.

Meanwhile, a total of eight soldiers died in separate incidents in London on 20 July 1982. A bomb exploded in Knightsbridge as mounted guards of the Blues and Royals, the Household Cavalry, were riding through Hyde Park. Two guardsmen were killed and seventeen civilians were injured. Only two hours later a second bomb exploded at the bandstand in Regent's Park, killing six bandsmen of the Royal Green Jackets and injuring twenty-four civilians. Three other people died later. On 17 December 1983 a bomb at Harrods killed six people and injured ninety. The British people were left in no doubt of the IRA's capacity and willingness to take human lives.

Another plan to kill Mrs Thatcher had been put to GHQ in 1983. The objective was to attack her while she attended the Conservative Party Conference. GHQ recommended the plan because the bomb would not only kill Margaret Thatcher but possibly wipe out her entire cabinet. The Army Council gave approval for work to begin on the project, and it was almost a year later before it was finalized. In 1984 the Tory Conference was scheduled for the Grand Hotel in Brighton. IRA bomb experts knew the hotel would be searched for explosives. The acquisition of long-delay switches made it possible for the IRA to construct a bomb which could be hidden in the Grand Hotel weeks before the conference. GHQ sent two explosives experts to Brighton to look at the hotel to determine the weight of explosives needed to cause maximum damage. On their return to Belfast they informed a member of GHQ that the building was structurally old, and a powerful device, using high explosives, would be effective if detonated within the building. I was told that the advice given to GHQ was that a bomb in the hotel 'would collapse it like a pack of cards'. GHQ doubted the advice of their explosives experts and identified an additional problem: which room would be allocated to Margaret Thatcher? They believed she would be confined to an upper floor where she would have privacy and heavy security. If they could get a bomb into the building, it should be concealed on an upper floor and timed to explode at night, making rescue operations extremely difficult.

Magee was the man chosen to plant the bomb, but was not, as reports later claimed, the explosives expert. Contrary to many stories, he was a 'bag man' who, more often than not, planted devices that he had not constructed. Magee was selected because he had been part of a team which had examined the feasibility of killing the Prime Minister in Blackpool in 1983.

At the beginning of September 1984 he was given a bogus passport, and told to travel to England and book into the Grand Hotel. He was advised to request a room on an upper floor, preferably one with a sea view. While he was there, an explosives expert would arrive with the bomb and prime it. Magee's task was to find somewhere to hide the device. On 15 September he booked into the hotel for a weekend and was allocated Room 629. He signed the register 'Roy Walsh', the name of one of the bombers in the Price sisters' team. During his stay he had only one meal in the hotel restaurant, preferring to eat in his room. The night before he left, he ordered a bottle of vodka for celebratory drinks with GHQ's explosives expert. Magee had found an ideal hiding place for the bomb. There was a partition wall separating the bathroom of Room 629 from Room 628.

The bomb contained 20–30 lb of Semtex, a high explosive which had no smell and was easily moulded into whatever shape the bomber considered appropriate. The IRA later claimed 100 lb of explosives were used because they did not want the security forces to know they had Semtex. In fact, the extent of the subsequent devastation did imply a large quantity of explosives, and security experts could not understand how the IRA could have smuggled such a large bomb into the hotel and hidden it in a wall cavity. Semtex is an ideal terrorist weapon, because dogs trained to sniff explosives, particularly gelignite which has a pungent smell, cannot detect it.

Magee was in Belfast in the early hours of 12 October when the bomb exploded, creating a fireball of 3,000°C. The death toll from the explosion was five, and thirty-four were injured, some of them seriously. Part of the hotel collapsed to the basement, and rescuers were forced to tear at the rubble in the darkness to find the dead, the dying and the injured. Margaret Thatcher escaped death and so did her cabinet. Ten years later, as one looks at the photographs of the bombed hotel, one is left pondering the changes which would have been made to history if the IRA had succeeded in its objective. The IRA issued a statement which contained a chilling reminder of the nature of continued IRA violence, not just for Margaret Thatcher, but for any political target: 'Today we were unlucky, but remember, we have only to be lucky once. You will have to be lucky always.'

While the intelligence community began its painstaking search for clues to the identity of the bombers, Magee returned to England to join others in a plan to bomb seaside resorts using long-delay timing switches. The discovery of similar devices in the terrorist dumps in the forests led anti-terrorist officers to suspect that the Grand Hotel bomb had been planted weeks before the atrocity. Detectives traced all but one person who had stayed in the hotel during a thirty-day period before the explosion. The missing person was Roy Walsh, with a bogus London address. Experts at Scotland Yard employed laser technology to extract the palm-print left by Roy Walsh on the hotel register. After three months the Anti-Terrorist Squad matched that print to one in the records kept by the police who had dealt with Magee when he was a teenager. But the intelligence community did not know where they might find Magee. The RUC's surveillance team reported no recent sightings of him in Northern Ireland. An alert was issued to all police forces in Britain to arrest him on sight. The only means of identification Scotland Yard could provide was a general description allied to one important piece of detail: a finger was missing on his right hand. However, other factors were about to come into play, and these would be vital to the discovery of Magee.

Scotland Yard was desperate to find him. They suspected he was in Britain planning the use of further long-delay bombs. It was a race against time to get to him before the devices were hidden in target areas. The Yard knew the explosion at the Grand Hotel could be repeated elsewhere in the country with devastating consequences. Luck was the missing element in the detective work until a Special Branch informer within the IRA warned of a planned meeting between a top IRA activist called Peter Sherry and someone in England.

IRA Internal Security had identified a problem with one of the members of the London unit. He was in the team with Magee that was planning attacks on seaside resorts. Donal Craig, a young man from Donegal, was mentally ill. Those who recruited him were unaware of his mental instability until a serious dispute developed between Craig and the leader of the London unit. GHQ was warned that he was a risk, and a decision was taken to 'deal with him', which in IRA parlance meant a bullet in the head. Magee was ordered to go to London and offer his own assessment of the risk. He used the London trip to plant a bomb at the Rubens Hotel near Buckingham Palace. In London, Magee told a courier to warn Dublin that Craig could jeopardize operations and they should send someone to eliminate the threat. Peter Sherry was the person selected by GHQ to deal with Craig; he was part of the team which ensured the internal security of IRA cells in Britain. Although he was overtly a member of Sinn Fein, his reputation for gunplay provided him with the covert role of an IRA sharpshooter. He was smuggled into Britain on a coal boat travelling from Belfast to Ayr in Scotland.

Contrary to later reports, the security forces did not know when, or in what manner, Sherry would enter Britain. Craig's depressive behaviour and drinking bouts were increasing, and his public boasts about his exploits were reported to Special Branch at Scotland Yard. Surveillance was placed on him, and as a consequence he led his watchers to Gerard McDonnell, the leader of the London unit, and Patrick Magee. Magee rented a flat in London and was observed in the company of Craig and McDonnell. On 22 June 1985 he took a train to Carlisle, and was kept under surveillance. He met Sherry at the W. H. Smith shop, and the two travelled to Glasgow. No attempt was made to arrest them because it was hoped they would lead the watchers to other IRA personnel. Magee and Sherry went to a flat where they met McDonnell and two couriers. The meeting was intended to finalize the details of sixteen bombings planned for English resorts and to discuss the risk posed by Donal Craig. The two couriers were twenty-three-year-old Martina Anderson, a former beauty queen from Derry, and Ella O'Dwyer, a university-educated woman who came from the Irish Republic, from a respectable middle-class family with no republican connections. While they discussed IRA business, policemen burst into the flat and arrested them. McDonnell was in possession of a list of the sixteen targets which included Bournemouth, Southend and Yarmouth. The women were to play the role of girlfriends to the members of the team who were tasked to plant the bombs. The Rubens Hotel was on the list, and a subsequent search uncovered the bomb. Craig was promptly arrested and was extremely co-operative. He identified another member of the London unit, and a house in Glasgow where the bombs intended for the campaign were hidden.

The discovery of several IRA units, weapons and explosives damaged IRA plans for a sustained campaign in Britain. GHQ made a detailed analysis of the reasons why so many people were apprehended. 'Brendan' argued that the IRA should plan the use of 'sleeper' agents, and gradually develop an organization in England which did not need to call upon volunteers at the last moment. According to 'Brendan', many mistakes were made because there was much haste in selecting and introducing volunteers into Britain. He favoured the gradual formation of a new cell structure, the 'England Department', which would be separate from all other IRA structures and planning. Knowledge of the department would be restricted to the Army Council, his small team in GHQ, and he would choose his own personnel to protect the department, which would have twenty people in England at all times. The teams sent to England would not have any contact with each other, and would be asked to plant bombs or provide a back-up service for larger operations. In the event of 'major jobs', specialists from the England Department would be sent to England to deal exclusively with one operation. A quartermaster, a bomb specialist and several well-trained shooters would always be available to enter England for specific operations. It was vital that the best operators were not retained inside England. When a cell was compromised, the loss would be sustainable. Each cell would consist of two volunteers and at most four. Their calibre would be such that if they were compromised they would not jeopardize all operatives, particularly the specialists. The specialist would be sent in to make the bombs and be out of the country by the time those bombs were allocated to the two-man teams that planted them.

In 1988, when I was researching for *The Dirty War*, I was told by IRA sources that I was the first person to learn of the existence of a new cell structure and its name, the England Department. I had requested a meeting with IRA intelligence, and was taken to an unknown destination, where I spent almost one day talking to people whose identities were unknown to me. One of the people who spoke to me was an extremely intelligent, articulate member of the IRA's GHQ staff. My enquiries covered the history of the Provisionals from 1970, and there were many things said to me which I was told I should never print. They were expressed in a context which was constructed to enable me to understand the thinking of the IRA. It is a difficult and disturbing experience for a writer to talk to members of the IRA for such a long time. There is always the implied, and sometimes direct, threat in relation to matters that must always remain private to such a meeting. Unfortunately, it was the only way of really understanding the mind-set and the long-term strategy of the Provisionals. I admit I was frightened, and was in no doubt that I should not compromise the people who talked to me. To do so would place my own life, and perhaps that of my family, in jeopardy. There was an unspoken rule that I knew the risks

I would incur if I stepped outside the brief agreed with them. When one talks to people who do not fit the archetypal image of the terrorist, it is easy to be lulled into a false sense of security – to believe that one is dealing with reasonable people. I was left in no doubt that they were determined men who were experienced in terrorism and would not fade away, like the IRA of the 1930s or the 1950s. They were too far down the political path of romantic republicanism to settle for anything less than their political objectives. They were very different from the older republicans I had interviewed in the early 1970s, who married ruthlessness with political intelligence.

The men I talked with in 1988 regarded the bombings in England as a way of 'focusing the British mind' on the need for a political settlement. They argued that Britain could cope with an 'acceptable level of violence' in Northern Ireland but would 'think twice' when that violence was exported to English cities. When I suggested that the violence of the pre-war campaign had achieved the opposite effect, they replied that the 1930s campaign did not have the military intelligence of the IRA of the 1980s, nor the components to sustain it – in other words, weapons, explosives and dedicated recruits. They said the political climate of the late 1980s was more conducive than the 1930s because Westminster had to take responsibility for all its actions and could no longer rely on, or blame, a Stormont government for its behaviour. There was no economic or political advantage to be gained by maintaining a Unionist veto on political change. Britain's international image had been damaged by Unionist misrule and British Army behaviour since August 1969. The British, they claimed, wanted to withdraw from Northern Ireland but they had to be pushed. A campaign in England, they argued, was economically damaging to the British economy and generated a loss of civil rights for British people who were opposed to a continued British presence in Northern Ireland.

After that meeting, I examined my notebooks and began to analyse the information which the IRA had not deemed unsuitable for inclusion in my book. It was then that I saw a reference to an 'England Department' and a description of its purpose. Having been in the company of the IRA for so many hours, I realized there were many things discussed which were absent from my mind until I scrutinized my notes. I was transfixed by my note on the new cell structure. I was worried about whether the information was not for publication. I asked myself whether I could have neglected to mark it as something that should not be printed. Had I perhaps made a note of something that should have been consigned to matters defined as secret by the IRA? I decided I could not go back and ask for permission to print. It was too important to ignore, and the likelihood was that they would tell me to erase it from my mind. I chose to risk publication. Subsequent events proved that the IRA was indeed constructing an 'England Department', and I am convinced they accidentally included discussion of it because so many issues were raised at the meeting, many of them off the record. My note on the England Department gave a valuable insight into the thinking of GHQ staff at that time, and was crucial to an analysis of the IRA when they mounted a massive bombing campaign in England two years later. This is what I was told:

The England Department is an entity kept separate from all other IRA operations. The Brits know that. It is their major target. The England Department is the most closely guarded cell structure within the IRA. It is the most tightly formed unit, with cells within cells. Even the IRA leadership is restricted with regard to knowledge of this department. The Brits put all their efforts into trying to get close to this department. They know that if they can get one breakthrough they are in business. We know that they expend so much effort and resources on man-to-man surveillance. They do that because they know we have learned a great deal. We also have technology. We are careful about the means by which we communicate. Therefore it all comes back to what may seem the simplest method but which, if successful, is the most devastating. For example – if, say, the Brits uncovered an operation like Gibraltar, it could happen this way. McCann, Savage or Farrell [the Gibraltar trio shot dead by the SAS] are not where the Brits expect them to be. If they do not appear on surveillance reports over a given period, the Brits become suspicious. The Brits devote every available effort into finding at least one of them. Word goes out to all their operatives and informers, or to the Gardai and Irish Special Branch, to find them. If they find one, they will concentrate on that person in the hope that he or she will lead them to the others and possibly a planned operation.

The creation of the England Department produced a spin-off with the emergence of a similar operation targeted at British diplomats, soldiers and military bases on the European continent. The cell structure for those operations was similar to that used by the England Department.

The European cells employed similar tactics, for example hiding their weapons and explosives in the Dutch and German countryside. One team was provided with a car which had been stolen in Northern Ireland, driven to London, where it was fitted with English number-plates, and taken by ferry to France and into Germany. That European cell was caught after they went to a wooded area off the Antwerp–Rotterdam road to examine their arms dump. They test-fired the guns and, in the process, alerted a father and his two sons who lived near by. Thinking the firing came from poachers, they went to investigate. The sons were former soldiers and showed no fear when they discovered a young couple who claimed they were lovers on holiday. One of the sons engaged the couple in conversation while his brother examined the surrounding area and found a bin containing four weapons. As he looked at the arms cache, a young man approached and then quickly ran off. The family alerted police, who arrested the couple soon afterwards and captured two more members of the cell, one of whom was on foot, the other being apprehended after he arrived in a car to pick up the straggler. A second cache found in the same area contained bombs made from Semtex. The cell had been operating for over a year, and it was their blunder and, for the police, sheer luck which led to their capture.

One of the forgotten tragedies of IRA violence in England is that Irish people living peacefully in Britain have often been subjected to verbal abuse in their places of work and in their neighbourhoods. They have also been the target of police scrutiny, some of it unwarranted and malicious. The scale of police searches and arrests over the last twenty-five years pales in comparison to the late 1930s, but it has been a problem for ordinary Irish families. Understandably, the level of IRA violence is such that members of the Irish community, and all those travelling to and from Ireland to Britain, will be filed on computer, and their movements liable to scrutiny. The cases of the Birmingham Six and the Guildford Four illustrate the potentially harmful nature of police procedures and the tendency of the judicial system to equate Irishness with terrorist intent.

However, there have been many cases which have not come to light in which scores of innocent people have been arrested under the Prevention of Terrorism Act, questioned and released. In periods of heightened tension in Britain, Scotland Yard, in particular, sought to convince the public that it was hot on the trail of the bombers and gunmen. It leaked information of a dubious nature to the press, named people who were not in the country and people who had never been in the country, and issued the registration numbers of cars which had left Britain for Ireland weeks before a tragedy. The obvious interpretation is that Scotland Yard was constantly under pressure to get results and the lack of success prompted staff at a senior level to create a smokescreen.

There have been documented examples of the abuse of police powers in that process. In 1979 members of an Irish society in Essex were arrested for questioning. Details of the arrests were leaked to the media, who speculated that those being questioned would soon be charged with bombings at Greenwich and Canvey Island. That story quickly faded from the news pages when it became clear that the Irish society members were law-abiding people with no republican connections. One of my RUC sources was forthright in condemning the attitudes of people he met at the Yard.

It is important to get things right, to target the right people and only arrest those you know have a role within or on the fringes of the Provos. It is stupid to antagonize the whole Irish community in Britain, especially when the vast majority couldn't give a damn about the IRA. I know Irish people in England and they have a hard enough job facing the embarrassment of being Irish when the IRA kills people in Birmingham and elsewhere. I was at the Yard on several occasions when raids were ordered on squats where Irish migrant workers were holed up. The operations were not based on hard information but were from my point of view a PR exercise. People were manhandled, arrested and questioned without any proper basis.

It looked good in the papers. People can say what they want about the RUC, and certainly we have not always been lily-white, but we have a bigger problem and the people we arrest are people known to be involved. The fact that we can't charge them is down to the rules of evidence. We arrest them to let them know we know what they're at. That keeps them jittery.

All the Irish people I have talked to who have lived peacefully in England throughout the present campaign of violence expressed abhorrence of the IRA, and the majority stressed that at times of tension in Britain they were embarrassed to admit they were Irish. They often felt the need to tell English friends and colleagues that being Irish did not mean they were republicans. One Irishman described to me what he considered to be the views of the Irish in Great Britain:

We live in England, we have made our lives here and we vote here. We don't harbour any resentment of the English, otherwise we wouldn't continue to remain here. Certainly there have been times like Bloody Sunday in Derry when the old prejudices come to light and you feel emotional. Even then it was not the English that many of us criticized but the army and those politicians who allowed it to happen. But it is difficult to criticize British policy in Ireland because people immediately think you're an IRA supporter. I can understand that because the English genuinely know nothing about the situation. It is not pleasant to be Irish and to arrive in work when an IRA bomb has just killed several people in an English pub. I talked to Irish friends about that and they found that they faced cold stares at work, in the local supermarket or in the street. It makes us feel guilty. Now that is difficult to convey to people – that we feel guilty about something we have no part of probably seems ludicrous. Probably we regret being Irish at those times and feel that our Irishness is something to be embarrassed about. The IRA will never understand what that is like because they don't care. When the bombs went off in Birmingham, I was reluctant to go to work. For days I could almost touch the resentment among guys who normally chatted away to me. I stopped going to Irish pubs because I thought that maybe I would be scrutinized and filed as someone who was republican. The Irish love their music and much of it is political but that does not mean those who listen to it are going to go out and kill innocent people. Friends told me to avoid places where the Irish congregate because it was likely everyone there would be a potential suspect.

During the IRA campaign in England in the 1990s – one of the most ruthless ever mounted by the Provisionals – the security in the City of London resembled Belfast and Derry. That was exactly what the IRA set out to achieve. The IRA has proved it can sustain a long campaign in mainland Britain. When one IRA cell was apprehended, often because of its mistakes, another was activated. The public was entitled to ask whether it was possible to win the war against the terrorists, and whether the intelligence war was already lost. Security was often imposed after the event, or in the expectation that something was going to happen. The terrorists had the upper hand because security was never foolproof, and security methods were generally static and predictable. On the other hand, the terrorists altered their targets, changed their personnel and routes, selected alternative dates and worked out ways of bypassing security. In large cities such as London, it was impossible to mount a security screen round every target. The IRA would as likely bomb a national monument, a bank, a museum or a hotel.

IRA cells comprised people who blended into the crowds on the Underground. They were indistinguishable from you and me. One of the problems with security over the years was that many people believed the tabloid image of the terrorist as a scruffy, wild-eyed criminal type who looked different from those around him. That was nonsense, just as an accent was no indication. British soldiers in Northern Ireland were taught to speak with a variety of Northern Irish dialects, and the IRA employed similar tactics. Public vigilance was important, but in large cities it was easy for terrorists to hide and survive; they were not living in tightly knit communities but in large areas where people tended to lead their own lives and did not pry into the movements and habits of others. The urban terrorist was adaptable because he or she generally derived from an urban background. Terrorists were also taught to lead quiet and uneventful lives in which they avoided contact with the British-Irish community and neighbours. The terrorists were mostly aged between eighteen and twenty-eight and were familiar with the style of dress and behaviour typical of that generation. There was no means of identifying the terrorist in a crowded Oxford Street, in a burger restaurant or in the cinema. The young woman carrying her weekly shopping could have been a member of Cumann na mBann armed with a Semtex bomb concealed under boxes of washing powder and cartons of milk.

Who would have suspected thirty-seven-year-old James Canning, who lived with sixty-year-old Ethel Lamb in her small bungalow in Northolt, West London. They looked an unlikely pair, but that did not cause neighbours to suspect them of being involved with terrorism. He was small and dark-haired and sported a moustache. She was overweight and looked depressed. Canning spoke with a Scots accent which he had acquired while living as a teenager in Scotland. He had a wife and five children, one of whom was born while he lived with Lamb. His wife and children lived in Crossmaglen near the Northern Ireland border with the Republic. He befriended Lamb when they met at a singles party in the Adam and Eve pub in Hayes in 1991. Lamb was trying to recover from a broken relationship, and Canning seized the opportunity to exploit her sadness and loneliness. He moved in with her, behaved like a doting lover, repaired the garden, where he built a secret hide, and played golf. He decorated her bungalow, and helped her spend her savings.

Ethel Lamb was unaware that her lover's trips to Ireland were to his wife and family. Once he had control of her life and affections, he began using the bungalow as a storage place for guns and bombs. In the hide at the bottom of the garden, under a rabbit hutch, was a cache containing Kalashnikov automatic rifles which the IRA intended to use in an assassination campaign. Under the lovers' bed were quantities of Semtex, ammunition and bomb-making components. Canning was the quartermaster for IRA cells in London. Lamb did know about the terrorist equipment which her lover assembled, but her fear of losing him prevented her from going to the police. She was suspicious that he had another woman in his life, and she followed him to Ireland, where she learned of the existence of his family. That was the beginning of a serious rift in their relationship. She threatened to betray him, but he warned her the IRA would kill her. The stress of a double life, and the knowledge that he was using her, drove her to confide in the police. Scotland Yard told her that her co-operation would result in a lighter sentence. She was encouraged to return to her home and act as if she were a willing accomplice. The Anti-Terrorist Squad targeted the bungalow with electronic surveillance, but moved in to arrest Canning when they felt he had become aware of their presence. He was arrested in April 1992, but he was only one person in a large terrorist network.

The IRA had many 'sleeper' agents in Britain whose only role was to provide accommodation for active service cells. Moreover, a terrorist with a job and a flat did not attract suspicion. It was the intention of those who created the 'England Department' to foresee the problems facing cells in Britain.

The only effective means of fighting terrorism is through hard intelligence which anticipates atrocities, and that requires the penetration of terrorism at every level. However, the casual observer of the campaign in Britain, during which the IRA fired mortar bombs into the garden of 10 Downing Street, would have been justified in asserting that the intelligence war was lost.

12

The Intelligence War

The war against the IRA in Britain was always fought against the background of rivalry and squabbling within the security apparatus, which includes the army, MI5, MI6, the Anti-Terrorist Squad at Scotland Yard and regional police forces. There was a lack of co-ordination of anti-terrorist policy and a feeling within each grouping that the others were inadequately shaped for combating the IRA. One could compare it to a large bureaucratic structure where inter-departmental rivalry results in the non-sharing of information. In England one big problem for security was Scotland Yard's belief that they were the experts and that the spooks at MI5 did not possess the expertise or the intelligence necessary to deal with the IRA's England Department. When the 1990s produced a more sustained IRA campaign, it was clear that Scotland Yard's anti-terrorist methods were inadequate because the IRA continued to move men, guns and explosives into England without incurring arrests. Each side accused the other of incompetence and failure to share information.

A former officer at the Yard explained the bitterness which existed between the Anti-Terrorist Squad and MI5.

We were across this issue when Five [MI5] was too busy watching Soviet diplomats and engaging in a lot of its other curious activities. We were on top of the problem and we didn't need interference from people in Five who did not have the expertise we had on the ground. We were dealing with one of the most experienced terrorist organizations in the world, and it was always going to be a task which would not produce immediate results. Of course there was a lack of co-ordination because they constantly refused to share information with us. They had their people in Ireland and it would have been valuable to us to have had constant access to intelligence which had a bearing on the IRA's activities over here. That was denied us time and time again. There was a feeling at the Yard that after the Cold War there was a lot of spare capacity in Five and they wanted to take up the slack by snatching control of the whole security apparatus which was targeted at the IRA. They were pointing the finger at us as though we were at fault for not stopping the IRA campaign in Britain. It was always a thankless and difficult task but we built up enormous expertise and intelligence. No-one will ask how much worse it would have been without our efforts. After all, Five and all the other organizations in Ireland have not been able to defeat terrorism.

I relayed those criticisms to a contact in MI5, who scornfully dismissed them as 'typical of the narrow attitudes of some people at the Yard'. He castigated Scotland Yard for failing to anticipate the IRA build-up of men and supplies in Britain at the beginning of the 1990s. I put it to him that ever since MI5 assumed the primary role in 1992 it too has proved incapable of eliminating the terror in Britain. He replied that greater co-ordination had not always shown visible signs of success, but in time people in Britain would recognize the value of MI5's role: 'There were grave consequences waiting in the wings if we had not been given the task of co-ordinating all intelligence and methods. Of course we restrict the flow of types of intelligence to the Yard. Our job is to lead, and in this we have to protect sources and agents. We knew that people at the Yard were leaking information to the media to damage us by alleging incompetence on our part. We value the expertise in the Yard, but it is just one part of an overall structure and effort.'

I believe the internecine struggles within the anti-terrorist community seriously limited its capacity to defeat the IRA. A senior IRA intelligence officer was quick to point out to me that the Provisionals benefited considerably from the friction among the various organizations. Within British Army HQ in Northern Ireland there were a number of groups preserving information for their own operations. They employed loyalist terrorists and targeted members of the IRA for assassination. There were psychological-warfare operatives, people involved in black propaganda and a Political Secretariat run first by MI6 and later by MI5. The military intelligence structure was wide-ranging, and comprised listed and unlisted units; the unlisted units were given titles such as 'Four Field Survey Troop, Royal Engineers', and the practice of using bogus titles persists to the present day. When covert bodies became what the intelligence community called 'public property', their names were changed, all documentation was destroyed, and some personnel were moved beyond the reach of investigating authorities such as the CID. Similar covert units were put in service in the last ten years with names such as 14th Intelligence Company, 14th Independent Company and Future Research Units. Most of them were trained by the SAS to gather intelligence, assassinate terrorists and run loyalist terrorist agents. Loyalist paramilitaries were supplied with intelligence files on members of the IRA to enable them to kill people considered a threat by the authorities. Employing loyalist hitmen was a clean and easy way for the intelligence community to distance itself from its own assassination campaign.

Intelligence gathering created more problems for government than any other aspect of the conflict. The problems could be categorized as lack of co-ordination and oversight. In many respects, the intelligence agencies mirrored the problems faced by the British Army when it lacked political direction. Too many short cuts were taken, and too many agents allowed to operate with impunity. The genesis of the problem went back to the early 1970s, and that was confirmed to me by a former general who said it was debilitating for the regular army to find that the two leading organizations, MI5 and MI6, were more concerned with their struggle for power than 'on-the-ground operations'.

The running of agents was another bizarre dimension to the intelligence war. Special Branch found that other organizations were running their agents without their knowledge, while military intelligence conferred with no-one about their recruitment policy. When the RUC was resurrected as a front-line force in the mid-to late Seventies, the situation became even more troubled and complex. The historical enmity between the RUC and the military surfaced once again, and information was not shared. The police regarded military intelligence as 'the long-haired wide boys in the business'. The use of agents and *agents provocateurs* by the military made life difficult for the police and also for MI5. In his official inquiry in the 1980s, the English policeman John Stalker tried to unravel that can of worms, but he ended up being branded as the friend of criminals, and serious attempts were made to hamper his investigations and to damage his reputation. He was examining a series of controversial shootings which had occurred in 1982 and which led to the allegation of a shoot-to-kill policy by the RUC.

At that time the RUC had its own covert units trained to fulfil the role of the SAS and military intelligence. They took over many of the army undercover operations in the Tyrone area and extended their work into other border counties. The RUC created a department known as E4, with separate cells trained to undertake tasks ranging from surveillance to photography, the planting of bugging devices and armed confrontation with terrorists. The cell dealing with surveillance was E4A but it relied heavily on MI5 technicians to plant bugging devices. MI5 was well equipped to provide expertise in a range of security matters. 'A Branch' in London comprised units such as A1A which specialized in break-ins, and A2A which transcribed bugs. Within 'F Branch', which dealt with surveillance on politicians, journalists, teachers, trade unions and other activists, there were separate units: F3 was responsible for analysing terrorism; F5 contained experts with knowledge of Irish terrorism; and FX ran agents in subversive organizations. MI5 had its own series of code-words for bugging operations: 'Cinnamon' was used to denote a telephone-bugging operation authorized by a warrant; and 'Azure' was the bugging of a building without a warrant. Despite MI5's expertise in this field, E4A was not happy about handing control of bugging operations to MI5 because it was obliged to provide the agency with first-hand knowledge of the sources of intelligence and the way in which they were used.

Often there were arguments between the RUC, its Special Branch, MI5 and MI6 about which organization should control a particular intelligence operation. MI5 and MI6 tended to take over when any electronic surveillance was required, but the RUC was then often left in the dark when covert operations, sometimes involving the SAS or other undercover groups, were taking place. Yet if anything went wrong – as happened in the cases investigated by Stalker, where unarmed republicans were shot dead – MI5 and MI6 were content to allow the RUC to take the blame. On several occasions RUC detectives were even denied access to personnel involved in undercover operations which had been approved by the Government, the British Army, MI5 and MI6 but of which it had little or no knowledge. The RUC was frequently not kept informed by its own Special Branch of E4 surveillance activities. In many instances the priority seemed to be to ensure that informers were protected, rather than to prevent IRA operations from taking place. RUC Special Branch and MI6 operatives passed information to journalists that I suspect was intended to obscure the identity of their top informant who was, I believe, still active inside the Provisional IRA long after the Stalker Report was completed – which is why so many attempts were made to hamper Stalker's inquiries.

My own investigations have revealed that some agents were used by their intelligence handlers to bring about the deaths of certain members of the IRA. This was the kind of political and military hornets' nest that Stalker encountered when he arrived in Northern Ireland in 1984. His inquiry, together with RUC anger at the denial of MI5 and MI6 involvement, created hostility between the police force and MI6 in particular. It was a further example of the way the intelligence war was reduced to internecine squabbling and dirty tricks. Once again the blame lay with the British government and with staff in the Home and Foreign Offices. The absence of proper guidelines permitted abuses in the employment of terrorists as sources and as *agents provocateurs*.

I know of one incident where a friend in the RUC was on a house raid in a republican area when he was confronted with such a problem. He told me: 'I went to the house with several colleagues and discovered a small arms cache. We radioed in and were ordered to return to base without the terrorist or his arms. I discovered the orders came from military intelligence. The guy was one of their agents, and he was also a Provo. The arms were not IRA weapons and one wonders what he intended to do with them.'

Many agents were sacrificed to IRA execution squads for the purpose of concealing the presence of more highly placed informants. The use of agents was an important part of the drive against terrorism, but there were no strictures on what those agents were allowed to do in the course of their work for the Government. In order to maintain their cover, should they have been permitted to shoot members of the security forces? Should they have been allowed to plant bombs which damaged property and killed or injured civilians? What price should a democracy pay for the defeat of terrorism? This issue demanded that the Government legislate to give freedom of action for the intelligence community within guidelines enshrining democratic principles such as the right to life. There could be no illegal killing.

The growing problems in the intelligence community in the 1980s and the failure of Scotland Yard's Anti-Terrorist Squad to eliminate the IRA threat in Britain made casual observers conclude that the intelligence war was being lost. With the end of the Cold War, MI5 began to seek a greater role in the fight against

Irish terrorism. The agency needed to convince the Government that the controversy relating to intelligence activities was due to a lack of co-ordination between the various groupings; that the failure to halt the IRA campaign in Britain was directly caused by the absence of a centralized method of analysing information; that there were operations in progress which might produce damaging revelations about the role of military intelligence; and that there were too many undercover groupings out of control. But MI5 required something more tangible to sustain its case, and it had just the solution at its disposal.

In 1993, MI5 dismissed an internal report by the RUC Chief Constable, Hugh Annesley, a former commissioner of special operations lists at Scotland Yard. Annesley argued that there should be a national anti-terrorist task force, modelled on the FBI. He believed such a body would be better suited to co-ordinate intelligence and train experts specifically for that role. His arguments pointed to a deterioration in the sharing of information. However, it was Annesley who provided MI5 with the crucial evidence that led to their take-over of all counter-intelligence in 1992.

The story of how MI5 achieved its goal of convincing the British government that it should be the agency in charge began in the wake of the Stalker inquiry. MI5 told Number 10 that the embarrassing revelations of the Stalker Report could have been avoided if there had been tighter control of the security network. Military intelligence and the Anti-Terrorist Squad disagreed, and pointed out that MI5 was not experienced in dealing with IRA terrorism. It did not possess the types of ground operative who could be placed under cover, or the man-to-man surveillance techniques developed by other groupings. MI5 warned the Government that damaging revelations concerning the use of terrorist agents were waiting in the wings. They had in mind the role of military intelligence, which for twenty years had been using loyalist organizations for counter-terror. MI5 emphasized that the Ulster Defence Regiment had been so deeply penetrated by both military intelligence and loyalist paramilitaries that the level of collusion would be obstructive in the event of moves towards a political settlement. I was told by an MI5 source that the Government appeared unmoved by the case being made, and that senior MI5 officers decided that public exposure of some of the issues would turn the tide in their request for control.

MI5 knew that military intelligence was running a UDA hitman, Brian Nelson. He was a former soldier with the Black Watch Regiment and had served for a short time in the Ulster Defence Regiment. In the early 1980s he took time off from his work as both an informant and a terrorist and went with his family to Germany. Nelson was a loss to the intelligence community because he was a senior figure in the UDA and its military wing, the Ulster Freedom Fighters (UFF). He was persuaded to return to Northern Ireland, and MI5 asked military intelligence to organize a meeting with him in a London hotel in 1987. They wanted a closer look at Nelson and to discuss the work he was about to undertake for the military. The meeting with Nelson was the beginning of an MI5 plan to expose the problems within the dirty war. Military intelligence persuaded Nelson to return to the UDA, and guaranteed him a regular income and a deposit for a house. In the spring of 1987 he rose within the ranks of the UDA/UFF and became their co-ordinator of intelligence.

Nelson's job was to provide loyalist murder squads with details of the lifestyles of republican sympathizers, members of Sinn Fein and those suspected of being IRA members. His military intelligence handlers supplied him with security forces' intelligence files on people in the Catholic community. Nelson fed the data into his home computer and built up extensive records on scores of targets. He passed files containing information and photographs to UFF gunmen. It was simply a case of the military employing Nelson to prepare death squads for them. In turn, he kept his handlers informed of UFF operations and those carried out jointly with the UVF.

Nelson was within a secret military intelligence unit with the bizarre title 'Future Research Units', a successor to other cover groupings I mentioned earlier. It typified the kind of body that would exist and subsequently disappear once its activities came to light. RUC CID discovered its existence in 1991 after a Catholic student at Queen's University was abducted in Belfast by armed men, taken to a room, interrogated about the political affiliations of his fellow students, subjected to electric shock treatment to his genitals, and dumped in an alleyway. The student reported his ordeal to the RUC, who were at first reluctant to believe him. Some detectives suggested that his captors were probably IRA, but one element of his story pointed elsewhere. From his description of the battery used to power the electrodes which were attached to his body, one detective concluded that this battery was of a type only used by the military. However, the army denied knowledge of any covert grouping within its ranks, and unofficially told one detective to be careful when asking questions about military intelligence. The RUC Chief Constable decided to conduct a secret investigation and a detective was ordered to carry out surveillance on military bases in Belfast, particularly the one attached to the RUC centre at Ladis Drive. One of the investigating officers told me what occurred:

> I went to see a colonel who was very pleasant but pointed out that it was not in his interests to discuss military intelligence work. He was not unpleasant but he made it clear that no-one would talk to me about that sort of thing. A Special Branch man who had just retired told me to look under my car if I continued to make inquiries. He was a friend, and he gave me the name of a special, classified grouping only known as Future Research Units. I placed surveillance on the military compound at Ladis Drive and discovered that the FRUs operated from there. They entered and left in Land Rovers and were never stopped. They used a series of special hand signals and torchlight signals to give them unhindered access to the base.

A special report was prepared for the Chief Constable, substantiating the student's claims and identifying the Future Research Units. He passed it on to MI5, giving them yet another illustration that there were groupings out of control. The Chief Constable explained to MI5 that a senior member of the nationalist SDLP knew about the episode; since the student was one of his constituents, he was not prepared to jeopardize the young man's life by going public. However, there was no absolute guarantee that the politician would maintain his silence, and public exposure of the matter would seriously damage the security forces.

In September 1989, MI5 moved ahead with their strategy to expose the weaknesses in the security system and convince the Government of its case. Events took on a controversial tone when loyalist paramilitaries, namely the UDA/UFF, provided journalists and public figures with evidence of collusion between the security forces and loyalist paramilitaries. One of those in receipt of evidence was on MI5's books as a willing conduit. Media reporting of the use of security forces' files by loyalist hit-squads led to renewed calls from the Republic and the Catholic community for a public inquiry.

MI5 encouraged the RUC Chief Constable, Hugh Annesley, personally to demand an inquiry on the grounds that it would clear the RUC. They did not tell him that it would seriously damage military intelligence and the Ulster Defence Regiment. For months, MI5 had been aware that Annesley wanted to highlight the inadequacies in security. His willingness to encourage public scrutiny suited their plan to publicize faults in the system in order to provoke a policy review. Reports that Annesley demanded an inquiry only after two terrorist files were taken from Dunmurry police station were incorrect, since those files were recovered by CID over a weekend, and Annesley was already determined to have the matter investigated. The Chief Constable therefore asked HM Inspectorate of Police to appoint an English policeman to set up an inquiry. Annesley acted honourably, and could not have known MI5's motives for supporting his actions or that they would seek to take control of security from the Home Office.

When John Stevens, Deputy Chief Constable of Cambridgeshire, was appointed to head the inquiry, his staff were not permitted to liaise with the RUC. MI5 helped set the parameters by identifying areas to be investigated. They knew it would not be to their advantage if too many issues were examined or exposed, because it would have the effect of damaging the war against the terrorists; only certain matters should be exposed to public scrutiny. MI5 pointed the inquiry in the direction of Nelson, who was picked up with many leading loyalist figures. Military intelligence were informed by MI5 that Nelson was on a list of people suspected of collusion. The tip-off enabled him to destroy many of his files and pass other documents to his handlers in military intelligence. Meetings took place between representatives of MI5, the Home Office and military intelligence. The military wanted immunity for Nelson, but Stevens told Home Office officials that he would run his own inquiry irrespective of pressures from the military. Stevens was an honest, tough and uncompromising officer and went about his task with vigour and resourcefulness. A leading member of the UDA, X, whom I knew well, asked Stevens if he would consider giving him immunity in return for evidence about his role as an agent for British intelligence; but Stevens rejected the offer.

In January 1990 the room in which Stevens and his team stored their files was set alight, telephone lines were cut and security cameras were made inoperative. The damage to the telephones prevented members of the Stevens team from summoning assistance to deal with the blaze. Although the RUC told reporters the fire had probably been caused by a cigarette end, that explanation stretched credulity. The room was in a heavily guarded police building and had electronic security devices. No-one was registered as being in the room when the fire began. The room had been locked for a considerable time before the fire was discovered. Some people in the intelligence community believed that Stevens had access to information which would have taken his inquiry into dangerous areas for the security forces. Could the fire, which damaged computerized records, have been the work of experts in burglary from 'A Branch' of MI5? Did the agency feel that the investigation was going outside the parameters it had been trying to establish? The fire occurred the night before Nelson was due to be arrested.

Stevens was angry when he discovered that one of those in receipt of evidence of collusion, Mr A, who was used as a conduit by MI5, had failed to tell police about dealings with the UDA. When Stevens interviewed Nelson and the other UDA leader, X, he found they had both been instrumental in providing journalists and others with documents proving collusion between elements of the security forces and loyalist terrorists. However, he learned that one individual,

Mr A, was so close to the UDA leadership that he had been present at a meeting where a decision was taken to go public with evidence of the links between the UDA/UFF and the security forces. Unknown to Stevens, Mr A was the MI5 conduit, but Stevens was angry that such a person in public life had been in that position and had lied about the manner in which he had acquired the documents which were used by the media. Stevens's team argued that Mr A should be questioned and, if possible, prosecuted. Before Stevens could act, however, MI5 used the Home Office to intervene: a phone call was made to the Stevens team ordering them not to proceed against Mr A.

There was a further twist in the story. Nelson's UDA colleague, X, was an MI5 informant. In one of his sessions with Stevens he admitted that he and Nelson had met Mr A in X's home and had shown him classified security forces' files to enable him to facilitate a story about collusion between loyalists, the military, and the UDR. X said they had fabricated evidence to implicate the RUC in the collusion allegations, and X also told Stevens that he would reveal who had ordered him to expose the security forces if he was granted immunity; as I have mentioned, Stevens rejected this proposition. When Stevens confronted Nelson with X's account of the meeting with Mr A, Nelson refused to explain why he had been willing to jeopardize the UDA's working arrangement with military intelligence by revealing the existence of the files he had been given by his handlers.

As the inquiry continued, Nelson began to feel vulnerable. He had never imagined that his employers in military intelligence would allow him to be arrested and imprisoned. Growing more desperate, he began to talk more freely to Stevens, and through a lawyer made it clear to his employers that he would reveal all if he was not granted immunity. The Director of Public Prosecutions was put under pressure to drop the case, but refused. An RUC source explained to me the reasons why immunity was not on offer to Nelson and to X.

Nelson began talking to Stevens the moment he realized that he was on his own. When he began talking, there was no way it could be hidden. Many people in the judicial and security systems still remembered the Stalker affair, and nobody wanted their fingerprints on a cover-up. He told Stevens that his handlers suggested that the UDA bomb Dublin in an operation codenamed 'Snowball'. The bombings would force the Dublin government to call for the extradition of the offenders, namely loyalists. That would expose the Irish government's own poor record on extradition and force them to seek conducive arrangements with London for a proper extradition arrangement. The plan was never put into action. There had to be one sacrificial lamb. —— [The other UDA leader] was not going to get a deal because he was not as important as Nelson. I think people on high knew that it wasn't in his interests to talk too much. His own people would take him out if he tried to expose his role. There was enough in the Nelson case for those who wanted it out. Let's put it this way: it was a strange way for certain people in the UDA to behave. It wasn't in their interests to expose their relationships with the security forces. Firstly, if, as some people suggested, the UDA was bitter about RUC pressure on them and decided not to compromise the RUC, the people running Nelson would have advised against that because it would lead to an investigation which would point the finger at them. Nelson met MI5 in London. We know —— [the other UDA leader] was being run by them, but was Nelson? I don't know, but let's put it this way: it was not uncommon for someone to be run by two agencies without one of them, or either of them, knowing the role of the other. Nelson was the big fish, and there were those who wanted what he had to say out in the public arena.

The Stevens team was puzzled that the UDA leadership, in particular Nelson and X, had made public their links with members of the security forces when they themselves were government agents, Nelson with military intelligence and X with 'British intelligence' (X still refused to name his employers as MI5 and Special Branch unless Stevens agreed to protect him).

Nelson eventually appeared in court and pleaded guilty to twenty offences, including five of conspiracy to murder. His guilty plea was part of a deal whereby other charges were dropped. On 22 September 1992 he was given a ten-year sentence after a colonel in military intelligence gave him a character reference: the colonel said Nelson had saved as many as 200 lives and was 'a courageous man whose mistakes were understandable'. How could an army colonel describe murder as 'understandable'? Nelson had been charged only with five cases of conspiracy to murder, but no full picture was given of his role as the man who identified a large number of victims and sent the killers on their way to the target.

One of the killings with which he was not charged was that of a solicitor, Pat Finucane, who had represented the families of the IRA trio shot dead by the SAS in 1988 in Gibraltar. Nelson knew the killers were en route to Finucane's home in North Belfast in February 1989 – as did military intelligence – but that information was never passed on to the RUC, who might have been able to prevent the death of the solicitor at the hands of the UFF. Finucane was an extremely able lawyer who frequently represented republicans or the families of IRA dead. In a divided society like Northern Ireland, lawyers on both sides act, without prejudice, for all the paramilitaries. Finucane had been highly successful in controversial cases involving IRA suspects. His ability, rather than his religious persuasion, was the cause of his death. I know of one Protestant solicitor who held regular meetings with the leaders of the UFF and UVF and was paid in cash for his extra-curricular services. He visited and acted for loyalist hitmen who were in custody, and his role was to discover if they had admitted guilt or divulged sensitive information to investigating detectives. His findings helped the UDA/UFF leaders to judge whether they needed to plug a leak in their security, or take action to silence a talkative terrorist. Pat

Finucane was not that kind of solicitor. He was marked down for assassination by the UDA, though some members of the RUC think the orders may have come from military intelligence. An RUC source told me: 'We were angry about the failure of military intelligence to inform us about Finucane and other people whom their agent, Nelson, was targeting. But then why should they have confided in us? We would have stopped it. That was not their objective. Some of our people have for years been warning about wide boys in this business and the Nelson case proved our point beyond reasonable doubt. It proved there was need for change.'

One of the striking aspects of the colonel's court appearance was his defence of Nelson's employment in this fashion and the reason for his involvement in murder. He told the judge that no guidelines existed for the running of agents who, in the context of Northern Ireland, were bound to become involved in criminality. Moral responsibility, he added, lay with the system, which had not yet found ways of coming to terms with the problems faced by an agent. So, after Stalker, there were still no guidelines, according to the colonel. After twenty years, parts of the military machine were out of control. No-one at government level cared to impose controls on certain aspects of the war.

During Margaret Thatcher's term of office as Prime Minister there was increased undercover activity of a nature that led to abuse. In 1979 she had sent the head of MI6, Sir Maurice Oldfield, to Stormont in an attempt to co-ordinate intelligence. He failed to do that, but, while he was there, his homosexuality was the subject of seedy stories which were malicious in their intent. The stories emanated from the ongoing conflict between MI5 and MI6. MI5 was angry that three years after they had finally ousted their rivals from the primary role, Thatcher should choose an MI6 chief to oversee their senior operatives in Northern Ireland. His appointment was tantamount to a public criticism of their work. MI5 used RUC Special Branch to circulate stories about Oldfield going to the town of Comber to pick up young men. Another angle offered to journalists was that the ageing spy chief was involved in the abuse of young boys from the Kincora boys' home in East Belfast. In my opinion Lady Thatcher's personal crusade against terrorism obscured the problems within the security forces and tainted her political judgement. She did not defeat terrorism, despite all her promises, and left no meaningful political legacy for Northern Ireland.

The Stevens inquiry had the effect of exonerating the RUC but exposed the problems within the British Army and the UDR. The result was an internal government review of intelligence policy, which led to the conclusion that MI5 was correct in its assessment of the need for change in the war against the IRA and the loyalists. The UDR was merged with another regiment and became the Royal Irish Regiment. But the most important development was that MI5 was granted overall control of intelligence gathering. Several journalists reported that the Home Office review which transferred control of counter-intelligence to MI5 imposed the criterion that the agency should share its information with the police. If such a concession was wrung from MI5, it was not apparent after that agency took over in 1992. It held the key to all intelligence and did not share it. RUC CID, Scotland Yard's Anti-Terrorist Squad and the regular police were continually denied access to information. In 1993 numerous requests for updated information on terrorist suspects were rejected, and relations between MI5 and Scotland Yard became strained. An insider who knew the workings of the RUC was bitter when he explained the problems:

It was all supposed to be happy in the garden when they took over. That's what the public thought and what some of us hoped, but that is not the reality. They have closed down so many avenues by which people normally sought information. Special Branch at the Yard and in Northern Ireland aren't particularly happy about it either, but they are closer to MI5 than anyone else. They have had their problems accessing information. People in the Branch are scared shitless to divulge information without permission from Five. In the past it was easy for CID or anti-terrorist people to contact colleagues in Special Branch and say: 'Look him up for me. Give me what you've got on that person or what's happening with that operation.' That's changed, and, while people understand the need for tight security in the flow and control of information, this is simply ridiculous. We are all in the same business. It appears to many of us that Five has decided that the future lies solely with them, and those of us in counter-terrorism failed and are relics of the past.

An RUC source confirmed those views and told me that CID could no longer visit Special Branch collators and ask to see files or request information:

> MI5 has its own staff at RUC HQ. They are mostly females and they are not permitted to associate with RUC staff. The Special Branch filing system is antiquated, and is still kept in cardboard folders. It is no longer possible to go down to the collators and ask for a file or for information. They are not allowed to facilitate you. They have to pass the request upwards. It's like a bureaucratic jungle. The Branch's filing system is now more complex. In order to protect the identity of agents, details are spread across numerous files and different indexes so that no one person has access to all the information to enable him or her to identify an informant.

It was a chill wind which blew through the corridors of all groupings involved in the gathering and processing of information. Special Branch was the organizational filter for the streamlining of MI5's policies. The Task Co-ordinating Group, which once contained representatives of all the security organizations, was now made up of Special Branch staff who ensured that all covert operations were co-ordinated through them and then passed on to MI5 for approval. MI5 also installed new procedures for the recruiting and handling of terrorist agents. Military intelligence was forced to consult Special Branch before it recruited terrorists; it was also required to set out in full detail the tasks for which terrorist agents were employed, and to update that information regularly. The days of organizations operating independently were believed to be over, and the 'wide boys' had been brought to heel.

However, MI5 learned the hard way that it was not staffed by the best and the brightest. I offer two examples of their lack of expertise in 1993. The supergrass system required the Government to reward many informers with a new life and a new identity. Many supergrasses proved to be incapable of living outside Northern Ireland or coping with large amounts of cash. Joe Bennett, the UVF supergrass, was provided with a new identity and sent to England. It was agreed that he could have £70,000, and this was lodged in a building society account. A limit was placed on his access to cash, allowing him to withdraw up to a maximum of £200 a day. Bennett withdrew that amount *every* day and spent it on gambling until the account was empty. His propensity to criminality led him to rob the betting shop where he spent all his money; and that took him back to prison.

Other supergrasses demanded a place in the sun, a home in a faraway country where the IRA could not reach them. That proved impossible because the CIA and other intelligence agencies throughout the world, including Australia, refused to co-operate with the relocation process because they were not prepared to relocate people with criminal records. Most supergrasses had led criminal lives before they forged links with paramilitaries, and while members of terrorist organizations they were also guilty of murder and maiming innocent people. That was allegedly the price for maintaining their cover. Relocation became a serious problem for the RUC's C14, the body which dealt with the security of supergrasses. They asked MI5 to use their influence with their counterparts overseas, but MI5 reported back that they had encountered a negative response from the CIA and similar bodies throughout the world.

C14 agreed to provide special protection for supergrasses until they were relocated, but said it was the responsibility of MI5 to find them new identities. When a supergrass was released or granted immunity, C14 ensured his safe passage to a house in England where he remained under guard until all the details of his new life were in place. No-one was allowed access to him or his family. But MI5 admitted to the RUC and C14 that it did not know how to fashion new identities for supergrasses or agents. An RUC source told me that he was amazed that an organization which demanded control of counter-intelligence could not handle relocation of agents. 'It was ludicrous that MI5, which everyone believes is the *crème de la crème* of the intelligence world, doesn't know how to hide agents. Surely they did it with the KGB when they turned them? C14 was left to do the job for them.' C14's method of creating new identities was not as complex as one might imagine. They used the computer of the Department of Social Security headquarters at Newcastle upon Tyne. Selected members of the DSS staff assist C14 in creating a new history for an agent, and security systems built into the computer prevent anyone tracing his identity or that of his wife and children.

Within a year of the 1992 take-over, MI5 had imposed on the intelligence services stringent rules about the handling of agents and the security of the information provided from those sources. They restricted access to intelligence to only those directly involved, and warned that handlers should not employ informants as *agents provocateurs*. There is no guarantee that the rules will be adhered to by everyone, though I came across a case in which the Director of Public Prosecutions maintained that the rules had been breached. An informant was asked by his Special Branch handlers to bring them an IRA mortar. He removed a mortar tube from an arms dump and gave it to his handlers, who used MI5 technicians to place a small bug inside it, before it was put back in the dump. The DPP demanded to know if the mortar was in a working condition when the agent returned it to the dump because he could not approve of a weapon being put back in service if it was capable of killing people. He argued that there was a moral as well as a legal dimension to the case. Special Branch were obliged to admit that it was in working condition, but claimed the return of the mortar could save lives. They made a valid point but were judged to have breached the new guidelines. It was an example of how MI5 were imposing restrictions on the handling of terrorist sources.

In the field of practical surveillance, the agency suffered its most serious embarrassment very soon after its take-over. Several of the national newspapers published a claim that MI5 agents lost track of a 1,000-lb bomb in Central London. The story was correct and had been leaked to the press by disgruntled Anti-Terrorist Squad officers at Scotland Yard, because MI5 had taken charge of the operation against the wishes of the anti-terrorist teams who were experts in man-to-man surveillance. For some time Scotland Yard had been warning that there were two teams of IRA personnel in London. One team did the 'small jobs' and the other did the 'big jobs'. There were sleepers and couriers in place, and an intermediary who was buying stolen fertilizer throughout England. MI5 agents were positioned in the boots of parked cars to watch two lorry-loads of explosives, each thought to contain 1,000 lb of fertilizer mix. The intelligence community has developed a number-plate which works like a two-way mirror. It is used on cars where the number-plate sits in a cavity between the bumper and the boot. Anyone looking at such a plate would never know that an agent was inside the car boot, watching and videotaping people in the street. With that type of equipment in place, the MI5 watchers failed to detect one of the bombs being moved. At Scotland Yard there was a degree of merriment as well as dismay that a large quantity of explosives was still available to the bombers.

Overall, however, MI5 have sought to institute new procedures which had been sorely needed for twenty-five years. If the British government had appointed MI5 to that role in the 1970s perhaps there would have been more accountability and less controversy.

13

A Trail of Terror

Before the end of the 1980s the IRA made clear its
intention to make the British mainland a major area
of operations. It firmly believed that a campaign of
terror in English cities would lead it to the conference
table. On a quiet morning in September 1989 ten
members of a Royal Marines band were killed
when a huge bomb made of Semtex exploded in
the rest room of the Regimental School of Music
at Deal in Kent. The bandsmen were rehearsing for
a performance in Strasbourg to celebrate the fortieth
anniversary of the Council of Europe. The death toll
could have been much higher because there were
seventy bandsmen in the room where the bomb was
concealed. Security at the barracks was in the hands of
a private company which employed unarmed guards.
The IRA bombers had little difficulty gaining access
to the site and did not distinguish between military
musicians and fighting personnel.

This mass killing was a warning of IRA intent and was followed within one year by the booby-trap killing of an army careers officer in London rush-hour traffic. He died as he got into his van, and a colleague was injured. Two months later, Ian Gow, a senior Tory MP who had befriended the Unionists and was a close friend of Margaret Thatcher, was killed by a bomb concealed under his car. He had been a constant critic of the IRA and before his death had remarked that the British government and people would never surrender to them. Two months after his murder, two IRA gunmen failed in an attempt to murder Sir Peter Terry at his Staffordshire home; he was high on the IRA's target list because he was Governor of Gibraltar at the time of the shooting there of the three members of an IRA cell by the SAS.

Political assassination was always favoured by the IRA, but their main aim for the 1990s was to bring terror to the heart of London with a ferocity never before experienced in the capital. The Army Council decided that selected assassinations were not a major priority unless the targets were cabinet ministers. They told GHQ that the targeting of individual politicians involved too many risks for active service personnel, and spectacular operations such as large bombs in London or the killing of John Major were a more effective way of proving that the IRA was a threat which could not be eliminated. They retained memories of the bombing of the Grand Hotel at Brighton and, far from regarding the operation as a failure, considered it an example of what was possible. Within the IRA psyche was the belief that a powerfully orchestrated campaign of terror was politically effective, particularly if the terror was in Great Britain. They knew they were the only terrorist organization in Western Europe to survive the rigours of operating against sophisticated intelligence operations.

The IRA could afford to lose individual cells or operatives because they were constantly training other volunteers for England operations. From the beginning of the 1990s, a large percentage of IRA intelligence planning was directed at the mainland campaign. They began to believe that the anti-terrorist structures in Britain were inadequate and overburdened by a bureaucracy that effectively reduced them to a follow-up role. A member of IRA intelligence told me that they did not feel too inhibited by the counter-terrorist efforts in Britain.

> Even by the beginning of the Nineties, we were aware that we could operate effectively in Britain. We were constantly devising means of putting personnel in, of hiding materials and plugging gaps when any of our people were lifted. We were always planning, always thinking, and we were ahead of them. They were always in the position of acting after the event. They love committees, grand code-names for operations, and each part of the structure wants its own independence, whereas our system is simple, has only one objective and is not complicated by rivalry.

During the late 1980s, Margaret Thatcher remained at the top of their hit-list, and after their failure to kill her at Brighton they continued to devise means of getting close to her. They considered driving a bomb into Downing Street, or leaving car bombs close to her route from Number 10 and detonating them by remote control when her official car was taking her to Parliament. The first option was dismissed when IRA intelligence reported to the Army Council that Downing Street security had been improved and the area was bristling with cameras and electronic devices. Margaret Thatcher and the security forces knew her life was in constant danger, and from 1989 even tighter security measures were introduced at Number 10 and in its immediate vicinity. Security advisers warned her that a car bomb was probably the means by which the IRA would attempt to assassinate her. Number 10 had been fitted with blast-proof materials, new electronic cameras and a front door reinforced with steel panels. The IRA's second option – parking car bombs on thoroughfares near Downing Street – was also dismissed by the Army Council, particularly those with Sinn Fein connections, who argued that it would risk the mass murder of civilians which would be politically counter-productive. Then GHQ came up with the concept of firing home-made mortar shells into the rear of the building. Although the IRA had used the mortar to kill nine policemen in Newry police station, the unpredictable trajectory generally made it an ineffective weapon. The mortar shells were constructed from gas cylinders, packed with home-made explosives and fitted into steel tubes fixed to a wooden or metal frame. The firing mechanism was electronically controlled and the range of the shells was between 200 and 400 yards.

In 1988 Scotland Yard Anti-Terrorist Squad detectives raided an IRA safe house, and among the finds were items for constructing mortars and technical details of the weapon's trajectory. No-one in the intelligence community in London sought to analyse the potential for the use of mortars in London. In the late summer of 1990, the Army Council sanctioned a GHQ plan to send a two-man team into London to carry out an attack on Number 10. One member of the team from the IRA's Belfast Brigade was familiar with the manufacture of mortars, and his companion was knowledgeable about their trajectory. Another team was given the task of purchasing a Ford Transit van and renting a lock-up garage. An IRA co-ordinator was sent to London to liaise with existing cell members and to acquire the explosives and other materials for the manufacture of the mortars. It was a sophisticated operation which involved considerable planning.

In the autumn the two-man team began the process of constructing the devices, and cutting a hole in the roof of the van so that the mortars could be fired through it towards the Prime Minister's residence. The critical issue for the IRA was selecting a location from which to fire the shells so that the trajectory would take them over the roof of Number 10 and into the garden which faced the Cabinet Office. The 'technical expert' and the bomb-maker made numerous trips to the Downing Street area and took mental notes of the distances from possible locations in Whitehall. Their task was to make the mortars ready and leave the country before the proposed attack. GHQ decided that they were valuable personnel and did not wish to risk their being caught in a follow-up security operation. Once the van was prepared, the mortars were in place and a firing location was selected, the task of carrying out the attack was to be the responsibility of a London cell. One of its members would drive the van, park it, activate the mortars and be ferried from the scene by a companion on a motor cycle. That form of transport was chosen because it would enable a quicker escape through London traffic and avoid the inevitable security alert which would be radioed to all policemen in Whitehall. The choice of date was left to the Army Council; a telephone message to the IRA co-ordinator would be sufficient to begin the operation.

In November 1990 John Major had replaced Margaret Thatcher as Prime Minister. On the morning of 7 February 1991 the British War Cabinet was due to meet at Number 10 to examine ways of sharing with its allies the costs of the Gulf conflict. The Cabinet Office faced a garden and a surrounding wall which was ringed with barbed wire and cameras. At 10 a.m. a white Ford Transit was driven to the junction of Whitehall and Horse Guards Avenue within sight of the Ministry of Defence building. Snow was falling, and the van and the motor cycle travelling alongside it failed to attract the attention of policemen. The van driver stopped his vehicle, quickly jumped into the rear and removed a makeshift cover from the roof, exposing three mortar tubes attached to a wooden frame. He activated a timing mechanism which was attached by wires to each mortar, leapt from the van and sped off on the motor cycle with his accomplice.

In the Cabinet Office, John Major, Douglas Hurd,

Peter Lilley, Tom King, Sir Patrick Mayhew, Sir Charles Powell, Sir Percy Craddock, Sir Robin Butler, Chief of the Defence Staff, Sir Percy Craig and a number of officials were listening to David Mellor, in his role as Chief Secretary to the Treasury, outlining details of a recent visit to the United Arab Emirates. Suddenly a mortar shell landed in the garden of Number 10 and exploded, shattering the windows of the Cabinet Office. Fortunately, a plastic covering on the windows prevented a lethal shower of glass splinters and no-one was injured. The Prime Minister, John Major, and his colleagues quickly left the room because of the risk of another explosion. There was no panic among the cabinet members, who were advised by Tom King to vacate the room; as a former Northern Ireland Secretary, he had an instinct for danger. Most of the windows at the rear of the Chancellor's residence at Number 11 took the force of the blast and were destroyed. There was also damage to Number 12. Two other mortar shells failed to explode and landed near the Ministry of Defence. The Ford Transit van burst into flames as panic spread among pedestrians in the vicinity of Whitehall. Fortunately, there were no fatalities, though four people, two of them police officers, were slightly injured. The audacious nature of the IRA operation and the lack of effective security measures in Whitehall were a stark illustration of the IRA's resourcefulness and apparent invincibility.

Two weeks later the tactics of the 1939–40 campaign were once again repeated when bombs were left in litter-bins at Victoria and Paddington stations. IRA coded warnings about the bombs proved adequate only at Paddington, where the first device exploded and no-one was injured. The IRA caller did not give precise details about the second device at Victoria, and it exploded without warning, killing one person and injuring thirty. Ten days later a bomb at London Bridge Station injured twenty-nine people. The attacks were part of an IRA policy to damage the Underground and railway network and to bring terror to the whole population.

I asked a senior IRA figure why they found it necessary to turn their attention to the general public, and he replied:

Your question is typical of people who think all we want to do is kill innocent civilians. If we wanted to kill masses of innocent people, we could have done that at any time and the death toll would not be what it is. People are going to get hurt in this type of conflict. Sometimes warnings are inadequate but that is not the intention. Sometimes the authorities misinterpret the warnings or are slow to act. The reason why we hit communications is to bring the place to a standstill. It damages London economically. It makes the British people aware of the conflict in Ireland. It affects tourism and it proves the Brits can't isolate the conflict. They would be happy to have their acceptable level of violence in Northern Ireland but when it is brought home to them that it is on their doorstep they take notice. It's really about getting their attention. London is one of the major cities in Europe and when we make it unstable that's when the talking begins.

That is the thesis, but the reality is that innocent people have died, and one is left with the realization that the IRA of the 1990s concentrated more of its efforts on tactics which it must have known would lead to loss of civilian lives.

Their enormous potential became clear in early 1992 when their target was the financial heart of London. For months the IRA's England Department had devoted its energies to acquiring a large quantity of fertilizer for two bombs. Vehicles were purchased and a bomb-maker arrived from Dublin to complete the mechanisms for the bombs which required quantities of Semtex as ignition charges and complex timing devices. When the bombs were ready to be moved towards their targets, he returned to Ireland. One bomb was placed near the Baltic Exchange in the City of London. The explosion killed three people and injured ninety-one. The cost of the devastation to property in the City was estimated at hundreds of millions of pounds. Some people assessed the bomb as containing 1,000 lb of explosives but the likelihood is that it was half that size. Massive property damage was due to the IRA's choice of location: in the narrow streets of the City with its high buildings, the destructive power of the device was enormously increased. The other bomb, which had been placed near the main junction with the M1 at Staples Corner, damaged a large store and a motorway bridge.

The general public, the financial mandarins and

workers in the City were shocked, yet the atrocity could have been forecast by an astute observer of IRA tactics. Four months later two more bombs bound for the centre of London did not reach their targets. The devices were similarly constructed to the one which shattered the Baltic Exchange. A surveillance operation by anti-terrorist officers resulted in the arrest of one man and a van-load of explosives. Another van bomb evaded detection because of a failure in communication between some of those involved in undercover surveillance.

The apprehension of terrorists is a dangerous business and frequently police forces throughout Britain have preferred to use their own personnel rather than experts from Scotland Yard. It is a case of 'This is our patch and we are capable of dealing with it without outside interference'. Whether that was what happened on 7 June 1992 we may never know, but the fatal episode that occurred epitomized the risks facing ordinary policemen encountering terrorists. In the early hours of 7 June, Special Constable Glenn Goodman and Police Constable Alexander Kelly stopped a Ford Sierra on a slip road at the A64 near Tadcaster in North Yorkshire. According to later reports, it was a routine check, yet the car contained one of the IRA's leading gunmen, Paul 'Dingus' Magee, and an accomplice, Michael O'Brien.

Magee was on police and army wanted lists, having been involved in numerous attacks on the security forces in Northern Ireland. He was highly trained in the use of weapons and was regarded as extremely dangerous. In 1980 he had become famous in republican circles for a stand-off with an SAS team in which its leader, Captain Herbert Westmacott, was shot dead. In that episode, Magee and several IRA men were in a house in North Belfast waiting to attack a passing army patrol. Their weapons included automatic rifles and the high-powered M60 machine-gun (now well known from Rambo films). The SAS team, acting on a tip-off, made an assault on the house but were forced to withdraw after Captain Westmacott was killed and a priest was summoned to mediate with the IRA unit. Joseph Doherty, who was later incarcerated for nine years in New York, where a street was named after him, was with Magee in the siege house; they and their accomplices became known as the M60 gang. After their arrest, they escaped from Crumlin Road prison in Belfast and shot their way to freedom, despite being surrounded by police and soldiers outside the prison. Magee fled to the sanctuary of the Irish Republic but was arrested and gaoled there in 1982 on arms charges. He was released seven years later and rearrested after the British government demanded his extradition to serve a life sentence, imposed in his absence, for the murder of Westmacott. The Irish courts freed him to await the extradition process and he disappeared from view. IRA GHQ decided he should remain in hiding in the Republic until they found use for his talents. In the autumn of 1991 the organizers of the England Department decided that Magee would be useful as an assassin, and he was moved, first to London and then to a location in the north of England. I was told that the IRA had a target list of former politicians and military personnel and Magee was assigned to make a selection based on a feasibility study of the security of each potential victim.

On 7 June, contrary to subsequent media reports that he was on his way to an operation, Magee was en route to conceal a handgun and an automatic rifle in a wooded area close to a selected target, namely a former politician. His accomplice was a long-term operator in England who often acted as a courier of documents or weapons. Special Constable Glenn Goodman was a novice to police work with only three weeks' experience. His regular job was lorry driving, but his ambition was to be a regular constable. When he and PC Kelly stopped the Sierra, O'Brien got out and during a lengthy conversation with the policemen failed to satisfy them about the ownership of the car or the previous whereabouts of himself and his companion. When it became clear to Magee that the police were not only suspicious but summoning assistance, he emerged with a handgun and killed Glenn Goodman with two bullets. He then fired four at PC Kelly, who survived, partly because a bullet luckily struck the radio he was carrying.

As the two IRA men sped off in the Sierra, they were pursued by another police car containing PC Mark Whitehouse and twenty-four-year-old Woman Police Constable Susan Larkin. Both were unarmed and, irrespective of the risk to their lives, they gave chase for several miles to the outskirts of the village of Burton Salmon. Suddenly the terrorists' car pulled to a halt and Magee emerged with a Kalashnikov automatic rifle. He fired the weapon in one automatic burst at the police car before the terrorists drove from the scene. Fortunately, the bullets did not find their target but they succeeded in preventing PC Whitehouse and

WPC Larkin from continuing their pursuit. Magee and O'Brien drove the Sierra into a wood and set the car alight. Then they spent several days sleeping rough in the countryside near Pontefract. They had an adequate supply of money, and after four days Magee decided they should separately go into Pontefract, buy new clothes and contact their IRA co-ordinator. He would arrange for them to be spirited out of the area to a safe house and, eventually, to Ireland. I was told by an IRA contact that if Magee had contacted his co-ordinator he would have been told he was 'on his own'.

In that situation the risks for other operations are too great. They were compromised, and they should have known that in those circumstances they are a danger to others operating in Britain. The mounting of a rescue would only take place if they found themselves in a situation where they were not cornered by the Brit forces. The rules of the game are clear. They were exposed, and anyone trying to contact them faced a similar risk. Let's just say, for the sake of argument, that the Brits knew roughly where they were and had surveillance on all main routes into the area. They might just wait to see who comes to extricate them or where they run. The people who work in England are well briefed about the risks. Once you are out in the cold it's difficult to bring you in. It's different from moving people in and out who have done jobs and are not at immediate risk, or special operatives who are only tasked for one job because of their technical expertise.

On 11 June, residents of Pontefract reported to the police that two men with Irish accents were trying to buy clothes using large-denomination banknotes. Public vigilance led to their immediate capture and, eventually, a life sentence for Magee and eighteen years' imprisonment for O'Brien.

As the IRA campaign of terror continued through the 1990s, ordinary English civilians who found their lives were at risk often wondered what exactly was the IRA's attitude towards the English people. Members of the republican movement mostly refer to 'the Brits', and I asked some of those I interviewed if their use of 'British' included the Welsh, Scots and Ulster Unionists. I received the reply that 'the British are the English'. The following is a transcript of an interview with a member of the IRA.

Author: Why do you talk about the Brits and not the English? 'Brits' denotes the peoples living in Britain and the Protestants of Northern Ireland who claim Britishness.

Interviewee: You've a point there but it's easier to talk about the Brits because historically and constitutionally we talk about the British Crown, the British Parliament and the British Army. It would be much easier if we could simply isolate it to make it the English. Don't get me wrong – we're not anti-English, because most English people want their army to get out and Westminster to cut itself adrift.

Author: Why have you not targeted Scotland and Wales?

Interviewee: They're Celtic peoples who, like us, were subjugated by the English.

Author: The Scots and the Welsh are also British and intrinsically support the Crown, Parliament and the army. Is it not a fact that within the IRA there is a bitterly anti-English mentality that extends to all who are British? That the exclusion of Wales and Scotland from your agenda of violence is a convenient ploy to concentrate your activities within England where you believe the major political decisions are made?

Interviewee: OK, we know that London is the centre of power and commerce, and that's the reason for the England campaign. We talk about the Brits but we really mean the English establishment. It would be counter-productive for us to target Wales or Scotland. There are many people in those countries who understand the Irish problem better than the English and there is no point in antagonizing peoples who secretly want their own forms of independence. Essentially, the balance of power in Britain means that neither the Scots nor the Welsh can effect any change in Ireland – hence we put pressure on the English.

Author: To kill people you must harbour a hatred of them. Is it not the case that there is a hatred of the English within the IRA?

Interviewee: That's too simplistic. We've no love of the English but our problem is not with the ordinary English person living in, say, Derby, provided he's not in the army patrolling the streets of the North of Ireland.

Author: I doubt if that argument would be accepted by the dead of Birmingham, Guildford or Warrington.

Interviewee: That's a typically emotive argument. This is a war and people are going to get killed. What about the dead of Ireland? Where is the English guilt about that?

Author: How do you know how English people feel about Ireland, if you don't talk to them? How do you know how ordinary Protestants in Northern Ireland, who claim Britishness, feel about the issues if you don't talk to them? Surely your problem is that you are rooted in a history in which blame is more important than progress, and in which responsibility for the violence must be shared by all?

Interviewee: Fine, let's all share in the blame but that's not the way the Brits see it. The British people are told by their own media that violence only comes from the IRA. Who cares about the hundreds of Catholics killed by the loyalists and the security forces? We're all for getting it out in the open. The only people who have said 'No surrender' over the years have been the Unionists. When we said it, we became the enemy. Lift the broadcasting ban and let us talk to the English people. Maybe that will widen the debate.

Author: Stop the killing and talk to them.

Interviewee: You prefer the simplistic approach as usual. After all the deaths, and our struggle, we don't trust the Brits, or maybe I should say the English establishment. When we are convinced of their sincerity to move forward there'll be a new ball game. They're too hung up on their own political problems. They've never been open with their own people, and they want to decide the rules of the game. That has to be agreed and everyone has to know what they are, including the Great British public.

Author: Could I just return to your view of the English whose cities you are bombing?

Interviewee: I'm not bombing cities so keep that in mind when you're talking to me.
Author: How many English people do you know?
Interviewee: Not many.
Author: How many?
Interviewee: Maybe one or two . . . but they were soldiers who arrested me.

It would be incorrect to claim that all members of the Provisional IRA share a hatred of the English, but such an element does exist within the IRA psyche. Undoubtedly there is a mistrust of British political leaders, and that is shared by the IRA, successive Dublin governments and the Ulster Unionists. One member of the IRA was unapologetic about his hatred of the English and explained that his views were shaped by Irish history.

It is not so long ago – the beginning of this century – that we fought the English to liberate part of this country, yet they continued to hold part of it and to allow their underlings at Stormont to treat the Catholic population like shit. They don't understand Ireland yet they persist in holding part of it. The English people have their army on our soil killing our people. This is Ireland but they persist with this colonial view of us. Ask people who were also colonized what they think of the English and they will be the same as me. Ask the English and the hatred is mutual. We're Paddies just like the French are Frogs, the Germans are Krauts and the Pakistanis are Pakis.

If people say I'm racist, I've a long way to go before I catch up with the English.

During conversations with the more senior republicans, however, I discovered that they were unconcerned about the English and did not have strong views about them. They focused their attention on British policy-making, the role of the British Army and the unification of Ireland. Most of them knew little of the English way of life, only a few had visited England, and the majority refused to be drawn about their opinions of the English. One of them offered a precise theory of why England and the English should be subjected to violence:

It's simple. Until they know what we have experienced, they will be content to have an acceptable level of violence in the north of Ireland. It's only when English people have deaths on their doorsteps, when their rail services are disrupted, when their political leaders can't feel safe, when a journey into Central London is risky, that they take notice. It's only then that the British press deals with the conflict and that politicians take note. It's all right when the violence is in somebody else's street, but when it comes into yours you want something done about it. We know that people in Britain would be happy to see Ireland float off into the Atlantic, and the more we hit them at home, the more they'll want their political leaders to get rid of the problem. Until we struck in England with a sustained campaign, the British establishment was happy to contain the violence.

It was over there and the British press could afford to ignore it. One small bomb in London creates headlines but one in Belfast might not even find a space in the papers. We took the war to England because throughout the Seventies it was clear that the British people wanted disengagement. The politicians and the military ignored the British public. We knew they couldn't ignore them when the violence was moved to England.

IRA operations in England in the early 1990s were characterized by GHQ's practice of constantly switching targeted locations and varying tactics. When security tightened in London, they moved teams to other parts of the country. They hid weapons in rural areas, made bombs in cities in the north of England or the Midlands and moved them into London. At least twenty experienced operatives were kept in England at all times, many of them divided into individual cells with different tasks and virtually no liaison between the cells. Co-ordinators were placed in different parts of England on a temporary basis to make links between different cells. When a major operation was planned, GHQ would send technical experts into England for short periods and remove them before the operation took place. They always had a hard core of experienced and dedicated operatives and others whom they recruited for tasks which did not involve great personal risk. The two distinct types of operative could be described as the 'real activists' and the 'helpers'. The IRA was always prepared to recruit 'helpers' for specific aspects of their operations, irrespective of whether those persons had a criminal background or were motivated by a naïve or romantic attachment to republicanism.

A typical example of a 'helper' or what the IRA internally defined as a 'sleeping agent' was twenty-nine-year-old Vincent Wood, an English sales executive married to an Irishwoman. He attended Irish-language classes in London and thereby met his future wife, a nurse from Dublin. Wood read avidly about Irish history, and in the shipping company where he worked he made no secret of his political views. He was an ideal target for IRA recruiters, who watched him when he made frequent visits to his wife's family in Ireland. He was respectable, English, and had no criminal record. Contrary to press reports, he was not asked by the IRA to take an oath which would have bound him to the organization's General Orders. He was not trained by the IRA or initiated as an active service operator. I was told the IRA believed he was naïve but would be useful as a 'helper'; they saw him as an ideal quartermaster who could store explosives for cells in England. Wood agreed to take possession of a tea-chest and later claimed he had been duped into thinking it contained someone's personal effects. Inside the tea-chest were a bomb-maker's kit of Semtex, timing devices, and a map showing the area and country residence of John Major. Wood moved the tea-chest from his home at Leytonstone in East London to a friend's shop in Essex. Staff at the shop became curious, opened it and informed the police of its contents. Scotland Yard anti-terrorist officers kept Wood under surveillance for almost two weeks. When it was apparent that no-one from the IRA was visiting him, they moved in and arrested him.

I learned that the IRA's GHQ became suspicious when Wood told them he had moved the tea-chest to another location. They considered the possibility that he had been caught with the Semtex and been recruited by British intelligence. Hence no-one contacted him during the period he was under surveillance. In reality, he had moved the Semtex because he was frightened. The IRA now believes he panicked when faced with the enormity of his role and the huge quantity of explosives in his home. In the shadowy world of terrorism, however, there is always the possibility that he was being exploited by clever and cunning men. At his Old Bailey trial, his defence lawyer claimed Wood had been duped into taking possession of the explosives by his Irish brother-in-law who had told him the tea-chest contained a friend's personal belongings.

The concept of the hard core and the helpers within the IRA England cells was again in evidence in February 1993 when GHQ temporarily switched attention to Nottinghamshire, with a plan to establish a new cell. Its first target was to be the gasworks at Warrington, over 80 miles from Nottingham. In a move typical of IRA GHQ, two experienced activists were selected to link up with two 'helpers' to form the new cell. GHQ chose forty-year-old Pairic MacFhloinn as its bomb-maker and cell leader. He worked for a Dublin law firm and his criminal record carried a conviction for IRA membership in 1975. His number two was a volunteer who used the alias Michael Timmins. Timmins's task was to liaise with another cell and acquire from them a quantity of explosives and weapons. He would also be required to find a suitable dump where the tools of terrorism could be safely stored. The 'helpers' were forty-nine-year-old John Kinsella and his twenty-five-year-old nephew Denis. The Kinsella family were not IRA personnel but were avowed republicans. John Kinsella had spent thirty years working in England and was known to police as a petty criminal with convictions for fraud. His nephew was a relatively new arrival on the scene and had travelled from Dublin in 1988 to look for work in Nottingham.

MacFhloinn and Timmins travelled from Dublin to Nottingham in the cab of a lorry. The first meeting of the experienced IRA activists and their two associates, John and the young Denis Kinsella, took place in a car park in Nottingham adjacent to Notts County football ground. MacFhloinn and Timmins were not familiar with the geography of the region, which is why the cell needed local involvement and knowledge. Denis and John Kinsella had already selected a number of targets and their role was to provide the hard core operators with a safe house, transport and details of the target sites. It was designed to be a typical IRA operation in England, similar in style to the workings of IRA units in 1938–9, when the bomb technicians were sent to England and sleeping agents of Irish descent were in a place to provide them with local knowledge, a safe house and a target list.

The IRA liaison officer, who used the alias 'Michael Timmins', made contact with another IRA cell based in Nottinghamshire and acquired several handguns, Semtex and bomb-timers. Denis Kinsella agreed to his flat being used for the manufacture of bombs, and his uncle provided an allotment in the city for storing extra supplies of Semtex and the guns. The IRA believed this cell could operate for a lengthy period and advised that their targets should not be within the area where they were based.

The first target was the Longford gas terminal at Warrington in Cheshire. Denis Kinsella drove MacFhloinn and Timmins to the site to enable them to assess the level of security, work out where explosives should be placed to create maximum damage and plan a suitable escape route. The bombers and their 'helpers' made several such trips before MacFhloinn decided to use three Semtex devices to blow up the massive gas tanks. The possibility of devastation and massive loss of life was not a consideration. MacFhloinn's orders were to create a 'spectacular', and exploding gas tanks would do just that. He decided to use the cover of darkness to attach the bombs to the massive gas-holders.

On the evening of 26 February 1993 Denis Kinsella drove the bombers and their deadly cargo to Warrington. MacFhloinn and Timmins told Kinsella to wait in his battered Mazda van while they entered the site and primed the bombs. They returned to the van to make the 80-mile return journey to Nottingham, while the bombs were set to explode when they were safely back at their base. The major flaw in their plan was that Denis Kinsella was nervous, and his van was in such a sorry state of repair that it was likely to attract police attention.

PC Mark Stoker was on duty in his patrol car in Liverpool Road, Warrington, just before midnight when he saw the battered white van approach traffic lights and stop. When the lights turned green, the van remained stationary and PC Stoker suspected the driver was under the influence of alcohol. He went up to the van, told Kinsella of his suspicions and breathalysed him. The test proved negative, yet PC Stoker's intuition warned him that there was something suspicious about the other man in the van. He used his radio to check that the van belonged to the driver, who gave his name as Denis Kinsella. A message came back from the police computer that the van was registered to the driver. In other circumstances a policeman might have allowed the van and its occupants to continue their journey. After all, Kinsella had explained that his indecision at the traffic lights was simply due to unfamiliarity with the locality; he was 'lost', he said.

Whether it was police training or a gut instinct, PC Stoker remained suspicious and asked the other men in the van to identify themselves. MacFhloinn gave him a false name and his companion offered what I believe to be the alias, Michael Timmins. PC Stoker was still not satisfied, and told them he wished to search the three men and their vehicle. Kinsella responded by producing the contents of his pockets. That was the ideal diversion for MacFhloinn to reach for a gun in a holdall. MacFhloinn, like 'Dingus' Magee, was a hardened activist who was determined not to be caught. PC Stoker saw MacFhloinn's movement towards the holdall and warned him to 'wait a minute, mate'. The warning came too late. MacFhloinn had a pistol in his right hand, and with the experience of a gunman had his left hand under the butt to steady it. Stoker was looking down the barrel of the weapon and he was in mortal danger. MacFhloinn was in a crouching position, and in those few seconds between the gun appearing and it being aimed with menace Stoker decided to run for his life, a split second before MacFhloinn opened fire. The first bullet struck the police constable in the stomach but he kept moving away from the threat. A second bullet struck his right thigh. He continued to stagger to safety until a third bullet embedded itself in his buttock and brought him down. He was about fifteen or twenty feet from the van when he hit the ground. He reached for his radio and announced that he had been shot and gave details of the van and its occupants. Fortunately, MacFhloinn made no attempt to get out of the vehicle to complete his handiwork. PC Stoker was still conscious and talking to colleagues as the terrorists drove away.

Knowing they would be easily traced because police had details of the van, MacFhloinn decided to hijack a car, hold the driver prisoner and get to safety where he could telephone for advice and assistance. Lee Wright, a nineteen-year-old salesman, was driving home when three men walked into the road and blocked his path. 'I had no choice but to slow down,' he said. 'When I pulled up, everything happened very fast, and a gun appeared through the window. I was told to get out.' The man with the gun was Denis Kinsella, who later claimed he had acted under duress. Timmins and MacFhloinn forced Lee Wright into the boot of his car and the three terrorists drove towards Manchester. Panic quickly set in among the bombers, who fired at a passing police car which immediately gave chase. Wright was another hero of that evening and showed great courage and ingenuity. With his life in danger, he had the presence of mind to disconnect the petrol gauge wire which ran through the car boot. The terrorists abandoned the car on the M62 and made off on foot. Kinsella and MacFhloinn were quickly arrested in a police follow-up operation but 'Timmins' escaped under cover of darkness. I was told he later linked up with another IRA cell in Nottinghamshire, and returned to Dublin within three months.

Early in the morning, after the bombers had been arrested, the bombs at the gasworks exploded, one penetrating a gas-holder. The efforts of the police and fire services prevented a massive blaze from extending to the other tanks and threatening the lives of families in a nearby housing estate. PC Stoker survived but was left with a residue of pain in his stomach and leg and the trauma of having come so close to death. MacFhloinn was gaoled for thirty-five years, Denis Kinsella for twenty-five and John Kinsella for twenty. At their Old Bailey trial in February 1994, Mr Justice McCullough remarked that the three bombs could have had effects 'far-reaching in the extreme'. He praised PC Stoker, and Lee Wright for his 'cool action'.

Before the trial, MacFhloinn was unco-operative with police. He was a typical IRA operator who was schooled in anti-interrogation techniques, but his accomplices were not resilient under questioning. John Kinsella, who enjoyed a reputation as a tough man in his neighbourhood, answered all police questions, and his nephew was equally responsive. When John Kinsella realized that his co-operation with the police investigation would make him a marked man, he attempted suicide by slashing his neck with the serrated edge of the lid of a food tin. He was placed in protective custody, with the fear that the IRA has 'a long memory'.

In the spring of 1993 the IRA constantly switched operations from one part of England to another, but the ferocity of the campaign increased. On 27 February a Semtex device was left in a rubbish bin in Camden Town in North London. When it exploded, one shopper was killed; eighteen people, including two children, were injured. Scotland Yard claimed the IRA warning of the bomb location was misleading, and police clearing the area unwittingly moved some people towards the site of the explosion.

It was obvious that the IRA's England cells, who frequently chose their own targets, were unconcerned that bombs in shopping thoroughfares were a serious risk to innocent life. That was apparent in the 1939 campaign and during twenty-five years of violence in Northern Ireland. In July 1972 in Belfast the IRA's decision to bomb a city centre led to what became known as 'Bloody Friday'. It was to be repeated many times, yet the IRA tried to justify their tactics by claiming that warnings were given to police but ignored. The task of clearing a High Street or a town centre during a bomb threat is a frightening experience for police and civilians. Frequently, IRA messages have not been exact about bomb locations. A general warning is phoned to a newspaper office with a code-word and then has to pass through several channels before it is acted upon. During that process, even a precise IRA message can result in a garbled version given to police on the streets. Police are sometimes only given the street name and little or no other information to help them identify the site of a planned explosion. I do not think, as some journalists suggest, that every IRA bomb is planted to cause civilian casualties. It is in the nature of terrorism that bombs in built-up areas are likely to lead to the deaths of innocent people. The IRA argument that they give warnings rings hollow in the history of their bombing campaign.

It was due to the IRA's failure to recognize the futility and inherent risks to life from bombing shopping centres that history repeated itself in March 1993, and reminded those who knew IRA history that the Coventry tragedy of 1939 was a lesson never learned by republicans.

At 11.38 a.m. on Saturday 20 March 1993, the Samaritans in Liverpool received a coded warning that a bomb had been left outside a Boots chemist's shop in the city. It is easy to conceive of the fear within a police force when they receive such a vague warning of the whereabouts of a device. They know it is ticking away while innocent civilians go about their daily lives. A police radio alert was circulated throughout the region, including Warrington in Cheshire. Thirty-four minutes after the IRA message, a bomb exploded without warning in Bridge Street in Warrington while families were buying Mother's Day gifts or simply window-shopping. In the midst of the ensuing panic and injury, a second bomb exploded near by. Both devices had been placed in cast-iron litter-bins attached to lamp-standards. Scores of people were injured, some of them maimed for life, but history will remember that day because the dead were children – three-year-old Johnathan Ball and Tim Parry, aged twelve. Perhaps Tim Parry's death will best symbolize the futility of violence because his parents later embarked on a journey to Ireland to try to understand their own pain and confusion.

The Warrington tragedy united reasonable people in both islands in a vociferous condemnation of violence. Those who knew the complexities of Irish politics and IRA history quietly accepted that indignation and condemnation would not lead to a cessation of the IRA's England campaign.

While newspapers carried denunciations of the IRA from churchmen and politicians, an IRA cell planned another massive explosion for the City of London. On the morning of Sunday 24 April 1993, two members of an IRA cell drove a ton of home-made explosives into Bishopsgate. They parked a tipper truck, walked to a car driven by an accomplice and left the vicinity. A short time later two policemen walked into the Hong Kong & Shanghai Bank and asked if anyone knew who was responsible for the truck parked outside. Any doubt about the risk to life and property was discounted when Sky Television received a coded warning about a bomb in the City. Unfortunately, there were no bomb-disposal officers readily accessible. When the device exploded it killed *News of the World* freelance photographer Edward Henty, aged thirty-four. He was just a journalist doing his job and was close to the seat of the explosion. The blast left the area deep in rubble and produced newspaper images which shocked Britain. Damage was first estimated at £1 billion but experts later downgraded the cost to half that figure. Much of the media coverage of the bombing realized the IRA's twofold objective of striking at the heart of the financial centre of the capital and generating paranoia about the inability of the security apparatus to combat terrorism.

Within months, a 'ring of steel' surrounded the City where over 7,000 vehicles used its access routes every hour of the working week. The cost of the bomb damage was only part of the overall monetary cost of trying to ensure the City would remain safe from further attacks. Dr Conor Cruise O'Brien, writing in *The Times*, made some valid observations about the real value of the increased security.

> The ring of steel increases the risk to the City in two ways. It increases the incentive to the IRA to strike, because of the propaganda value to be derived from penetrating that loudly trumpeted ring. The other way in which the charade increases the risk to the City is that it diminishes manpower available to counter the IRA threat. Fixed road-blocks need a lot of trained manpower.

The bombing of cities also deprives people of basic civil liberties such as freedom of movement and freedom from suspicion. It makes everyone a potential suspect and encroaches on the lives of the public. Ever since the IRA's mainland bombing campaign got under way in the 1970s people regularly face search procedures in public buildings, and every time a new campaign begins people's movements are restricted further. That is an objective of terrorism.

On the same day as the Bishopsgate bomb, two minicab drivers were hijacked and bombs placed in their vehicles. One was told to drive to New Scotland

Yard and the other to Downing Street. In each incident, the cab driver was told that IRA personnel would follow his vehicle to ensure he carried out their instructions. Fortunately, both men abandoned their vehicles and informed the police. Subsequently the bombs exploded, one in Finsbury Park and the other near King's Cross. It was almost one year from the MI5 take-over of security, and the three explosions were proof that the IRA could still operate with impunity.

When security was stepped up in the wake of the Bishopsgate explosion, GHQ ordered the familiar change of location, and activated one of its units based within striking distance of the north-east of England. The target was a gas-holder at Gateshead on Tyneside. It was the second attack in the area within a matter of weeks, a previous one having been made at an Esso terminal at North Shields. At Gateshead the IRA carried out an operation similar to the bombing of the gas-holders at Warrington. Three bombs were used, and an explosion led to the evacuation of 400 people living near the site. Fortunately, the gas-holders themselves did not explode and, according to a spokesman for British Gas, were capable of resisting a wartime bombing. Once again, however, the terrorists experienced no difficulty in gaining access to their target. An Esso official explained that vast areas of land surrounded gas and oil complexes. It was impossible to restrict access. The Assistant Chief Constable for Northumbria said the IRA's aim was maximum damage and not loss of life, although he admitted that where petrol and gas were involved there were 'potentially tremendous implications'. As usual, when the IRA struck at Tyneside they used timing devices to allow operatives to return to bases well removed from the target sites. The overall terrorist objective was to damage the north-east of England, which was attracting new industry, and to prove that the IRA could strike anywhere in England. The repeated change of location also kept the security authorities constantly guessing where the terrorists would next strike – which left the initiative with the IRA.

After a lull in the summer of 1993, the IRA returned to targets in London and exploded five bombs on 4 October. The explosions occurred at 6.30 a.m. and caused massive traffic disruption. Two went off near a YMCA in Crouch End Road, two on the A1 at Archway near Highgate Tube station, and a fifth at an art gallery in Highgate Street. A sixth device failed to explode and was defused. Fortunately, there were no injuries. The bombs were small and crudely constructed with a timing device attached to a small quantity of Semtex.

At the close of 1993, the IRA ordered a scale-down of operations in Britain because Sinn Fein was desperate to convince everyone that they were committed to peace. However, they kept up the terror by using code-words for bomb hoaxes which temporarily paralysed the rail and Underground networks. Cells were told to continue planning while Sinn Fein and the IRA appeared to debate the Anglo-Irish Declaration which was signed by the British and Irish Prime Ministers on 15 December at Downing Street. In March 1994, the Army Council gave GHQ permission for a special operation in London to coincide with a parliamentary debate on the renewal of the Prevention of Terrorism Act.

Following the launch of the mortar attack on 10 Downing Street in 1991, the IRA continued to favour a similar operation. A direct repeat was vetoed because of the unreliability of home-made mortars, the risk of the mass killing of civilians and the lack of a suitable target. Before Christmas 1993, however, a London cell had proposed a mortar attack on one of the runways at Heathrow Airport. I talked to an IRA source about the way in which the IRA selected targets.

People think that a bomb is only there to kill people or damage property. That's naïve. It can have the effect of demonstrating that we can strike at anything. A lot of discussion takes place before a major operation is sanctioned such as the attack on Downing Street. We proved, like we did with Thatcher, that no-one is safe while the war goes on . . .

The bombs in the City of London were to hit the economic heart of Britain. There are always the other operations but there is constant planning for the big one. We could have thrown mortars at the House of Commons, but what does that achieve? Why kill a lot of civilians and MPs? We'll always select individual members of the British establishment for assassination because they make themselves part of the war. They publicly advocate shooting and hanging our people. That makes them legitimate targets. The spectacular operations let people know what we are capable of and that we are there. They illustrate just how serious a threat we are. If they want the threat to go away, they can talk directly to us. They know our terms of reference for a meaningful dialogue.

The *raison d'être* for the bombing of Heathrow fell within the above category.

Five days before mortar bombs were launched into the airport surrounds, an IRA cell stole a Nissan Micra car and fitted it out for launching four mortar shells. They welded a plate to the floor of the car and attached the mortar tubes to it. Their knowledge of the target enabled them to adjust the angle of the mortars to fire their explosives the necessary half-mile to take them over Heathrow police station and into the airport. Contrary to claims from Unionist politicians, the mortars were made in England and not in the Irish Republic. They were easily constructed from steel tubing. The shell of the type fired at Heathrow was 18 inches in length with fins attached to the rear. Each shell was packed with Semtex explosives and designed to explode on impact with a hard surface.

For the Heathrow operation, the Nissan car was fitted with false number–plates and the mortar tubes placed to fire through the rear window of the vehicle. A fifth tube carried a small explosive device timed to go off after the mortars were fired. Its purpose was to destroy the interior of the car and remove both human fingerprints and 'bomb fingerprints' which might indicate the identity of the IRA explosives expert. The mortars were on a relay-timing mechanism which discharged them almost simultaneously.

The Nissan and its deadly cargo were driven to the car park of the Excelsior Hotel opposite the airport. The timer for the mortars and the other device were activated, and the IRA personnel left the area. At 5.56 p.m. on 9 March 1994, three mortars landed close to the northern runway, and a fourth appeared to disintegrate. Fortunately, they failed to explode. The small device in the Nissan car went off, destroying much of the vehicle and setting light to others near by. The failure of the mortar shells may have been due to the smaller device exploding simultaneously with their discharge and damaging their nose cones.

Just after midnight on 11 March, the IRA struck again at Heathrow, sending four mortar shells towards the southern runway. They failed to explode, creating speculation that the IRA had ensured the shells would not create damage on impact. A third attack on the morning of 13 March made a mockery of security. The mortar tubes and their metal base were found half buried in waste ground; the top of each mortar launcher was scarcely visible. A timing device had enabled the terrorists to bury the third launcher days before the attack. Speculation that none of the attacks was intended to cause injury did not accord with the fact that all the shells carried explosive charges.

The IRA made it clear it was still in business. Its message was that it continued to pose a serious threat to Britain. The mortar attacks seemed to be evidence that the IRA had finally rejected the Downing Street Declaration signed by John Major and Irish Prime

Minister Albert Reynolds on 15 December 1993. The declaration was an attempt by both governments to institute a peace process, and it came into being after three years of secret dialogue designed to bring 'the enemy within' out of the cold.

14

Talking amid the Carnage

Talking, negotiating or having a dialogue with terrorists is not a new phenomenon but is always a risky venture. Most Western governments, and in particular British governments throughout the period of colonial rule, have used a variety of words and phrases to explain their political contacts with terrorist movements, or to cloak the nature of those contacts. In democracies, the concept of dialogue with those who terrorize you is abhorrent, but the reality is that governments often find that it is the only means of eliminating a threat which cannot be eradicated by security measures. Terrorists know that violence leads to political dialogue and negotiation, and are therefore reluctant to relinquish violence until they achieve their goals. Contemporary history, particularly in the Middle East, demonstrates that even the most powerful governments will eventually concede to terrorism, and recognize within it a political thesis which can be accommodated.

The major problem for democratic regimes is convincing their people that the organizations they have vowed to destroy cannot be extirpated and should be drawn into a political process. This requires a policy to persuade the electorate that a strategy that has been contrary to previous government objectives is now morally and politically worth pursuing. Because of the risks involved, the critical dilemma facing governments is whether to begin the process in secret before making a public admission that terrorists are about to be accorded political recognition. If details of the government's intentions suddenly become public knowledge, that serves to weaken the moral authority of the administration and to confuse the public. If the procedure fails, the terrorists are then able to make public the whole process, thus embarrassing the government and the security apparatus. The terrorists and their cause are also given legitimacy because of the government's willingness to consult them. Given those circumstances, governments inevitably respond by telling the public that there was no negotiation, no dialogue and no talks. Other responses may take the form of phrases such as: 'They asked how they could stop the violence and we gave them advice'; 'The contact we had with them was a means of conveying our distaste for violence'; or 'We exchanged letters with them in which we made clear our position that we would not talk to them or invite them into the political process until they renounced and ended their campaign'.

During the last twenty-five years, successive British governments have negotiated with the IRA, talked to the IRA, had dialogue with the IRA, maintained contacts with the IRA, sought clarification from the IRA of its political and military objectives, and used intermediaries from political parties and the churches to find grounds for an exchange of views. In some instances, the intentions of the governments were sincere, but in each case the procedure failed. The dialogue in the mid-1970s, however, was more of an attempt to destroy the IRA than to draw it towards a political process. In 1972 the Whitelaw talks were seriously flawed and led to even greater violence.

Whatever terminology British governments use to describe their contacts with the IRA, I believe the public can be assured that the truth lies somewhere between the words 'contacts' and 'dialogue'. Since the mid-1970s there have been instances where contact was established with and by the IRA. The procedure was infrequent and inconsequential. It was not dialogue but a method by which intermediaries such as churchmen or politicians were used to discover the IRA's terms for ending violence and entering a political process. Throughout the 1980s the Provisionals made clear their distrust of the British. The young leadership which emerged after the débâcle of the 1974–5 truce recognized the dangers of negotiation, and the hunger strikes created a bitterness and a desire for revenge which made contacts between the Thatcher regime and the IRA impossible.

Nevertheless, the IRA strategy of concentrating many of its operations in Great Britain forced the British government to re-establish contact. The Provisionals have never been more dangerous than in the past six years. The campaign in mainland Britain proved how lethal was the threat they posed. History may show that the extension of terror to Britain was a catalyst in a renewal of contact between the IRA and Downing Street, however unpalatable that may be for many who lost loved ones, or who lost their livelihoods.

The British government has claimed that the IRA sought a way of ending its campaign and asked for help. In the opinion of one who has studied the Provisionals and their strategy over twenty-five years, that is simply nonsense. Why should terrorists who believe they cannot be defeated, and who are committed to a republican ideal, 'seek a way out of the conflict'? They have never asked for penance, for absolution or for advice. They appear to know where they are going and will bomb and shoot to get there. The nature of the dialogue between Downing Street and the IRA from 1991 shows that the IRA, far from asking for advice, was exchanging opinions with a government which sought a way of drawing the IRA into a new political framework in Ireland. I make reference to Downing Street because dialogue of the nature I am about to describe could only have been authorized from within a cabinet committee dealing specifically with Ireland policy.

Margaret Thatcher's government was responsible for opening lines of communication with the IRA. One of the imponderables in any examination of her reasoning is her publicly avowed detestation of the Provisionals. There were two possible motives for her taking a step which was at variance with her declared aim to defeat the IRA. She may have been advised that overtures to Sinn Fein could drive a wedge between the political and military arms of the Provisional movement. Such a thesis could have been formulated on an analysis of the mid-1970s IRA truce which almost wrecked the organization. The advice to Margaret Thatcher may have been along the following lines:

'Let's suck Sinn Fein into a dialogue which appears to offer them political progress. The Adams leadership is keen to resurrect the fortunes of Sinn Fein, and may be attracted towards such a dialogue. We should encourage them to the view that we have no long-term strategic interest in remaining in Northern Ireland. That would force Adams and his fellow travellers in Sinn Fein to instigate a debate within the IRA. Now, Prime Minister, we know historically that political debates within the IRA open cracks between those who favour the gun and others who seek a more progressive political route. Adams and elements of Sinn Fein have become intrinsically involved in politics.

'Let us appear to give them something which leads them to believe that the IRA should at least suspend operations while talking takes place. We know from the mid-Seventies experience that the Labour government of Harold Wilson almost achieved the defeat of the IRA by lulling them into the belief that they were about to be offered something substantial. Our strategy would be to concentrate on Sinn Fein with a process of secret negotiations. Once we suck them into the process we should begin to demand a sign of their sincerity to negotiate. Our bottom line should be a temporary ceasefire from the IRA as a demonstration of good faith on their part. That will be our opening gambit and, as the stakes are raised by us, we will demand an extended ceasefire. We know that in 1974-5 an extended ceasefire damaged the

IRA's military capability. The Wilson government suspended communications with them when it was clear that there was no purpose in proceeding. We have to be more cautious. We must not jump too quickly. Our real purpose will be to weaken them by detaching the Sinn Fein leadership from the military side of the organization and thereby create such a massive split that it will impair the Provisionals for a sufficient time for us to find agreement with Dublin and the constitutional parties.'

The problem with that scenario, if it was indeed the motivation for Thatcher's decision to renew contact with the IRA, is that the leadership of the Provisionals was politically and militarily cohesive. They had learned from the débâcle of the mid-Seventies and were conscious that such a tactic might be used by the British government.

I prefer an alternative scenario: that Margaret Thatcher, the political heavyweight, reckoned she could play the international game of politics by demonstrating her ability to resolve the Irish question in parallel with efforts to solve the Palestinian issue. In other words, she genuinely felt that a meaningful dialogue could be orchestrated to encourage the IRA to seek a political path. Irrespective of her role as the scourge of the IRA, she was responsible for the 1985 Anglo-Irish Agreement, which reaffirmed the Protestant veto on a united Ireland but also established the means whereby the British and Irish governments could meet to consider Northern Ireland issues. It is possible she believed she could go much further and offer Sinn Fein a real opportunity to pursue their objectives peacefully. Whatever her reasoning, her successor, John Major, inherited the strategy of contact with the IRA and pursued it in a way which produced some startling results.

The story began in the late summer of 1990. Raids on an IRA safe house in Clapham and another in West Belfast uncovered a list of 235 politicians, generals, judges and other prominent figures whom the Provisionals proposed to assassinate. In July they murdered Ian Gow and their potential became frighteningly apparent. Only nine months earlier they had killed the ten Royal Marine bandsmen at Deal.

It was ironic that in the midst of carnage a dormant communication line was quietly reactivated. The mechanism was a person who both sides knew would always be available as the first point of contact should either consider it necessary to re-establish 'relations': a dialogue, orally or in written form. The intermediary was known to the IRA and acceptable as a bona fide agent for government messages to Sinn Fein. He received a telephone call from a British government representative at Stormont Castle who said he wished to meet Martin McGuinness, generally accepted as a foremost leader of the Provisional movement and closer to IRA strategy than Gerry Adams. McGuinness was part of the triumvirate with Adams and Danny Morrison who had resurrected IRA and Sinn Fein fortunes in the late 1970s and early 1980s. While Adams established his position as the political spokesman for the movement, McGuinness and Morrison were major players in overall Provisional strategy.

The purpose of a meeting with McGuinness was twofold. The British government representative wished to announce that he was retiring and that his replacement would be available to develop communication. The prospect of a renewal of contact worried the Provisionals, and the matter was discussed within Sinn Fein and the IRA. McGuinness was granted permission to attend a meeting in the capacity of observer, and advised that he was not to speak on behalf of Sinn Fein or the IRA. Adams, McGuinness and Morrison were sceptical about the overture, while the Army Council were unanimously hostile to it. But Adams, Morrison and McGuinness convinced the Provisional leadership that there was nothing to be lost from such a meeting because policy discussion would not be on the agenda.

The meeting took place in October 1990 and was attended by McGuinness, the intermediary and the outgoing government diplomat. It lasted several hours, during which the contact and the diplomat discussed British–Irish relations, the changing face of European politics and the need for new political concepts in Britain and Ireland. McGuinness obeyed his brief to listen and not comment. He was told that the incoming government representative would be available to reopen a secret and meaningful exchange of positions.

After the meeting, the contact received an advance copy of a speech due to be made by Peter Brooke, then Secretary of State for Northern Ireland. He was asked to pass it on to Sinn Fein. The speech adopted a more moderate tone towards the republican position, and hinted that British government policy was now politically flexible towards Sinn Fein. The deliberate leaking of that speech was the Government's opening gambit to convince the Provos of their sincerity and draw them into a process of communication. There was no further exchange for two months, but among the Provisionals there was a vigorous debate over whether Peter Brooke's statement about the future was the beginning of a new and flexible British approach.

In February 1991 the IRA launched mortars at Downing Street in an attempt to kill the new Prime Minister, John Major. The mortar attack was a clear signal that the IRA's Army Council was not only sceptical about the prospect of dialogue but openly hostile to it.

Nevertheless, two months later the retired diplomat was able to inform the intermediary, and subsequently the IRA, that loyalist paramilitaries were about to call a ceasefire to facilitate inter-party talks. The purpose of the communication may have been an attempt to elicit from the Provos a similar cessation of violence or to put pressure on them to do so. It is worth noting that the loyalist paramilitaries, whose violence was rarely accorded the same column inches in British newspapers, were rapidly becoming a major terrorist force whose objective was simply to kill Catholics. In June 1991 the intermediary met a new government representative, who identified himself with a letter signed by Peter Brooke. The Provisionals and the intermediary knew they were dealing with a serious approach, and were in a position to verify the status of the British government appointee. He was an MI6 officer with a wide experience of politics and methods for handling secret and sensitive negotiations. The Provisionals relied on the intermediary to inform them of ongoing telephone discussions and meetings with the British government representative. Sinn Fein admits that the IRA was suspicious of the British government's overtures and only reluctantly agreed to allow Sinn Fein to reciprocate.

In November 1991 the intermediary told McGuinness that the British government was keen to use the home of a retired civil servant in Derry as the venue for a meeting. But the Provisionals were not interested in meetings, and GHQ continued to plan operations in Britain.

In January 1992 the Provisionals and the British government exchanged letters about a peace initiative put forward by Gerry Adams and John Hume, leader of the Catholic nationalist SDLP. Hume provided an interesting dimension to the overall process. He himself had been an intermediary during talks between the IRA and the British government on several occasions, particularly during the 1970s. In the early 1980s he and Adams took part in a BBC radio programme that I produced in which they discussed nationalism and republicanism. A few minutes before the end of the programme, Hume derided Adams as being a message boy for the IRA, and said he would rather talk to the real men. Adams looked at the studio clock, realized there was one minute to the end of the programme, and presented Hume with a dilemma: 'Are you saying, Mr Hume, that you would rather meet the real men?' Hume asked him to clarify the phrase 'the real men', and Adams defined them as the Army Council. Hume could not extricate himself from this predicament and agreed to meet the IRA Army Council. The subsequent meeting was a failure because the IRA demanded that it be videotaped and Hume refused.

None the less, John Hume was always a peacemaker and an ideal intermediary. During the late 1980s it was apparent that he believed that Sinn Fein were moving towards a less militaristic position, with public statements which implied they were softening their approach to finding a solution only through violence. It was easy for Hume to seek out Gerry Adams. When it became public that he was talking to the Provisionals, there was no condemnation from the British or Irish governments. At the time, I was convinced that both governments were keen on his decision to reopen a line of communication with the IRA. The Dublin government was kept informed of his progress. One should not necessarily connect the two processes, yet it is difficult to avoid concluding there was some linkage between Hume's talks with Adams and the British government's dialogue with Sinn Fein.

In April 1992 the massive bomb at the Baltic Exchange in the City of London killed three, injured ninety-one and caused huge devastation. In May, the intermediary told the Provisionals that the British government hoped they would make greater use of the line of communication. From an IRA viewpoint, that message was interpreted as a clear signal that their policy of bombing London was the catalyst for generating dialogue. It appeared to them that violence had a real purpose. The government representative sent a document to the IRA through the joint 'contact'. It concentrated on the prospect of an IRA Christmas ceasefire, an annual event when for reasons known only to the IRA they celebrated the birth of Christ with a limited cessation of hostilities. The British government believed there might be an opportunity for an extended ceasefire, and they were keen to relay to the IRA the government response to such a prospect:

> The Secretary of State may also at this stage wish to note that, as last year, it may be necessary to make a quick — and potentially far-reaching — political decision in the immediate run-up to Christmas and we may need to set up machinery and short-term contingency plans for this. I say this because we cannot rule out a sequence which goes something like this: Provisional IRA calls a Christmas ceasefire; we respond with some security de-escalatory measures; Sinn Fein asks for a dialogue with Government on political issues — this dialogue to be linked to a continuing absence of hostilities. Alternatively, some third party or parties may elicit a response from the Provisionals with similar implications.

This paragraph in the document was a clever way of indicating to the IRA that if they extended their Christmas ceasefire the British government would respond by easing security. There was a suggestion that the Government would also use a 'third party', which I suspect would have been the Irish government, to encourage Downing Street to respond positively to a call from the Provisionals for political dialogue. That would have allowed the British government to hide behind a third party if it decided to engage in dialogue. The outcome would be publicly perceived as emanating from the 'third party or parties', perhaps the British Labour Party, and not John Major's government. The document also indicated that the RUC Chief Constable and the British Army Commander in Northern Ireland were being kept informed of the communications with the IRA.

In October 1992 the intermediary was given an internal document from the British government which was passed to the Provisionals. It dealt with the current state of the Australian diplomat Sir Ninian Stephen's attempts to encourage the Northern Ireland constitutional parties to reach a settlement. The vital element in the document was that the British government was pessimistic about reaching a settlement through the inter-party process, and the British and Irish governments were considering an imposed solution. I believe the significance of that admission for the Provisionals was that they were subtly being encouraged to believe that the British government was being radical, and that an imposed solution would require a new framework, one to which Sinn Fein could contribute. An imposed solution would need their approval, otherwise it would be made unworkable by violence. The concept of both governments imposing a settlement implied an end to the status quo, particularly an end to the Unionist veto on political developments in the province. The British government was offering the Provos a sweetener, but was it being honest? My analysis is that it was a ploy to suck Sinn Fein into the process of dialogue with the prospect of new horizons. British governments never favoured imposed settlements, and history proved they did not work.

In the same month, Sinn Fein was given a preview of a speech to be made by Peter Brooke's successor, Sir Patrick Mayhew. There were no startling revelations within it, though it restated the view that the IRA and Sinn Fein would be free to assume a role in the community if they renounced violence. However, in what appeared to be a reversal of policy, the speech contained the assertion that Her Majesty's Government did not seek to impose a solution on the constitutional parties. The only olive branch in the speech was the statement that a genuine cessation of violence would lead to the Government re-evaluating its own range of activities and responses to the IRA. The latter was a coded message to the Provisionals that the situation was still politically fluid. However, Mayhew's speech increased the stakes if Sinn Fein was to move towards that position. Mayhew defined a cessation not as an extended ceasefire but as 'a genuine and established cessation of violence'. Suddenly the concept of political movement in response to an extended Christmas ceasefire was radically changed. Mayhew's wording suggested that only after what could be defined as a genuine cessation, established as such, would the Government respond.

The IRA Army Council was angry with what it regarded as a subtle attempt by the British to redefine the terms of reference. Adams was told by the IRA that its patience was running out. It had quietly scaled down England operations to show good faith, but that situation would not be maintained if the British continued to change the ground rules. None the less, the

IRA's response to the Mayhew speech was concealed from the British government: Sinn Fein replied that the speech was 'interesting' and suggested better methods of communication between both sides.

In December 1992, the Government's representative made it clear to Sinn Fein that there were considerable risks for the Government in its lines of communication with the Provisionals. Government, he said, was serious about the dialogue, but meetings could only take place in the right location and with proper security. He enquired about a unilateral ceasefire, and whether the IRA would ease off its violence if talks were held. Sinn Fein replied that they could not answer his queries without consulting the Army Council.

At the beginning of January 1993 the Army Council told Sinn Fein it was reactivating planned operations in Britain, with some 'spectaculars'. The Army Council also informed Sinn Fein that it did not perceive a seriousness in the government communiqués. The unanimous view within the Army Council was that an upsurge in England operations was the only way to force the British government to apply greater urgency to a process they had initiated.

On 12 January the government representative told Sinn Fein that talks could begin without a major gesture from the IRA. He said that an easing of IRA violence could be the catalyst for a progression towards talks. Sinn Fein was non-committal but agreed to seek advice from its military colleagues. On 20 February the Provisionals, in a speech by Martin McGuinness sanctioned by the Army Council, adopted a moderate tone. They called on the British and Irish governments to instigate a talks process which would be 'inclusive' of all political opinion. The speech invited the British government to talk to Sinn Fein, adding that the private conviction of the British was that such a process would be acceptable. Despite the obvious manoeuvring and the machinations of both sides, the McGuinness speech clearly established their terms for talks:

> If both governments have the courage of their private convictions, they should now finally meet with Sinn Fein. For our part we recognize that such a scenario would place a great deal of responsibility on us. We would approach any serious talks accepting that we haven't got all the answers but we most certainly believe that we have some of them. The British government and others demand dramatic initiatives from us before we can be involved in talks. Whilst rejecting any pre-conditions on our participation we are quite prepared to be open and flexible to serious proposals which can lead to a realistic agreement . . .

Even the most ardent IRA critic would concede that the above constituted a position whereby the Provisionals moved from a policy of uniting Ireland by force to an acceptance that talks were required to create a new framework in Ireland. The speech was intended for the Dublin and London governments who had already expressed the view to John Hume that talks with Sinn Fein were essential for a resolution of the conflict.

In November 1993, when details of the exchanges with the Provisionals became public, the British government claimed that its advance copy of the McGuinness speech had been received with a note from him containing the following: 'The conflict is over but we need your advice on how to bring it to a close.' The most naïve student of the period would find it hard to believe that the IRA, through McGuinness, had made such a statement. The reason such a bogus note was produced in November 1993 was to fool the British public into believing that the only reason the Government continued exchanges in 1993 was the IRA's desire to end its campaign. I believe that on 20 February 1993 John Major and his cabinet were elated by the McGuinness speech. Four days later, the government representative told Sinn Fein that Her Majesty's Government accepted that a three-week cessation of IRA violence would be sufficient to initiate talks. There would be an immediate government response to the cessation. British troops would be withdrawn to barracks and checkpoints would be removed. Security levels would be maintained to combat the continuing threat to Catholics from the UDA and UVF.

It was noticeable that the British government was willing to respond to a cessation of violence in terms of the military but did not set any deadline for talks. The Army Council unanimously agreed that there was insufficient substance to the promises made by the government representative. It concluded there was still a risk that it would be drawn into a ceasefire; that the British would prevaricate about talks and demand a further extension of the ceasefire; and that the situation would be a parallel with the 1974–5 truce.

On 26 February 1993 the government appointee met with the intermediary, and covered the following points: he said the Government had agreed to talks with Sinn Fein; there was need for a two-to-three-week suspension of violence but there was to be no public declaration that the cessation was taking place; Her Majesty's Government believed it could, within that period, convince the Provisionals that violence was redundant; and if talks proceeded positively, they could be moved to a secret location in Sweden, Norway, Denmark, Scotland or the Isle of Man. But the Army Council decided that there was no point in easing off the violence in Britain until 'the British provided greater proof of their sincerity'.

That day the gasworks in Warrington were blown up and on 27 February a bomb in Camden Town in London killed one shopper and injured eighteen others. Despite the carnage, there was an oral message from the government representative that 23 March was scheduled for a meeting to examine potential venues for talks, the security that would be needed, and who would be assigned to represent each side. On 5 March Sinn Fein confirmed to the representative that Martin McGuinness and Gerry Kelly would be available for 'an exploratory' meeting as soon as possible. The government representative was told the Provisionals welcomed the proposal for a meeting. Perhaps, on reflection, someone in the Government thought events were moving too fast, and that the atrocity in Camden demanded a re-evaluation of events.

On 11 March it was made clear to Sinn Fein that an exploratory meeting was not possible 'in the light of the continued violence'. 'There must be some evidence of consistency between word and deed,' Sinn Fein was informed.

On 19 March, the Government sent Sinn Fein a nine-paragraph document outlining its basis for dialogue. Paragraph 4 read:

> It must be understood, though, that once a halt to activity became public, the British government would have to acknowledge and defend its entry into dialogue. It would do so by pointing out that its agreement to exploratory dialogue about the possibility of an inclusive process had been given because – and only because – it had received a private assurance that organized violence had been brought to an end.

Implicit in this paragraph was a government which was covering its back. In November 1993 Sir Patrick Mayhew disputed the Sinn Fein copy of this document and produced another, with different wording. One of the significant differences was a form of words which implied that the Government's document had been produced in response to a request from the Provisionals for advice. In the aftermath of the dialogue between the two sides, Sir Patrick Mayhew and John Major tried damage limitation to disguise the fact that there had been a process of dialogue, and communication with the IRA. They wanted to make the public believe there was no such dialogue and they were merely responding to the Provos' desire to find a way of ending the conflict.

Some people might say Sir Patrick Mayhew and the Cabinet would have difficulty persuading relatives of the dead children of Warrington that the Government was merely answering a plea from the IRA to end the conflict. Twenty-four hours after the IRA received the nine-paragraph outline of the Government's position, two bomb explosions tore through shoppers in Bridge Street in Warrington, and the world was shocked. The deaths of Johnathan Ball and Tim Parry did not stop the dialogue but the incident did force the Government to change the style and content of the meeting due to take place between the two sides three days later. Martin McGuinness and Gerry Kelly turned up at the venue and were met by the government representative. It was an upbeat meeting and Sinn Fein later communicated, in writing, that it had been 'most useful'. They must have been pleased that, despite the dead of Warrington, the Government was still prepared to continue the dialogue. The Sinn Fein internal report of that meeting reads as follows:

The British government representative said Martin McGuinness's address to the Sinn Fein Ard Fheis '93 had been read and triggered Government action. Mayhew had tried marginalization, defeating the IRA etc. That's gone. The Coleraine speech [by Mayhew] was a significant move. Mayhew is now determined. He wants Sinn Fein to play a part not because he likes Sinn Fein but because it cannot work without them. Any settlement not involving all of the people North and South won't work. A North/South settlement that won't frighten Unionists. The final solution is Union. It is going to happen anyway. The historical train – Europe – determines that. We are committed to Europe. Unionists will have to change. This island will be as one. He outlined the situation of talks at the level of delegations. The politicians, he said, were moving. This opportunity must be grasped. Next week, if possible. British government is sincere. No cheating is involved. He mentioned the Rees letter to Wilson: 'We set out to con them and we did' [a reference to the 1974–5 truce when Merlyn Rees was Secretary of State and Wilson was Prime Minister]. The two weeks for talks proposed was repeated. He alleged that John Chilcott [Permanent Under-Secretary and liaison between the Secretary of State, Mayhew, and the Cabinet Sub-Committee on Northern Ireland] had instructed him to inform Sinn Fein that if this was agreed at six-o-clock that clearance for the meetings at the level of delegations would be forthcoming by one minute past six. Confidentiality was of the utmost importance. Only Major, Mayhew, Hurd and the Cabinet Secretary knew all of this. The British side would probably be led by Quentin Thomas [Northern Ireland Civil Service representative at Whitehall] with John Chilcott down the line. This issue of location for meetings was raised again.

In February 1994 Sir Patrick Mayhew refused to deny claims that this meeting and another face to face with McGuinness took place. However, he said no official was ever authorized to give an undertaking to Sinn Fein that government policy was aimed at a united Ireland. Irrespective of his denial, the meeting happened three days after the Warrington tragedy and did not take place without approval at the highest political levels.

John Hume's talks with Gerry Adams were also continuing in March, and it is impossible not to consider that there must have been a link between those and the Sinn Fein dialogue with the British government. The Irish government was kept informed about Hume's progress, and believed his exchanges with Adams were bearing fruit. On 24 April Hume and Adams issued a joint statement and the IRA bombed Bishopsgate, killing a *News of the World* photographer and again causing massive damage in the City of London.

The IRA had no intention of allowing a let-up in the violence, no matter who was talking or issuing statements. I asked a senior Provisional why they continued the bombing campaign, and he replied: 'There was no incentive for us to stop. The dialogue which involved all sides to the conflict was in its infancy. If we stopped, there would have been no incentive for the Brits to talk to us. It would have been a return to the dark days of 1974–5. We needed something substantial in place and constant reminders to the Brits that we were still there. They had every reason to negotiate after the bombs in the financial centre of London.'

The Hume–Adams statement on the day of the bombing confirmed that the SDLP and Sinn Fein had returned to a dialogue they had abandoned in 1988. It presented a republican analysis that a solution confined to Northern Ireland was not viable, and that it was essential to deal with 'all the relationships at the heart of the problem'. It added: 'We accept that the Irish people as a whole have a right to national self-determination. This is a view shared by the majority of the people of this island though not by all its people.' Adams and Hume were both convinced that any political settlement should be in an all-Ireland context, that a united Ireland could be achieved by peaceful means, and that there should be a process of national reconciliation. They were advocating an all-Ireland solution which would, in effect, remove the Unionist right of veto over the future of Northern Ireland, and potentially change the constitutional position of the province.

The outcome of Hume's discussions with Adams encouraged the British and Irish governments to be optimistic about leading the Provisionals towards a cessation of violence, and holding inclusive talks. Much depended on the British government's moving towards the Hume—Adams analysis, which was shared by the Irish government. It demanded from John Major a policy of persuading the Unionists that their future lay in a new Ireland. Two days after the Bishopsgate explosion, a meeting took place between the intermediary 'contact' and two representatives of the British government. A Sinn Fein internal memorandum of the meeting read:

> They confirmed their commitment to the delegation meetings notwithstanding events on the ground at that time. They were told that Sinn Fein would be providing a policy outline which would be their basis for entering into dialogue at that level. The British government

was asked to come forward with the logistics for the meetings as soon as possible.

The British government now denies a claim by Sinn Fein that it sent an oral message to the government representative, asking why there was no response to their request for information on plans for delegation meetings. Sinn Fein claim they also included the following written query: 'Are you still serious about this? Are there problems?' If the Government had later admitted to such a communication, it would have been tantamount to telling the public that it had been instrumental in setting up a formal talks process.

A written communication from the Government on 5 May 1993 was also later the subject of dispute when the whole process came under press and public scrutiny. The Sinn Fein copy of the government document read as follows:

1. Events on the ground are crucial, as we have constantly made clear. We cannot conceivably disregard them. We gave advice in good faith taking what we were told at face value. It is difficult to reconcile that with recent events.
2. None the less we confirm that we stand by the 9-paragraph document which we prepared as that advice.
3. We have not received the necessary private assurance that organized violence has been brought to an end as, without that, further progress cannot be made.

The government version differed in two significant ways, supporting the later contention that they were merely responding to pleas for advice: Paragraph 1 above read: 'We gave in good faith the advice which was sought . . .'; Paragraph 2 read: '. . . which we prepared in response to that request for advice'. The Government later expected people to believe that the IRA's bombings in England were really a cry for help and that the IRA wanted a way out of the conflict.

At the end of the first week of May 1993, the Army Council told Sinn Fein it would agree to a two-week suspension of violence to facilitate a two-week dialogue. This was communicated to the government representative along with a policy document which the Provisionals defined as their basis for entering dialogue. It presented an analysis of the conflict similar to the views expressed in the statement from Hume and Adams. The Provisionals also asked for someone from the British side to liaise with Martin McGuinness on agendas for the two weeks of meetings, and to identify the representatives from both camps and the venue.

The subsequent events of May 1993 are disputed by both sides, but one fact emerges, and that is that information was leaked about the secret exchanges. The information surfaced in Washington, and the Provisionals claim they brought this to the attention of the British government representative, and received a reply that government press personnel would dismiss any journalistic queries following from the leak. The Government maintains there was no such communication from Sinn Fein, or with Sinn Fein in respect of the alleged leak. Information was leaked, and one must ask who could have been responsible, and who could have gained from it. During the early 1970s, the British Army's black propaganda experts and members of the intelligence community often leaked information about government policy when they believed it was detrimental to the war against the IRA. In order to disguise the source of the leaks, information was frequently conveyed to journalists living abroad.

In 1993 there were many people who knew about the secret dialogue, and disapproved of it. At Stormont there were civil servants of a Unionist persuasion who, I was told, were appalled by the concept of inviting the IRA to the conference table. There were others, directly involved in combating terrorism, who were angry that their avowed enemy was bombing its way to talks. There were people in the higher echelons of the Tory Party who believed that the process was flawed and that the British public would not accept a reversal of government policy. Within the Cabinet too there were some with serious reservations. The Government needed the support of the Unionists in the House of Commons, and an open dialogue with the IRA would remove that support. The person or persons responsible for the leak intended sabotaging the communications with the IRA. Could it have been part of a government policy to end the process?

On 25 May the intermediary between the two sides, who the Provisionals prefer people to believe was a female, spent almost two hours with the government representative in a hotel suite, while he outlined the debate taking place within the Cabinet, the reservations of some about the viability of the communications, whether the IRA could guarantee that a ceasefire would hold, and the political risks for the Government. The intermediary was told that John Major had made a decision on 18 May that he would agree to talks with the Provisionals. He would announce his decision to Parliament provided the IRA agreed to a longer-than-two-week cessation of violence, and provided any talks were preceded by meetings between British government representatives and the Provisionals to agree logistics. According to the intermediary, the representative said John Major had told the Cabinet that this was his personal plan for furthering the process. But on 19 May the plan was put aside after cabinet colleagues convinced the Prime Minister that it was too risky in the current political climate.

On 3 June it became clear the Government was indeed worried about the whole business and was looking for either a way out of it or a means of avoiding any serious commitment to its enemy. The government representative conveyed a written message to Sinn Fein outlining government thinking:

The Government was working out a response which, because it was radical, needed careful crafting. This meant deliberate (but not artificially slow) work at the highest levels. One of the reasons why it was necessary to proceed so carefully was the recognition that any response must remove existing doubts, misconceptions and suspicions. Before that process could be completed, renewed violence on a serious scale took place – with the inevitable consequence that the process itself had to be halted. Since then there have of course been changes in the Government. It would be possible for further considerations of this to be resumed after the Whitsun recess. The outcome will, as always, be affected by events on the ground. This is not a threat, merely a statement of reality.

The Government later denied that the above message existed, and produced a document in which the 'Provisional Leadership' offered a total cessation of violence.

I believe this document was flawed, because there was no reason for the IRA to make such an offer at that stage. They had nothing to gain politically from offering something which they had refused up to that point. Nothing was said to them, no guarantees were given which would have encouraged the Army Council to make such an offer. I believe the British government changed the document to convince the British public in November 1993 that its dealings with the IRA after Warrington and Bishopsgate were, once again, based on the IRA's desperate desire to end the conflict – the same IRA that was still meticulously planning England operations and attacks on the security forces in Northern Ireland.

The most enlightening document which conveys the sudden disintegration of the communication process was received by Sinn Fein on 3 June. It was a personal, rather than authorized, communication from the government representative who had joined the process after the retirement of his colleague. It contained references to

Major as 'National Chairman' and Mayhew as 'Local Chairman'. He used 'Bank' as a coded expression for the Foreign Office/MI6. The author of the letter referred to 'economic issues' meaning political issues, and used 'Board' instead of Cabinet. The letter read as follows:

There is depression and anger here at our failure to respond to your brave and straightforward offer. None feel it more than I do for obvious reasons. I appreciate, as do those most closely involved, the position this puts you in. It also contrasts with all that you have heard earlier. You have my word that all that was conveyed was done so honestly and accurately at the time. There would have been no quotation from 1975 [his leak of the comments of Merlyn Rees to Harold Wilson] if the intention was to copy that bad example and I for one would not be party to it. The present position is that the local Chairman had accepted your offer, but such a vital economic issue had to go to the Board. We had miscalculated in assuming that the National Chairman would simply give it the nod of approval. Recent economic events have made him nervous of bold steps and your unfortunate headline events of April have made acceptance of your offer more risky for him. You and I may think this should not matter, but the fact is that it does and it is that which is holding things up – if you like, human characteristics rather than anything more sinister. We all hope that you and your colleagues can bear with the situation – you are certainly being asked for a lot, but there is will on both sides to complete the loan and we must succeed . . .

We have our struggles and pressures from individuals as perhaps you do. There is a proposal worked out (the National Chairman's own and new idea of 18 May) which delayed us, and was then in turn put to one side on 19 May. I know that you feel for our Bank 'the time is never right', but this time it will be. I cannot tell you when – our wheels turn far too slowly, but that is the way of the Bank, not any notion of stringing the other side along. If delay were a ploy it is certainly taking up our attention as much as yours. I can only ask for patience for all our sakes. You will carry out your own financial policy, and it would be impertinent for me to suggest anything otherwise (as well as being counter-productive); but in economic terms headline stuff knocks us back because the National Chairman is then wary of proceeding and it gives support to those who are against such a step. I hope you will not mind me ending with a new meaning to Tiochfaidh ar la.

The last three words of Gaelic translate as 'Our day will come'. They were and remain a phrase often used by the Provisionals. The letter explained the political dilemmas faced by John Major after the bombing of Bishopsgate on 24 April. The writer identified the general political climate, 'economic events', which deterred the Prime Minister from proceeding with his own plan, and confirmed that John Major was serious about the authorized dialogue with the Provisionals.

On 10 June Sinn Fein complained to the British government that it had not responded to its policy outline dated 10 May. Four days later, a text marked 'Secret' was passed to Sinn Fein by the government representative. It revealed that the British Cabinet knew the substance of the Hume–Adams dialogue which was becoming known as 'the Irish peace initiative'. By the beginning of July, Sinn Fein was exasperated by the failure of the other side to make serious proposals for the future of the dialogue. Seven days later, they contacted the government representative and handed him a letter which outlined their concern about press leaks, and the fact that the RUC had privately briefed a local journalist about the extent of the exchanges.

The Government ignored the Sinn Fein complaint about press leaks in a message it sent to the Provisionals on 17 July. The message explained that the delay in responding was due to the critical need for additional time to provide a considered reply. It also pointed out that 'events on the ground in March', an obvious reference to the bombings in Warrington, had halted progress, as had the local elections in May. A merely temporary halt in violence would be unacceptable, and inclusive talks could only begin when there was an assurance from the Provisionals that organized violence was brought to an end. The statement appeared to be contrary to the pre-May position – that a limited suspension of violence would be enough to facilitate talks.

The Army Council was angry with Sinn Fein, pointing out that the British were changing the ground rules and therefore might not be serious about the process. I was told that in August 1993 a senior meeting of Provisionals took place and there were angry exchanges about the changing character of the communication between the two sides. Those present unanimously agreed that the British were increasing the stakes, and wanted an assurance that the conflict was over before they would continue the peace process. On 14 August the Provisionals expressed that view in a letter to the Government:

We are concerned at the inflexibility of your most recent communication. It does not reflect, in tone, or content, the pre-May 10 position. This coupled with recent political statements must raise a serious question over your commitment to a real peace process . . . The purpose of a dialogue about peace is to bring all organized violence by all parties to the conflict to an end . . .

The Sinn Fein communication speculated that 'internal and domestic party political reasons' were deterring the Government from developing the dialogue. 'We are not interested in playing games,' Sinn Fein told the Government. The violence on the ground in Northern Ireland was increasing and the main culprits were not the IRA but the loyalist paramilitaries who killed more people in 1993 than republicans. However, it was the bombings and deaths in Britain which most concerned 10 Downing Street. In the aftermath of Warrington and Bishopsgate, it would have been politically disastrous for John Major's cabinet to authorize talks with the IRA or to concede that there was an ongoing dialogue.

News of the exchanges between the two sides reached the public via two *Sunday Times* reports, particularly an article on 22 August 1993. Sinn Fein told the Government it was concerned with the newspaper developments. Ten days later, the government representative conveyed a message to the Provisionals which denied that the Government had ever conceded that a two-week suspension would be sufficient to guarantee a successful peace process. 'On the contrary,' the message added, 'it had been the consistent position that violence must be brought to an end before any process could begin.' That was incorrect, but it was a vivid illustration of the Government's recognition that its pre-May stance was clearly a non-starter after the Warrington tragedy. In another message two days later, the Government denied any involvement in the press leaks, and stressed that 'maximum confidentiality' was essential to the two-way communications.

The British government representative spoke to the intermediary on 6 September and offered advice which he asked to be conveyed to the Provisionals. He said it would be advantageous to both sides if the Provisionals publicly commented on the accord between the PLO and the Israelis. They should say: 'If they can come to an agreement in Israel, why not here?' Gerry Adams, in an interview on Radio 4, followed that advice. The Government later denied that any such advice had ever been given. On 10 September the Provos again wrote to the Government, expressing their commitment to a peace process and their scepticism about the Government's commitment. Gerry Adams and John Hume issued a joint statement about their initiative on

25 September, saying they were convinced their private discussions would lead to a solid peace agreement.

I believe that after the bombings in the spring of 1993 the advice given to the Cabinet was that the Government could not ask the British public to accept an open dialogue with the Provisionals. There was a danger of antagonizing the Unionists, losing their support in Westminster and weakening the Government's parliamentary strength. I also contend there was a process of damage limitation which took several forms. First, the communications from the Government demanded an end to violence so that, if there was ever public scrutiny of the private exchanges, the Government would appear morally clean on the issue. Second, there was a black propaganda exercise to change the wording of earlier government correspondence, and the creation of documents which appeared to have come from the Provisionals. In conjunction with those procedures, there was a gradual leaking of information about the history of the dialogue between the two sides.

Inherent in the overall strategy was a recognition that the process was over and the Government needed to win the propaganda war when the matter finally became public. It was important for the Government to bring it to the public's attention quietly, rather than risk a scenario in which the IRA would gain maximum value by exposing the Government's participation in secret exchanges with its enemy. The Cabinet decided that the only way of avoiding a public outcry was to be pro-active in seeking an accord with Dublin. That would override the Hume–Adams initiative and place both governments at the forefront of the quest for peace, overshadowing any public disquiet about previous contacts with the Provisionals. It was a clever strategy in damage limitation, and was a method of isolating the Provisionals. An inter-governmental peace accord would turn the spotlight on Sinn Fein and question their real commitment to peace. It might also drive a wedge between the doves and the hawks within the republican movement.

In the autumn of 1993 the British government made a dramatic diplomatic assault on Dublin in search of an agreed process for peace. I talked to a contact in Foreign Affairs in Dublin, and he explained the series of events which began in the autumn:

> Both governments were kept informed of the ongoing exchanges with the Provisionals, and the nature of the Hume–Adams peace initiative. We suspected that John Major would end up with egg on his face because he was within a weak government, and the IRA were making his life a misery. He did not have the political strength to move quickly in the dialogue with Sinn Fein. He also faced considerable opposition from elements within the ranks of civil servants at Stormont, from within his cabinet, and within the inner sanctum of the Tory Party. We felt that after Warrington there was no way he could concede to any public dialogue with Sinn Fein unless the IRA called off its campaign. We felt that before Warrington there was a slight possibility that secret talks could be held, with a temporary suspension of violence. We felt that the British had

a real opportunity to use a two-week dialogue to encourage the IRA to call a truce, which would have provided a platform for meaningful discussion. Sinn Fein may complain that the British changed the terms of reference after Warrington, but what did they expect? You cannot kill your opponent's children, and destroy his economy, and then expect him to be reasonable.

Major was serious about his dealings with Sinn Fein. The Foreign Office felt it was viable but a prime minister with a gun or bomb to his head was not going to commit political hara-kiri. The British are masters at deception, and after April 1993 they used that expertise to extricate themselves from an embarrassing situation. Jesus, they were clever about it, and what would you expect? I admired the way they set about doctoring communications to prepare a case for the public. We knew they were leaking details on a drip-feed system. That left the Provos vulnerable because they couldn't prove it was the British. While the Provos were still serious about developing the process, the British were spending their time destroying it. The Provos were being slowly weakened because they did not know what was happening.

The British were in the driving seat. They pressed the Dublin government. They praised the Hume–Adams talks but in reality they were intent on marginalizing them. I felt the personal relationship between Major and Albert Reynolds was a crucial factor. We knew Major was in a terrible dilemma, and if he went down on the issue there would be no future for peace. He needed us to assist him but we needed him if there was ever to be an end to the conflict. His dealings with Sinn Fein before the spring of '93 were illustrative of a sensitivity about the Irish question, and we could not walk away from that. The Irish government was buoyant about the prospects for peace because of what John Hume was telling us. He believed that Adams could carry the day and deliver the Provisionals towards a process. We began to talk to the British and there was a serious commitment to a peace accord which began in the autumn.

At the beginning of November a senior civil servant at Stormont gave a copy of one of the secret communiqués to a member of Paisley's Democratic Unionist Party. The chosen recipient was from a party which the Government knew would readily expect treachery, and make the matter public. On 8 November Eamon Mallie, the Irish journalist and author, broke the story of the contacts between the two sides.

Sir Patrick Mayhew denied that there had been negotiations with Sinn Fein and that any official had been authorized to talk to them. The use of the word 'negotiations' was a deliberate ploy to obscure the truth of the exchanges, but was honest in so far as dialogue did not constitute negotiation. The Government knew that, once the matter became public, the language chosen by members of the Cabinet was crucial to a policy of obscuring the reality.

On 20 November John Major told the House of Commons that the prospect of talking to Adams would turn his stomach. The press was biting at the Government's heels to get to the truth, and received an admission that there had been contact with Sinn Fein only because they had sought advice on how to end the conflict. That assertion required proof, and it was produced in the form of copies of some of the joint communications. Several of the communiqués, as I pointed out earlier in this chapter, contained changes in wording to support the Government's contention that it was only responding to a plea from the IRA for assistance and advice on how to end its campaign. Sir Patrick Mayhew also produced a message which he claimed had been sent by the 'Provisional Leadership' to the Government on 2 November, and a copy of the Government's reply. Interestingly, Sinn Fein received a copy of their letter and the Government's reply on the same day, 5 November. It was an ingenious ploy by the Government, occurring in advance of the major press leaks. Both documents eventually gave the impression that the Government's contact with the Provisionals was a genuine moral response to a cry for help. The reply document contained the following paragraph:

You ask about the sequence of events in the event of a total end to hostilities. If, as you have offered, you were to give us an unequivocal assurance that violence has indeed been brought to a permanent end, and that accordingly Sinn Fein is committed to political progress by peaceful and democratic means alone, we will make clear publicly our commitment to enter exploratory dialogue with you. Our public statement will make clear that provided your private assurance is promptly confirmed publicly after our public statement and after events on the ground are fully consistent with this, a first meeting for exploratory dialogue will take place within a week of Parliament's return in January.

The reply also stressed that the Government was talking about exploratory dialogue merely to examine whether Sinn Fein could even be admitted to inclusive political dialogue.

The 'Provisional Leadership' communication of 2 November which Sir Patrick Mayhew proudly displayed had a peculiar history. The Provisionals maintain they never sent such a message. The facts support a contention that such a message was inconsistent with the view of the leadership of the IRA and Sinn Fein at that time and since. It provided a solid basis for the government claim that it was morally justified in its dealings with people who wanted to end violence. Any government could not ignore such a 'plea'. The document was faxed from London to the intermediary on 3 November at 6.18 p.m. He assumed that it was genuine and was coming from Sinn Fein, even though the method by which he received it was contrary to established practice. Normally all documentation issued by both sides was passed through him. Since he had just returned to Ireland after spending a week out of the country he assumed that Sinn Fein had acted differently in his absence. A wily detective seeking the source of the letter of 2 November in the light of the controversy surrounding it would first ask who benefited from its public exposure.

The answer is easy: it was dated close to the period when the leaks increased and the Government was busy with its damage limitation exercise.

On 29 November Sir Patrick Mayhew lodged a series of documents in the House of Commons claiming they represented the totality of the exchanges with Sinn Fein during the period from 22 February to 5 November 1993. He was obliged to concede that there were typographical errors in some of the correspondence.

While Sinn Fein scurried from one location to another to prepare a response, the Government was successful with its strategy. The Provisionals kept all copies of their documents, and written notes on meetings, in secure dumps, and it took them a considerable time to resurrect them and prepare a propaganda counter-attack. They were unsuccessful because political events overtook them. The London and Dublin governments were preparing a peace initiative which would make the Hume–Adams talks redundant and obscure the history of exchanges with the Provisionals. There was genuine euphoria in Dublin that the British were prepared to move quickly and with far-reaching proposals. The Taoiseach talked about peace before Christmas. The active involvement of Dublin sidelined the Provisionals. They were busy screaming 'Foul!' but no-one was listening. Hume kept Adams on track with promises that a new accord between the two governments would go some way towards satisfying Sinn Fein demands. The Dublin government privately told Sinn Fein it would be part of a new political process.

My contact in Foreign Affairs in Dublin summed up the events which led to the Downing Street Declaration between the two prime ministers on 15 December 1993:

The British moved very quickly, and Sinn Fein was left behind. However, they could not immediately reject that Declaration because of our involvement. They were hoisted by their assertion that they wanted peace, and both governments were publicly declaring their intention to seek it. I think our government moved too quickly and created a euphoria which was misplaced. We were convinced by the British, and by John Hume, that peace was on the horizon. We moved too fast.

The British were intent on damage limitation and not real progress because the Declaration contained nothing startling for Northern Catholics and Sinn Fein. It had similar characteristics to the Anglo-Irish Agreement in that it recognized both identities in Ulster but within a British Unionist framework. Maybe it should have gone for joint sovereignty over Ulster, to placate both communities. The British would not go that far and we did not press them. The British resided within the principle that it was part of the UK and the Unionists were the only people with a right to self-determination. The Declaration did not ask the Unionists to compromise, yet it demanded Catholic nationalists should accept the status quo. It was a return to an internal settlement and left no-one with much room to manoeuvre. The prospect of success in inter-party talks is as far away as ever. The two governments effectively showed they have no policies. Where were their policies in the Declaration? It was a great media exercise and people loved it.

The Downing Street Declaration was not immediately rejected by the IRA. From the beginning of January 1994 there was speculation that the IRA was split, with Adams marginalized. That was valuable propaganda for the British government but untrue. I talked to a senior Provisional in January 1994 and he told me about what the media termed 'the debate and splits within the Provisionals':

Outright rejection would have damaged us and allowed the British a major propaganda coup. They had cleverly outplayed us, deceived the public and left us stranded. The Army Council pointed out that it was par for the course with the Brits and it should have been clear from the spring of '93. It was unanimously agreed that we should not be seen to reject the Declaration because that would undermine our claim that we wanted peace. We decided to continue to ask the Brits to clarify the Declaration because we knew they couldn't. There was damn all in it for us. We laughed about the press speculation that there was a debate and splits within the movement about the Declaration. There was no debate. We rejected it when we saw it. The Army Council knew that talking was over but like the Brits we were also in the business of winning the propaganda war. We got Gerry into America, despite British opposition to his trip, and embarrassed them. The Army Council said the war would go on and that in Britain it would be stepped up until the Brits realized that they could not defeat us with a useless political accord with Dublin.

Gerry Adams's trip to the United States was opposed by the State Department under pressure from the British government. I was told that John Hume used his contacts with senior Democrats to convince President Clinton that the visit was valuable. He told contacts in Washington that Sinn Fein was still interested in peace and should not be left out in the cold. Adams's visit was a huge propaganda success for the Provisionals and angered the British Cabinet. Hume believed his dialogue with Adams and the Downing Street Declaration were still the basis for finding a lasting peace. He tried to persuade the IRA that the Declaration was a historic document, and said the British government should agree to a Sinn Fein request for clarification. Hume was playing an American political card which he believed would eventually be central to a peace process in Ireland.

The IRA finally gave its answer to the Declaration in March 1994 with mortar attacks on Heathrow Airport. That was its declaration that war would continue.

Epilogue

When the British Prime Minister, John Major, and his Irish counterpart, Albert Reynolds, presented the Downing Street Declaration to the people of both islands in December 1993, many observers thought the opening of a peace process signalled an end to violence and a swift solution. I reminded myself that it was dangerous to make predictions about the Irish problem and that, over twenty-five years, many generals, politicians and optimists have declared that it would be over in five weeks or five years. The initiative of the two governments appeared ingenious, but it was flawed because political policies require the common consent of those for whom they are intended.

The IRA, whom the British government regarded as the major obstacle to peace, pretended to debate the Downing Street Declaration. Privately, though, the IRA leadership disapproved of the Declaration because they felt the accord did not confront the issue of the partition of Ireland and place it firmly on the political agenda. However, Provisional Sinn Fein leaders Gerry Adams and Martin McGuinness did not wish the republican movement to be perceived as resistant to peace; and the IRA Army Council also feared that an outright rejection of the peace process in general would damage the organization in the British Isles and the United States. The internal debate within the Provisionals can best be summed up by an analysis presented to me by a senior Provisional:

We saw the Downing Street Declaration as part of the overall move towards a long-term solution, but we were disillusioned that once again the British failed to address the central issue of partition. While Britain continues to defend the 1920 Government of Ireland Act which copper-fastens partition, there is little point in believing they are serious about eventually detaching themselves from Ireland. We were asking for a *negotiated* settlement, not an *immediate* settlement. We detected the euphoria surrounding the Declaration which provided the Brits with a much-needed breather and a propaganda coup. We knew we had to stick in there and not be seen to be the only people out in the cold. That would have suited the Brits, who would have said, 'Here we go again – the IRA doesn't want peace', and that would have allowed them to continue on their merry way of avoiding the real issues and returning to their old policy of finding an internal UK solution, which has never worked. We laughed at all the media hype about how the Provisionals were in turmoil and how Adams was being marginalized. Some of the British papers talked about the hawks and the doves, about Adams being sidelined. We knew what we were at. We reminded the Brits of our seriousness when they became casual . . . we threw a few mortars into Heathrow. It was a classic warning that we should not be dismissed. This is not over until a proper settlement is negotiated.

That statement contained some significant and disturbing admissions. First, the Provisionals, the umbrella name for the organization which is essentially the Irish Republican Army, have been held together by extremely determined men with twenty-five years' experience of politics. The average person watching television or reading the papers is inclined to believe that Gerry Adams and Martin McGuinness speak their own thoughts, but that is incorrect. They speak for all the men and women of the republican movement including the military wing. General Army Orders make it imperative that members of the republican movement adhere to the principles and ideals of the organization, and policy is not shaped by one or two individuals. Within the Provisionals there was a debate about the peace process but no evident dissent or deviation from an approach established at the highest levels of the organization.

In fact, the IRA/Sinn Fein reluctance to denounce the Downing Street Declaration was a propaganda ploy as well as a political strategy to maintain pressure on the British and Irish governments to consider radical options. The IRA knew that the Declaration was a product of its own willingness to seek a solution and was based on a belief that, if IRA violence ended, a solution would be quickly found. It could be argued that the decision of the British and the Irish governments to put Northern Ireland high on the political agenda was, itself, confirmation for the IRA of its assertion that it was the crucial factor in any future negotiated settlement. The senior Provisional who spoke to me about the Downing Street Declaration mentioned the IRA's potential for striking in Britain at any time. That fact remains prominent in the minds of those who are seeking dialogue with the IRA and leads to the oft-stated view that violence pays. No writer about conflict, myself included, would deny that IRA violence, particularly in mainland Britain, has changed the political landscape perhaps more than any other series of events in the last twenty-five years.

The nature of the threat was made clear at the Old Bailey on Friday, 13 May 1994, when two members of an IRA England cell were gaoled for thirty years. Both were English and had no previous convictions for terrorism or any known links with the IRA or other republican groupings. They were forty-one-year-old Patrick Hayes, who was a computer programmer with a degree from Central London Polytechnic, and Jan Taylor, aged fifty-one, a former British Army corporal who had served with the Royal Signals Corps. They were part of a cell which carried out a series of attacks in London, including the bombing at Harrods in January 1993 which injured four people. They also bombed a Network Southeast train, causing extensive damage. Hayes and Taylor were dangerous men because they were 'sleepers' who were not on the security forces' lists of suspects and had no obvious connections with Ireland. At the time of their arrest they were assembling a list of targets which included public buildings, senior military figures and politicians. They were caught because a security camera had recorded their movements after they planted the Harrods bomb in January 1993. Their associates in the IRA cell were not apprehended, but it was clear that others had supplied Hayes and Taylor with cash, explosives, weapons and transport. Their presence in the Old Bailey illustrated the type of people recruited by the Provisionals and the kind of targets they threaten.

John Major personally knew the extent of the IRA threat after the mortar bomb attack on 10 Downing Street and consequently understood the need to find a political solution. There is little doubt that Major is the first British Prime Minister to place the Ireland problem at the forefront of British politics. However, weak British governments tend to create instability in Northern Ireland, since they are vulnerable to Unionist pressure because of the size of the Unionist vote at Westminster. If there is to be a resolution, John Major may have to seek agreement across the Commons for a policy whereby neither Labour nor the Tories would ever again be content to play the Unionist card for political gain.

Albert Reynolds is also the first Irish Prime Minister to step outside the straitjacket of Irish politics and consider making major concessions to the Unionists by abandoning the Irish constitutional claim to jurisdiction over Northern Ireland. In the spring of 1994, while the IRA 'debated' the Declaration, and loyalist terrorists increased their campaign of sectarian killing, Reynolds moved quickly behind the scenes to encourage John Major to clarify aspects of the Declaration for the Provisionals. One senior British politician told me that in the spring and early summer of 1994 the British Cabinet became increasingly worried that the Irish government was moving too fast.

> We were not very happy when [Reynolds] decided to lift the broadcasting ban [in the Republic] because the Provisionals are now being heard in Northern Ireland courtesy of the Irish broadcasting network, RTE. We would prefer that concessions such as that are negotiated in return for something. In Cabinet there was a feeling that he was acting unilaterally. For example, he went to the United States to meet Clinton and while he was there made comments without consulting us. He was, after all, talking about part of the United Kingdom, and that is our responsibility. We were also dismayed when Gerry Adams was allowed into the United States in what became a propaganda coup for the IRA. Reynolds could have supported us when we asked the American State Department to ask Clinton to deny Adams a visa. Of course Reynolds's support might not have mattered – after all, Clinton was more interested in listening to leading Democrats whom he needed to support his wife's Health Reform Bill . . . and to people like John Hume who had the ear of those Democrats who lobbied for the visa for Adams. We all have

to be careful. The IRA wants to dismember part of the United Kingdom and that is something we should not be prepared to do. Concessions can be made to the Catholics in Northern Ireland without us relinquishing sovereignty, and the Unionists will have to learn that.

The Irish government and nationalist leaders such as John Hume have been at the forefront of the peace initiatives and have indicated their desire to have a meaningful dialogue with the Unionists to find a common solution. The Provisionals have abandoned the demands they made to the British government in 1972 which included immediate British withdrawal and the ending of partition. They now appear to be willing to engage in a process of negotiation, and to agree that they cannot arrive at a conference table in the middle of a campaign of violence. John Hume's pact with Gerry Adams enhanced the stature of the Provisionals, but there may come a time when Hume is forced to walk away from them. Should they abandon dialogue for the politics of the gun, he would be obliged to distance himself from them, and that could lead to the end of any IRA debate about peace and a return to republican violence. In that event a new leadership could emerge and men like Gerry Adams could be consigned to a distant history.

The Unionists fear change and do not have the political intelligence to see that British policy is moving inexorably towards disengagement. Unionist politics has, for long, lacked shrewd and decisive leadership, and the fracturing of Unionism by Paisleyism added to

Unionists' inability to formulate a strategy for protecting the rights of their people and coping with reality. It will be no longer possible for Unionists to fight Britain for the right to be British, particularly if Britain prefers a solution within an all-Ireland context, and my belief is that British policy is proceeding in that direction. While writing this book, I spoke to many influential figures in politics and the diplomatic service, and they confirmed a British desire to extricate themselves from Ireland. British policy-making in Ireland has failed, and the political and military blunders are too numerous to catalogue. A solution will have to be found within the island of Ireland, and concessions will have to be made by everyone, because all of us born there share responsibility for what has happened.

Yet I believe we are all equally capable of solving the problem. I do not think a solution can be found until the gun is taken out of politics and new relationships are created both within the island and between the two islands. It must be achieved first with an end to violence on all sides and then with a proper forum for the political ideas and aspirations of all the people of the island of Ireland. There will have to be a healing period during which all parties to the problem in both islands have an opportunity to talk seriously and sincerely to each other, not necessarily with a set political agenda.

For Unionists, sharing power in the same island with those who are Irish should not mean an abandonment of their cultural identity or political links with Britain, which can be reshaped in a positive way. For nationalists, an Ireland solution should not automatically guarantee an Ireland united in one culture or one political institution. The sharing of power may eventually become the mechanism for finding an Ireland solution in which part of the island is accorded a significant degree of autonomy whereby differences are firmly accommodated.

Whatever the political structures, the history of Ireland is one of bloodshed and it is difficult to be optimistic. From a British viewpoint, the enemy within is likely to remain just that until politics overcomes prejudice, ignorance, intolerance and political apathy.

Appendix: The Green Book

What follows is the constitution, aims, objectives and disciplinary procedures of the IRA. Known as 'The Green Book', it is the IRA's official handbook. Any errors of spelling, grammar or of sense can be attributed to the original.

CONSTITUTION OF OGLAIGH NA hEIREANN

1. Title:

The Army shall be known as Oglaigh na hEireann.

2. Membership:

1   Enlistment in Oglaigh na hEireann shall be open to all those over the age of 17 who accept its objects as stated in the Constitution and who make the following pledge:

'I . . . (name) . . . promise that I will promote the objects of Oglaigh na hEireann to the best of my knowledge and ability and that I will obey all orders and regulations issued to me by the Army Authority and by my superior officer.'

2   Participation in Stormont or Westminster and in any other subservient parliament, if any, is strictly forbidden.

3   Enlistment shall be at the discretion of the Army Authority.

3. Objects:

1   To guard the honour and uphold the sovereignty and unity of the Republic of Ireland.

2   To support the establishment of an Irish Socialist Republic based on the 1916 Proclamation.

3   To support the establishment of, and uphold, a lawful government in sole and absolute control of the Republic.

4   To secure and defend civil and religious liberties and equal rights and equal opportunities for all citizens.

5   To promote the revival of the Irish language as the everyday language of the people.

4. Means:

1   To organise Oglaigh na hEireann for victory.

2   To build on a spirit of comradeship.

3   To wage revolutionary armed struggle.

4   To encourage popular resistance, political mobilisation and political action in support of these objectives.

5   To assist, as directed by the Army Authority, all organisations working for the same objectives.

5. Army Control:

1 The General Army Convention shall be the Supreme Army Authority.

2 The Army Council shall be the Supreme Authority when a General Convention is not in session.

3 The Army Council, only after Convention, shall have power to delegate its powers to a government which is actively endeavouring to function as the de facto government of the Republic.

4 When a government is functioning as the de facto government of the Republic, a General Army Convention shall be convened to give the allegiance of Oglaigh na hEireann to such a government.

5 All personnel and all armaments, equipment and other resources of Oglaigh na hEireann shall be at the disposal of and subject to the Army Authority, to be employed and utilised as the Army Authority shall direct.

6. General Army Convention:

1 A General Army Convention of Delegates (selected as set out hereinafter) shall meet every two years unless the majority of these delegates notify the Army Council that they it better for military purposes to postpone it. When a General Army Convention is postponed, it shall be summoned to meet as soon as the majority of the delegates shall notify the Army Council that they deem it advisable.

2 An Extraordinary General Army Convention and that the urgency of the issue for the Convention does not permit of the selection of delegates as prescribed, that the delegates to the previous General Army

Convention constitute the Extraordinary General Army Convention. When for any reason a delegate to the previous General Army Convention has become ineligible, or is not available, the Battalion Council shall elect a delegate in his/her stead. Every active Volunteer in the Battalion shall be eligible to stand as a delegate.

4 When the Army is engaged on active service, no Unit or General Army Convention shall be held until a reasonable time after hostilities have terminated, unless the Army Authority decides otherwise.

5 An Executive of twelve members shall be elected by ballot at the General Army Convention: at least eight of these members shall be delegates to the Convention: Four members may be elected from active Volunteers who are not delegates. The next six in line shall, however, be eligible as substitutes to the Executive in order of their election. The Executive shall always have six substitutes in readiness.

6 No member of the Executive may also be a member of the Army Council and members of the Executive subsequently elected to the Army Council will resign from the Executive. Vacant positions on the Executive arising in such a way shall be filled by those substitutes next in line from the Convention elections.

7 The following shall be entitled to attend and vote at the General Army Convention:
Delegates selected by Battalion Convention.
Delegates selected by General Headquarters Staff and Staffs of Brigades, Divisions and Commands.

Two members of the Executive.

All members of the Army Council.

The Chief of Staff, the Adjutant-General and the Quartermaster-General.

8 Only Volunteers on the Active List shall be eligible as delegates to the General Army Convention.

9 A majority of the General Army Convention may invite anyone whom they wish to attend to speak.

10 The Chairperson of the General Army Convention shall be chosen by the General Convention.

7. Duties and Powers of the Executive:

1 The Chairperson of the General Army Convention or his/her representative shall, within forty-eight hours of the termination of the Conventions, summon a meeting of the Army Executive over which he/she shall preside during the election of a Chairperson and Secretary. The Army Executive shall then proceed with the election of an Army Council of seven members.

2 The Army Executive shall meet at least once every six months. The Secretary of the Executive shall be responsible for the summoning of the members.

3 It shall be the duty of the Executive to advise the Army Council on all matters concerning the Army.

4 The Executive shall have powers, by a majority vote, to summon an Extraordinary General Army Convention.

5 A member of the Executive who, for any reason, ceases to be an active member of Oglaigh na hEireann shall cease to be a member of the Executive.

6   Casual vacancies on the Executive shall be filled by co-operation after any substitutes that may be elected by the General Army Convention have been exhausted. Vacancies shall be filled within a period of one month.

7   The Executive shall hold office until the following General Army Convention shall elect a new Executive.

8   An extraordinary meeting of the Executive shall be summoned by the secretary of the Executive when a majority of the Army Council or a majority of the Executive so decide.

9   Two-thirds of the available members shall constitute a quorum of the Executive, for co-option purposes only. Full Executive powers shall not be vested in less than five members.

8. Duties and Powers of the Army Council:

1   The Chairperson of the Army Executive or his/her representative shall, as soon as possible after the election of the Army Council, summon a meeting of the Army Council, over which he/she shall preside, until a Chairperson and Secretary have been elected.

2   The Army Council shall meet at least once a month.

3   Vacancies occurring in the Army Council shall be filled from substitutes elected by the Executive or co-opted by the Army Council in advance. Co-options by the Army Council must be ratified by the Executive at its next meeting.

4   Any active Volunteer shall be eligible for membership of the Army Council.

The Army Council shall have power to:

1 Conclude peace or declare war when a majority of the Council so decide. The conclusion of peace must be ratified by a Convention.

2 Appoint a Chief of Staff and ratify all appointments to the Commissioned ranks.

3 Make regulations regarding organisation, training, discipline, equipment and operations, such as will ensure that the Army will be as efficient as possible.

4 Take all necessary steps to secure co-ordination with other republican organisations.

5 Keep in touch with all foreign organisations and countries which may help the Army in any way.

6 Arrange for the care of wounded Volunteers and their dependants and the dependants of Volunteers killed, imprisoned or on active-service.

The Chief of Staff, Adjutant-General and Quartermaster-General shall be entitled to attend and speak at all meetings of the Army Council but not be entitled to vote unless they are members of the Army Council.

Four members shall constitute a quorum of the Army Council.

A member of the Army Council who, for any reason, ceases to be an active Volunteer, shall cease to be a member of the Army Council.

9. Selection of Delegates:

Delegates to the Command Conventions shall be elected by ballot as follows:

1 At each parade called for the purpose, each unit in

Command Area shall elect a delegate to attend the Command Convention.

2 One member of the Command Staff, elected by the Staff at a special meeting called for the purpose.

3 The Command OC shall be entitled to attend and vote at the Command Convention.

4 Each Command Convention shall meet when instructed by the Army Authority and elect one delegate when the total number of Volunteers who parade for Unit Conventions do not exceed twenty, and two when the number of Volunteers do not exceed fifty, and one delegate for each twenty additional Volunteers on parade at Unit Conventions.

Brigade Conventions:

Where the Independent Unit is a Brigade, a Brigade Convention may be held consisting of the delegates elected by the Units, Battalion Staffs and the Brigade Staff, with the power to pass or reject any resolution brought forward by these delegates. The delegates from each Battalion shall each elect their own delegates to the Army Convention.

Election of Brigade, Divisional and Command Staff delegates to the General army Convention.

Two delegates shall be elected at a meeting of General Headquarters Staff officers, with the exception of the Chief of Staff, Adjutant-General and Quarter master-General.

Resolutions to General Army Convention:

Command Conventions and the meetings of GHQ Staff for the election of delegates to General Army Convention shall have power to discuss any matter relating to the Army or to the Nation and to pass resolutions regarding such matters. These resolutions shall be forwarded to GHQ within the time specified by the Army Authority and shall appear on the agenda for the General Army Convention.

10. Changes to the Constitution:
It shall require a two-thirds majority of a General Army Convention to change articles in this Constitution.

OGLAIGH NA hEIREANN (IRISH REPUBLICAN ARMY) GENERAL HEADQUARTERS GENERAL ARMY ORDERS (REVISED 1987)

General Order No. 1
1   Membership of the Army is only possible through being an active member of any army Unit or directly attached to General Headquarters. Any person who ceases to be an active member of a Unit or working directly with General Headquarters, automatically ceases to be a member of the Army. There is no reserve in the Army. All Volunteers must be active.
2   The duties of a Volunteer shall be at the discretion of the Unit Commander. If for a good and genuine reason a Volunteer is unable to carry out the normal duties and routine which obtains in the Unit, the OC may allot him/her some special duties. So long as he/she performs these duties satisfactorily and makes regular reports he/she shall be considered as an active Volunteer.

3   Leave of absence may be granted to a Volunteer in the case of illness or for other valid reason.
4   A Volunteer who, for any reason, ceases to maintain contact with his/her Unit or with General Headquarters for a period of three months shall automatically cease to be a member of the Army.
5   The provision of this General Order does not apply to Volunteers in prison.

General Order No. 2

Volunteers when making the Army Declaration promise '. . . to obey all orders and regulations issued by the Army Authority and any superior officers.'
1   Where an order issued by a duly accredited officer has been disobeyed, the Volunteer in question must be suspended immediately, pending investigation of the case.
2   Any Volunteer carrying out an unofficial operation is automatically dismissed from the Army and is liable to immidate repudiation.
    Minimum penalty for breach of this order: Dismissal.

General Order No. 3

1   All applications for re-admission by those who were dismissed or who resigned from the Army, must be submitted to the Army Council or delegated authority, who alone have the power to sanction reinstatement.
2   Where a Volunteer is summarily dismissed from the Army he/she may apply to his/her Unit OC to have his/her case tried by Court-martial. Such application

must be made within seven days from the date of receipt of notification of dismissal.

3   Once a Court-martial has confirmed such a dismissal, then as in all other cases, any further appeal or application for reinstatement must be forwarded to the Army Council through the Unit Commander.

General Order No. 4
No member of Oglaigh na hEireann may be a member of a political party which recognises the partition institutions of government as sovereign authorities for the Irish people.

General Order No. 5

PART 1
A Volunteer shall not:
1   Swear or pledge allegiance or recognition to the partition institutions of government of the Six or Twenty Six County states.
2   Swear or pledge recognition of their legitimacy as sovereign governing bodies for the Irish people.
3   Swear or pledge himself/herself in any way to refrain from using arms or other methods of struggle to overthrow British rule in Ireland.
    Minimum penalty for breaches: Dismissal.

PART 2
When arrested a Volunteer shall:
1   Remain silent.
2   Refuse to give any account of his/her movements, activities or associates, when any of these have any

relation to the organisation or personnel of Oglaigh na hEireann.

3   Refuse to make or sign any statements.

PART 3

A Volunteer shall:

1   Refuse to obey any order issued by the partitionist authorities requiring him/her to leave Ireland or reside inside or outside a specified area in Ireland.

2   Refuse to give any undertakings about his/her future behaviour. Volunteers released from prison on ticket-of-leave are bound by this.
    Minimum penalty for breaches: Dismissal.

PART 4

Any Volunteer committed to prison forfeits all previous rank and shall report into the Oglaigh na hEireann structure for de-briefing and further instructions.

A Volunteer's attitude in court shall be at the discretion of the Army Authority. Maximum penalty for breaches which are not also a breach of orders in Part 1: Dismissal with ignominy.

PART 5

No Volunteer should succumb to approaches or overtures, blackmail or bribery attempts, made by the enemy and should report such approaches as soon as possible.

Volunteers who engage in loose talk shall be dismissed.

Volunteers found guilty of treason face the death penalty.

General Order No. 6
Committees under Army control will have their terms of reference clearly laid out for them. They will adhere strictly to these terms of reference. In case of departure from these the individual or individuals responsible will be removed from the Committee. The Army Authority has the right to remove any member of such Committees from the Committee at any time.

General Order No. 7
Volunteers are forbidden to undertake hunger-strikes without the express sanction of General Headquarters. Maximum penalty for breach: Dismissal.

General Order No. 8
1   Volunteers are strictly forbidden to take any military action against 26 County forces under any circumstances whatsoever. The importance of this order in present circumstances especially in the border areas cannot be over-emphasised.
2   Minimum arms shall be used in training in the 26 County area. In the event of a raid, every effort shall be made to get the arms away safely. If this fails, the arms shall be rendered useless and abandoned.
3   Maximum security precautions must be taken when training. Scouts must always be posted to warn of emergency. Volunteers arrested during the training or in possession of arms will point out that the arms were for use against the British forces of occupation only. This statement should be repeated at all subsequent Court proceedings.

4   At all times Volunteers must make it clear that the policy of the Army is to drive the British forces of occupation out of Ireland.

General Order No. 9
Firing parties at funerals are only allowed in the case of Volunteers who die on active service or as a direct result of enemy action. General Headquarters permission must be obtained.

General Order No. 10
No member of Oglaigh na hEireann shall make any statement either verbally or in writing to the Press or Mass Media without General Headquarters permission. Volunteers are forbidden to advocate anything inconsistent with Army policy. Minimum penalty for breaches: Dismissal with ignominy.

General Order No. 11
Any Volunteer who seizes or is party to the seizure of arms, ammunition or explosives which are being held under Army control, shall be deemed guilty of treachery. A duly constituted Court-martial shall try all cases.
Penalty for breach of this order: Death.
NOTE: As in all other cases of death penalty, sentence must be ratified by the Army Council.

General Order No. 12
A Volunteer with knowledge of the whereabouts of Army property which is not under Army control shall

report such information immediately to his/her OC. Minimum penalty for failure to do this: Dismissal.

General Order No. 13

1   Any Volunteer who attempts to lower the morals or undermine the confidence of other Volunteers in Army leadership or in any individual in the Army control shall be deemed guilty of treachery.

2   Any Volunteer taking part in a campaign of slander and denigration against another Volunteer thereby weakening authority and discipline, and bringing the Army into disrepute, shall likewise be deemed guilty of treachery.
    Minimum penalty: Dismissal with ignominy.

3   All Volunteers are expected to act in an honourable way so as the struggle is not harmed or undermined. Any volunteer who brings the Army into disrepute by his/her behaviour may be guilty of a breach of his/her duties and responsibilities as a Volunteer in Oglaigh na hEireann and may be dismissed.

General Order No. 14

Oglaigh na hEireann is a voluntary organisation and Volunteers resign membership by giving notice to the relevant Army authority. However, no Volunteer or former Volunteer may join any other military organisation where his/her training, experience and knowledge gained in Oglaigh na hEireann could be used by that organisation.

General Order No. 15

No Volunteer convicted by a Court-martial on a capital offence can be executed if that Volunteer can show that he did not receive instructions in the Green Book. The officer(s) responsible for recruiting this Volunteer and clearing his/her application shall be held responsible for neglect and being in breach of this order.

COURTS OF INQUIRY

1 A Court of Inquiry may be set up to investigate allegations against any member of the Army, any alleged irregularity, or any other matter affecting the Army.

2 The Court may be convened by the OC or any Unit or by the CS. The Convening Authority should supply the Court with specific terms of reference in writing, setting out the precise nature of the matters to be investigated.

3 The Court shall consist of three members, one of who will be appointed President by the Convening Officer of his/her representative. Any active Volunteer may be appointed to sit on a Court of Inquiry.

4 The powers and duties of a Court of Inquiry are: to examine all witnesses who appear before it and having considered all the evidence, to make specific recommendations to the Convening Authority. It has no power to bring in any verdict or to pass any sentence. It may recommend Court-martial proceedings, but decision on this point rests with the Convening Authority.

NOTE: The powers and duties of the Court of

Inquiry should be made clear to the members of the Court and to all witnesses appearing before it, by the Convening Authority or his/her representative.

5 The members of the Court, should be supplied with copies of all General Army Orders, as they may be required for the drawing up of recommendations.

6 Witnesses summoned to appear before the Court should be accommodated in a separate room to that in which the Court is held. They should be cautioned before hand that they are not to discuss the matters being investigated, among themselves. An officer should be detailed to remain in the room with the witnesses. The witnesses will be called singly before the Court to testify.

7 Evidence should be taken on oath which will be administered to each witness by the President. Should a witness object to testifying on oath, he/she must state the objections, to the Court. Unsworn testimony may be taken, but will not carry the same weight as sworn testimony. Once a witness has been examined, he/she may be recalled as often as the Court requires, to answer any further questions the Court wishes to put. For this reason, witnesses will not be allowed to leave the precincts of the Court except with express permission of the Court.

8 If the Court so decided, it may call for additional witnesses to those summoned by the Convening Authority.

9 The recommendations of the Court shall be made in writing and signed by the three members of the Court. These recommendations together

with a record of the proceedings and all documents connected with the inquiry, shall be forwarded to the Competent Authority by the President.

NOTE: The President appoints one member of the Court to record the proceedings unless a note-take or other means of recording is specially provided by the Competent Authority.

OATHS FOR COURTS OF INQUIRY

To be taken by each member of the court.

I . . . swear by the Almight God that I will conduct this Inquiry without fear, favour or affection.

And I swear that I will not disclose the vote or opinion of any member of the court unless required to do so by the Competent Authority. And I swear not to disclose the recommendations of the Court until they have disclosed by the Competent Authority.

To be taken by each witness:

I . . . swear by Almighty God that my evidence to the Court shall be the truth, the whole truth and nothing but the truth.

To be taken by the official note-taker:

I . . . swear by Almighty God that I will maintain inviolate the proceedings of this Court, and that I will not disclose its proceedings unless required to do so by the Competent Authority.

COURT MARTIAL

1 A Court-martial is set up by the OC of any Unit or by the CS, to try any Volunteer on a specific charge or charges.

2 The Court shall consist of three members of equal rank or higher than the accused.

3 The Convening Officer will appoint one member of the Court as President.

4 When a Court-martial is set up by a Unit OC, the Adjutant of the Unit, or some members of the Unit delegated by the Adjutant to do so, will act as Prosecuting Council. When the Convening Authority is the CS, he/she may appoint any officer other than the Adjutant-General to act as Prosecuting Counsel.

5 The accused may call on any Volunteer to act as his/her Defence Counsel, or if he/she desires, may defend the case himself/herself.

6 A copy of the charge shall be supplied to the accused in reasonable time before the case is heard to enable him/her to prepare defence. The Convening Authority may either supply the accused with a summary of the evidence it is proposed to place before the Court, or arrange for a preliminary hearing at which witnesses for the prosecution will give on oath, a summary of their testimony. At such preliminary hearings, neither defence nor prosecution counsel will be present, but the accused may cross-examine the witnesses. The evidence shall be taken down in writing from each witness, shall be read over to the accused and shall be signed by him/her. If the accused wishes to make a statement or give evidence on oath, he/she must be cautioned that anything he/she says may be taken down and used in evidence at any subsequent hearing of the case.

7 If the accused objects to any of the three officers

comprising the Court, the objection will be examined by the remaining two members and, if upheld, the member objected to will be replaced.

8   The Convening Authority will supply the Court with a copy of the charges and with copies of General Army Orders.

9   The Convening Authority will ensure that the Prosecuting Counsel is in possession of all the facts relevant to the case and that all prosecution witnesses are present at the Court.

10 During the hearing of the case, all witnesses will be kept in separate rooms as in the case of a Court of Inquiry. The only persons present in the Court shall be the members of the Court, the accused, the Defence Counsel (if any), Prosecuting Counsel and note-taker (if any) and the witness under examination.

11 Evidence should be taken on oath which will be administered to each witness by the President. Should a witness object to testifying on oath, he/she must state the objections, to the Court. Unsworn testimony may be taken, but will not carry the same weight as sworn testimony. Once a witness has been examined, he/she may be recalled as often as the Court requires, to answer any further questions the Court wishes to put. For this reason, witnesses will not be allowed to leave the precincts of the Court except with the express permission of the Court.

12 At the start of the case, the President will read each charge to the accused and ask the accused if he/she pleads guilty to the charge.

13 Witnesses when called to testify will be cross-examined first by the Prosecuting Counsel and then by the Defence Counsel, or by the accused if conducting his/her own defence. Witnesses may be questioned by any member of the Court. Should either Counsel wish to recall a witness who has already testified, permission of the Court must first be obtained. The Court may recall any witness. Witnesses may not leave the precincts of the Court without permission from the Court.

14 At any time it so desires, the Court may go into private session to decide on points which may arise, such as the admissability of evidence.

15 When all witnesses have testified. Defence Counsel will sum up and make closing address to Court. This will be followed by summing up and closing address of the Prosecuting Counsel. The Court then goes into private session to consider its verdict and sentence.

16 For a breach of any General Army Order, the Court shall not have power to impose a lesser penalty than that laid down in such order.

17 The verdict and sentence of the Court shall be set down in writing and signed by the three members. This, together with a summary of the evidence must be forwarded by the President of the Convening Authority. Sentence is subject to the ratification of the Convening Authority.

NOTE: In the case of the death penalty sentence must be ratified by the A/C. (Army Council)

18 The accused may forward an appeal against the

verdict or sentence or both to the Adjutant-General who will place it before the Competent Authority. The appeal should be forwarded by accused through his/her OC, who in turn will forward it to the Adjutant-General with a signed copy of verdict and sentence and a summary of the evidence. The Competent Authority may order a new trial or reduce the penalty, but may not increase the penalty imposed by the Court.

NOTE: The President appoints one member of the Court to as recorder, unless a note-taker or other means of recording the proceedings is specially provided by the Convening Authority.

OATHS FOR COURT-MARTIAL

To be taken by each member of the court:

I . . . swear by Almighty God that I will try the accused on the issues presented to the Court without fear, favour or affection.

And I swear that I will not disclose the vote or opinion of any member of the Court or any proceedings of the Court unless required to do so by the Competent Authority.

And I swear not to disclose the verdict or sentence of the Court until they have been disclosed by the Competent Authority.

To be taken by each witness:

I . . . swear by Almighty God that my evidence to the Court shall be the truth, the whole truth and nothing but the truth.

To be taken by the official note-taker:

I . . . swear by Almighty God that I will maintain

inviolate the proceedings of this Court and that I will not disclose its proceedings unless required to do so by the Competent Authority.

NOTES FOR COURT-MARTIAL

1 On the Court assembling, the Convening Authority or his/her representative reads the order convening the Court.

2 The President asks the accused if he/she has any objection to any member of the Court. Members of the Court retire and consider any objections, and decide whether objection is to be upheld or rejected.

3 If any objection is upheld, the Convening Authority or his/her representative nominates another member.

4 The President appoints one member of the Court to record the proceedings, unless a note-taker is specially appointed by the Convening Authority.

5 The President then reads the charge or charges to the accused and asks him/her to plead to each separate charge.

6 The Prosecutor presents his/her authority to the Court and makes the opening statement for the prosecution, outlining the charges.

7 The Prosecutor then calls witnesses to substantiate case for the prosecution.

8 Accused or his/her Counsel cross-examine witness for the prosecution.

9 When evidence for the prosecution is closed, the accused or his/her Counsel makes opening statement for the defence.

10 Witnesses for the defence are then called.
11 Accused or his/her Counsel makes closing statement for the Defence.
12 Prosecutor makes closing statement for the prosecution.
13 Court may ask for records as to the character and record of the accused.
14 The Court retires to consider the findings on each charge and to award the sentence.

The Court may award a separate sentence or punishment on each charge on which the accused is found guilty of, or one sentence or punishment, to cover more than one charge.
15 Where different sentences are proposed, the Court shall vote first on the lesser sentence proposed.
16 Members of the Court shall vote on sentence according to their seniority, the junior members voting first.
17 The President of the Court shall be responsible for forwarding to the Competent Authority.

(a) The written records or other records of the proceedings of the Court and all documents connected with the trial.

(b) The findings and sentence of the Court.
18 The oath to witnesses shall be administered by the President of the Court.

CODE OF CONDUCT
(Issued in 1987)

No serious guerrilla organisation can exist or hope to achieve victory without a number of prerequisites.

One one side of the coin these include comradeship, an internal structure (or infrastructure), rules and regulations, an ability to recruit, and a brief in achieving objectives. On the other side there has to be public support and the commanding of the admiration and respect of the public.

Where comradeship is lacking and where there are no rules and regulations one can see from past INLA feuds how disagreements can degenerate into anarchy and demoralise one's base of support.

The Irish Republican Army is one of the oldest and surviving guerilla armies in the world. It has a long tradition of struggle but at certain times in its history a number of the prerequisites for success were absent – conditions were not right, but most importantly nationalist opinion in the North was not ripe for a sustained armed struggle. All this changed in the 1960s with the attempted repression of the Civil Rights Movement and from then until now the struggle has taken on a steady momentum of its own.

The IRA's objectives are set down in a written constitution (which can only be amended by General Army Convention: the last IRA Convention was in 1986). The IRA however, is regulated by a set of General Army Orders (which can be amended at any time by an Army Council). Volunteers have always been expected to be familiar with the Constitution and General Army Orders, but in recent years familiar also with the Green Book which is a further breakdown of the aims and objectives of the organisation, the tactics of how to conduct oneself during interrogation.

Enemy

The British government has attempted to undermine the struggle, deter people from fighting and sap the morale of Volunteers and supporters through a number of measures.

It kills people, it jails people, it consistently repeats that it will not give way to the IRA, it ridicules one's objectives as being unrealistic and unachievable. It attacks the methods such as the commandeering of cars, the taking over houses, fighting a war in the streets in which people live, the execution of informers, etc. All of this is so much hypocrisy compared to the commandeering of a country and British institutionalised violence and sectarianism. Most objective people — and not necessarily sympathetic people — can see through this hypocrisy, and only ongoing politicisation and publicity can really counter it.

It is IRA successes that demoralise the British and undermine their case. Ongoing IRA successes reinforce the belief in victory which in turn will lead to increased support.

Behaviour

No organisation and no organisation's members are above reproach. The behaviour of Volunteers on operations and how republicans conduct themselves in their private lives will, where exploitable, be used by the British, the media, and the SDLP, and the Movement's other detractors to undermine the Movement in the minds of the general public.

When Mao's Red Army was fighting the revolution in

China its Code of Conduct was summed up succinctly, (if idealistically) as follows:

Three General Rules of Discipline
1. Obey orders in all actions.
2. Do not take a single needle or piece of thread from the people.
3. Hand all booty over to headquarters.

And the Eight Reminders
1. Talk to people politely.
2. Be fair in all business dealings.
3. Return everything you have borrowed.
4. Pay for anything you have damaged.
5. Don't beat or bully people.
6. Don't damage crops.
7. Don't flirt with women.
8. Don't illtreat prisoners of war.

This is somewhat idealistic but one gets the drift about striving for the optimum in good behaviour and the necessity of avoiding scandal. Given the pervasiveness of the media in everyone's lives nowadays it is therefore even more essential for republicans to consider the effect of their attitudes and behaviour on supporters. To be conscious of how their behaviour could be used to ridicule the Movement and thus unjustifiably bring the struggle into disrepute.

The Republican Movement relies on a voluntary code of conduct (though Volunteers can still be dismissed under General Army Orders for blatant actions which bring the Movement into disrepute) and below are some of the guidelines expected of members:

1 Republican Volunteers are expected to be truthful in their dealings with other comrades and other sections of the Movement.

2 They are expected to be honest in all matters relating to the public, both in terms of official and private business. Whilst the majority of members are from working-class backgrounds, a business-person (who is also a known republican activist) who provides a poor serviced to the public or who exploits the public in business dealings is no asset to the republican cause.

3 Republicanism stands for equality and an end to sexism. Male Volunteers who mistreat or exploit their partners are flying in the face of this principle. Volunteers must practice domestically what the Movement preaches publicly.

4 Anyone promoting sectarianism or displaying sectarian attitudes should immediately be disciplined.

5 Republicanism has an international dimension which means respecting as equals other nationalities and races. Anyone who pays lip service to international solidarity and then slips into mimicking the racist attitudes which are typical of an imperialist mentality should be immediately upbraided. All people are equal and everyone has an international duty to oppose racism and oppression from wherever it emanates.

6 Our culture is something of which we should be proud, it is part of our identity and it can also be used, not in a chauvinistic sense, but against the British to show the separateness of our identity

as an individual nation. Republicans who do not subscribe, to Irish culture, or who have no interest in promoting the Irish language, should respect those who are making progress on this front against considerable odds. It is simply laziness which prevents people from attempting to learn their native language: no-one is that busy!

7 The Green Book makes reference to people who take alcohol urging them to be extremely careful. Under excessive drinking people's tongues loosen, people whom one wouldn't normally trust become 'great friends', and one is vulnerable to the temptation of engaging in 'loose talk'.

Apart from the security risk, a drunken republican is hardly the best example of a freedom fighter, he or she is open to ridicule from the Movement's detractors.

The activities of republicans even engaged in innocent celebrations would be used by the enemy, so vulnerable are ambassadors of freedom struggle on this issue! So be moderate and be careful and remember what you represent. If you need to 'let off steam' then be discreet.

8 Alcohol affects different people in different ways, turning some aggressive people into affectionate doves, and making some normally pleasant people nasty and unbearable!

Under alcohol people's attitudes can also undergo unpleasant changes: respect towards others, one's partner, the Movement, can temporarily diminish leaving one with a lot of apologising and more than a hangover the following day. Dependency on alcohol is also a major weakness which the Special Branch will be quick to exploit.

The code set out here represents mere commonsense and is a reminder to all activists of their responsibilities. No-one has been press-ganged into republicanism. If you cannot do the struggle the honour of your service, then do not do it the dishonour of a disservice. It is as simple as that.

Volunteer' Rights
(issued in 1988)

Volunteers should be well versed in General Army Orders and Court of Inquiry and Court Martial procedures. They should understand that they are aimed not only at ensuring the IRA runs smoothly within these agreed disciplinary codes, but also at protecting the rights of Volunteers. While everyone is accountabled to disciplinary process under General Army Orders, this is not their only function. They are there to protect the Army and as the Army is its Volunteers, they must serve to protect the Volunteers as well.

Communications within the Army are of vital importance. Thus all Volunteers should: be aware of how the Army structure works and of how a Volunteer can and should pass grievances or observations upwards. The onus is on the Volunteer to do this in a non-disruptive way, working through and using the proper channels all the time. All Volunteers should have access to their immediate superiors. This is through normal Army channels to GHQ. If this is unsatisfactory then there is access through GHQ to Army Council. The onus is on each tier, if requested, to pass requests upwards.

Security permitting, a Volunteer should always get an answer. Whether the Volunteer agrees with the answer is irrelevant: once Volunteers exhaust the channels, Army discipline demands that the answer be accepted. Final redress can be sought through the Army Council. Issues which are not important enough to warrant this should not be permitted to cause disruption or harmful dissensions. The onus is on the Volunteers to behave at all times in a correct, positive and responsible manner avoiding personal conflict or diversions from our main task.

Suspension of Volunteers should be conducted sparingly. Where suspensions are necessary they should not be of lengthy duration. Except in special circumstances Volunteers should not normally be suspended, unless facing charges, eg a Volunteer facing a court of inquiry should not normally be suspended. However, when a court of inquiry decided to press charges, this would normally involve suspension until the charges are adjudicated on. Special circumstances where a volunteer could be suspended by a competent senior authority could for example, include a refusal to obey an Army Order.

The above deals with suspension of membership of the Army. Suspension of a Volunteer from specific duties or a position in the Army is permissable at the discretion of a competent senior authority. Again the normal right to appeal applies. Summary dismissal of a Volunteer should be avoided except in the most extreme circumstances. Every Volunteer has the right to a court of inquiry. It should be noted that such a court, arising out of a summary dismissal, is a court, where those responsible for the dismissal will have to stand over their actions. They are not permitted to introduce new evidence other than that on which the dismissal was based. Volunteers summarily dismissed have seven days in which to appeal against the dismissal.

Courts are established by the Army Authority. Thus recommendations by courts must be agreed on by the Army Authority before they are acted on, or made known to other Volunteers.

All of the above places a heavy responsibility on those holding positions within the Army. The Adjutant General is responsible for discipline. The Adjutant General or those to whom he/she has delegated responsibility should be consulted in all cases involving the possible dismissal of Volunteers.

An organisation like ours which seeks political objectives based upon the principles of justice and freedom, must ensure that these principles are applied internally and in our dealings with one and other.

Volunteers, and this includes everyone from the CS to the Unit Volunteer, must be treated in a fair and overhand way.

Index

Aberdeen, bomb 1939, 16
Abwehr, 48–9, 50, 51
Adams, Gerry, 159
   talks with William Whitelaw,
     155, 156, 157
   and IRA, 195, 196, 197, 313
   peace initiative, 307, 309–10
   talks with John Hume, 321,
     322, 334, 335, 349
   interview on Radio Four,
     332
   visit to United States, 342,
     348
   and Downing Street
     Declaration, 344
Agents Provocateurs, 262, 243
Aldershot
   Parachute Regiment base,
     147–52
   bomb 1974, 192
Alliance Party, 178

Alnwick (Northumberland),
   bomb 1939, 12, 13
Anderson, Martina, 222
Anglo–Irish Agreement 1938, 3
Anglo–Irish Agreement 1985,
   305
Anglo–Irish Declaration 1993,
   see Downing Street
   Declaration
Anglo–Irish Treaty 1921, 2
Annersley Forest
   (Nottinghamshire), arms
   dump, 213, 214
Annesley, Sir Hugh, 245,
   249–50
Ansell, Elsie, 41–2
Anti-Terrorist Squad
   and London car bombs 1973,
     172, 173
   bombs 1974, 187

Anti-Terrorist Squad (*continued*)
  and Balcombe Street gang, 205
  and Canning cell, 235
  rivalries, 237, 238, 258, 262–3
  failure in 1980s, 244
  denied information, 258
Apprentice Boys'
  march 1969, 109–15
  marches 1971, 135
Arbuckle, Constable, 124
Ardoyne area, Belfast, violence, 117
Arlow, Revd William, 190
Armagh, Gough Barracks, 79–80
arms dumps in England, 213
Armstrong, William, 166, 168, 171, 173
Army
  sent to Northern Ireland 1969, 106–7
  ignorance of urban unrest, 107, 121
  moved into Derry, 115
  in Belfast, 118–21
  problems of control, 123
  Provisional attitude towards, 125
  brutality of, 125–6
  and Conservative government, 127–8
  search, Lower Falls area, 128–30
  relations with RUC, 133
shooting of two non-IRA youths in Derry, 134
  and internment policy, 137–9
  Bloody Sunday, Derry, 1972, 142–3
  and William Whitelaw, 156, 159
  and UDA, 158–9
  after 1972 breakdown, 161–2
  role under Wilson government 1974, 178–81
  intelligence, and rivalry, 237, 239–40
Arnott, John, 41–2
Attlee, Clement, 64, 73
'attrition' campaign against IRA, 131

B Specials (Ulster Special Constabulary), 56–7, 58, 84, 87, 88
  and Belfast/Derry march 1969, 103
  aid from British troops, 106
  mobilized for Derry Apprentice Boys' march, 113, 115–16
  West Belfast violence, 116, 120
  disbanded, 123
Baker, George, 127, 130, 140
Balcombe Street siege, London, 203–5
Ball, Johnathan, death, 291, 319
balloon bombs, 36, 48
Baltic Exchange 1992, 272, 310
Barnes, Peter, 43–4, 46–7
Barry, Tom, 4–5, 6
Beattie, Desmond, 134
Belfast, 115–16
  target for Luftwaffe, 57
  Bloody Friday 1972, 160, 290
  see also Ardoyne; Falls; Lower Falls; Shankill
Bell, Ivor, 157
Bennett, Joe, 260
Berehaven port, 2, 3

Best, Ranger William, 153, 154
Birmingham
  bombs 1939–40, 12, 16, 48
  bombs 1973–4, 176
  pub bombings 1974, 188
  'Birmingham Six', 188–9, 207,
    229
Bishopsgate bomb, London
  1993, 292, 321
Blandford (Dorset) army base,
  raided, 90
Blaney, Neil, 114, 123, 184
'Bloody Friday', Belfast, July
  1972, 160, 290
'Bloody Sunday', Derry, 30
  January 1972, 142–4
Bloomfield, Kenneth, 135–6
Bogside (Derry), 111–15
Boland, Kevin, 114
bomb-making, 34, 36–8
  'finger-prints' of makers,
    198–9
bomb warnings, 188, 271,
  290–91, 292
Border, sealing suggestion 1971,
  132
Bradford, coach bomb, 176
Brady, Martin, 166, 167, 168,
  170, 172–3
'Brendan', GHQ mastermind,
  206, 209, 211, 213, 223
Brighton, Grand Hotel bombing
  1984, 217–20
Britain, and Northern Ireland
  conscription, 51
British government
  Cabinet attacked by mortar,
    270
  talks with IRA, 301–3
  no imposed solution, 313
  wants end to violence,
    314–17

ready for talks, 317
talks with Sinn Fein, 319–21,
  323–4, 326–31
leak of news of talks, 324–5
demands non-violence, 332,
  333
see also Conservative
  government; Heath,
  Edward; Wilson, Harold
Brooke, Sir Basil, 63–4
Brooke, Peter, 307–8
Brookeborough Police Station,
  raided 1956, 86
Burns, Francis James, 32
Burntollet March 1969, 103
Burrows, PC George, 171
Butler, Edward, 182–3, 187,
  198, 200, 208

Cabinet, British, attacked by
  mortar, Downing Street,
  270
Cahill, Joe, 108, 190
Calabresi, Luigi, 165
Callaghan, James, 104
  sends troops to Northern
    Ireland 1969, 106
  and Derry Apprentice Boys'
    march 1969, 110, 114
  and the Army in Northern
    Ireland, 124
Campbell, Jim, xxiii
Canaris, Admiral Wilhelm, 59
Canning, Chief Constable, 21
Canning, James, 234–5
Canning, Manus, 77–9
car bombs, London 1973, 167,
  168–9, 170, 171–2, 174
Carrington, Lord, 135, 136–7,
  139

Carver, Michael, Field Marshal
    Lord Carver, 132–3, 135,
    136–7, 179
  and special treatment, 139,
    140
  and Army behaviour, 143
Casement, Sir Roger, 47
Casey, Charles James, 28, 29,
    30–1, 32, 39
Catholic Church, 141, 154
Catholics (in Irish Republic),
    and the IRA, 93
Catholics (in Northern Ireland),
    9, 73
  and RUC, 57
  and IRA, 58, 93
  isolation, 62, 64
  and partition, 66
  and electoral boundaries, 66
  and education, 66–7
  and conscription, 51
  flags not allowed, 81
  and Orange marches, 82–3
  protection by the Army, 115,
    124
  attacked in West Belfast,
    116–19
  welcome to the Army in
    Belfast, 118
  and internment 1971, 137–8
  Parliamentary opposition, 72
  against the Army, 125–6, 130,
    180
Chamberlain, Neville, and
    Northern Ireland, 55
Chelsea Barracks, bombs 1981,
    213
Chichester-Clark, Major James,
    104, 113, 118
Churchill, Winston, and de
    Valera, 55, 56, 60, 61

CIA (Central Intelligence
    Agency), and supergrasses,
    260–1
Citizens' Defence Committees,
    Belfast, 120, 122
civil rights
  and IRA, 99–100, 102
  march to Derry 5 October
    1968, 101
  internment of activists, 138
  march to Derry 30 January
    1972, 142–3
Clann na Poblachta, 68–9, 73,
    77
Clarke, Mrs Ada, 42, 43
Clay, James, 41, 42
Cleary, Michael, see Mason,
    Michael Joseph
Clinton, President Bill, 342, 348
coalition governments, Irish
    Republic, 69, 73, 77, 91
Cobh port, 2, 3
Conley, PC Stanley, 171
Connolly, James, 94
Connolly Association, 94
Conservative Government from
    1970
  and Army, 127, 142–3
  GEN 42 Cabinet Committee,
    132, 134–5
  and internment, 136–7
  thinks of settlement 1972,
    154
Conservative Party, bombed at
    Brighton 1984, 217–19
Cordner, Police Sergeant, 87
Corish, Brendan, 150
Costello, John A., 73–4
Costello, Seamus, and Parachute
    Regiment attack, 147–50,
    151
  death, 152

Council of Ireland, proposed,
    178
counter-insurgency, 131, 161
couriers, IRA, 38, 211–12
Coventry, bomb 1939, 41–7,
    148
Craig, Donal, 221–3
Craigavon, Lord, 55, 63
Crossman, R.H.S., diaries, 104,
    110
Crumlin district (Belfast),
    violence, 117
Crumlin Road prison, internees,
    139
CS gas, 112, 129
Cumann na mBann, 10, 164,
    212
Curragh concentration camp,
    World War II, 52–4, 91–2
Currie, Austin, MP, 99–100,
    102, 190
Cusack, Seamus, 134

Dail Eireann, possible Northern
    Ireland Catholic
    representatives, 69
Daily Telegraph, 1939, 15, 18
Daly, Edward, Bishop of Derry,
    142
'Dave', Provisional activist, 166,
    168, 170, 173
de Valera, Eamon
    talks with Britain, 2–3, 55
    neutrality policy, 2–3, 54–5
    and IRA, 6–7, 16
    against the IRA, 17, 48,
        50–1, 54, 58, 91
    and Northern Ireland
        conscription, 51
    and internment, 52
    and hunger strikes, 54
    and Germany, 60

condemned by Churchill, 61
postwar problems, 69
Prime Minister again, 77, 91
Deal (Kent), bombing 1990,
    264, 306
de-escalation, against IRA, 131
Democratic Unionist Party, 336
Derry
    target for Luftwaffe, 57
    civil rights march 5 October
        1968, 101
    student march, 1969, 102–3
    flashpoint for Orange
        marches, 109
    Apprentice Boys' march
        1969, 109–16
    Army shooting of two boys,
        134
    rise of Provisionals, 141, 153
    see also Bogside
Derry Unit, IRA, 76
Devlin, Bernadette, MP (later
    Mrs McAliskey), 68, 112
Devlin, Paddy (SDLP), 134, 155
Doherty, Hugh, 183, 187, 198,
    200, 201
    sentenced, 208
Doherty, Joseph, 274
Dowdeswell, Detective
    Inspector, 203
Downing Street, 267
    attacked by mortar, 268–70,
        308
Downing Street declaration,
    December 1993, 295, 298,
    340–1, 344–6
Dublin, bombs December 1972,
    160
Dublin government, *see* Irish
    Republic
Dublin, British Embassy, 144

Duffy, Eion (alias Oskar Pfaus), 49
Duggan, Harry, 181–2, 185–6, 187–8, 198, 201, 202–3
    sentenced, 208
Duignan, Michael, 150–2

Ebrington naval base, 76
Edgeworth, Margaret, 39
education, Northern Ireland, 66–7
Education Act 1947, 66–7
Edwards, Inspector Ronald, 171
Eire
    neutrality with Germany, 48, 51, 60, 62
    and the Second World War, 62
    postwar economic decline, 62
    republic 1948, 64
    neutrality under attack from British, 55
    see also Ireland, Republic of; Irish Government
Emergency Powers Act, 52
emigration, from Irish Republic, 77
'England Department', 223–8, 272
EOKA contacts, 90
ETA links with IRA, 186
Europe, IRA cells, 213, 228–9
explosives, 34, 36–8
    see also bomb making
External Relations Act (Ireland), repealed, 73

Fairley, Professor Hamilton, 199–200
Falls district (Belfast), 116, 117–19

Farrar-Hockley, Lieutenant-General Sir Anthony, 115, 127, 131
    and interrogation, 139
Farrell, Mairead, 227
Farrell, Michael, 138
Faulkner, Brian (later Lord Faulkner), 83
    Prime Minister, 132
    and UDR, 133
    demands internment, 134
    presses Heath government, 135–7
    and Bloody Sunday 1972, 142
    resignation, 145
    Chief Executive, Northern Ireland Executive, 178
Feeney, Hugh, 164, 166, 168–70, 172, 173, 174
    hunger strike, 177
Felsted Barracks (Essex), 77–8
fertilizer, for bombs, 211, 263
Fianna Fail party, 4, 69, 76, 77, 122
Fine Gael party, 69
Finucane, Pat, 255–6
Fisk, Robert, xxiii
Fitt, Gerry (later Lord Fitt), 178
Fitzpatrick, Daniel, 32
Flemming, Patrick (alias Michael Preston), 14, 28, 29, 30, 31
Foreign Office, 181, 189, 197
Foster, Superintendent A.G., 21
franchise, Northern Ireland, 65
Fraser, Sir Hugh, MP, 199
Freeland, Lieutenant-General Sir Ian, 106, 112–13, 114, 121, 127, 129
    replaced, 132
Future Research Units, 247–8

Gallagher, Molly, 38–9

Garland, Sean, 80, 86–7, 151, 152
Gateshead, target 1993, 294
gelignite, 37–8
GEN 42 Cabinet Committee, 132, 134–5
Gentle, Rex, 41–2
Germany, 3
 and IRA, 8
 and Eire's neutrality, 48, 50
Gibraltar, SAS killings 1988, 255, 265
Glenn, Mary, 24–5, 31
Goad, Captain Roger, 198
Gonne, Maud, 68
Goodman, Special Constable Glenn, 273, 275
Goulding, Cahal, 78–9, 92–3, 94–6, 98
 and civil rights, 99–100
 refuses arms 1969, 108–9
 gives guns, 109, 120–1
 and Belfast violence 1969, 120
 and new campaign, 147, 152
Government, British, see British government; Conservative government; Heath, Edward; Wilson, Harold
Government of Ireland Act 1920, 5, 107, 344
Gow, Ian, death 1990, 265, 306
Grand Hotel, Brighton, 217–19
Griffiths, Helen, 214
Grogan, Lawrence, 4
Guildford, bombs 1974, 188
'Guildford Four', 189, 207, 229

Halifax, Lord, 11–12, 55
Harrods bombs 1973 and 1993, 175, 346
Hasler, John, 150

Haughey, Charles, 114
Havers, Sir Michael, home bombed, 213
Hayes, Patrick, 346
Hayes, Stephen, 14
Healey, Denis (later Lord Healey), 110, 123
Healy, John, 26, 28, 31
Heap, Charles, 23–4
Heath, (Sir) Edward
 and Northern Ireland, 128, 133, 135
 and Brian Faulkner, 136–7
 agrees to internment, 137
 and interrogation, 140
 and Army's role, 143
 direct rule in Northern Ireland, 144–5
 and Sunningdale Pact 1973, 178
 IRA target, 192, 200
Heathrow mortar attack 1993, 296, 297–8, 342
Henty, Edward, 292
HM Inspectors of Explosives, 21
Hewart, Lord Chief Justice, 34–5
Hewitt, James and Mary, 43–4, 45
Hinsley, Archbishop of Westminster, 19
Holmes, Paul, 166–7, 168, 170, 173
Home Office, and 1970s intelligence, 181
housing, Northern Ireland, 64–5
Hughes, Brendan, 196
Hume, John (SDLP), 100, 102, 155, 190
 peace initiative 1992, 309, 315

Hume, John (SDLP) (*continued*)
  talks with Gerry Adams, 321,
    321–2, 333, 335, 349
  supporter of Adams' trip to
    USA, 342, 348
Humphreys, Mr Justice, 29,
  30–7, 39–40
hunger strikes, 54, 177
Hunt, Peter, 179
Huntley, Commander Robert,
  172

incident centres, 194, 197
Information Policy Unit, 160
Insight team (*Sunday Times*),
  xxiii, 106
Intelligence (British), 133, 161,
  180
  use of technology, 193, 211
  and deaths in Northern
    Ireland, 196
  surveillance, 215
  against the IRA, 237–63
  problems, 237ff
  MI5 takeover, 245–59
  not sharing information,
    257–8
Internal Security (organization),
  211, 214, 221
internment without trial
  Eire, World War II, 52–3
  1950s, 91–2
  1970s, request for, 132,
    135–6
  special treatment of internees
    (interrogation), 139–41
  opposition to, 141
  political status of internees,
    155
  should be phased out, 193
  used as political weapon, 195

interrogation of internees,
  139–40
Ireland
  partition, 344
  re-unification, 3, 70
Ireland, Republic of
  inaugurated 1949, 73
  not crucial to Britain, 70
  neutrality, 70
  General Election 1951, 77
  foreign investment policy, 95
  for earlier period, see heading
    Eire
Ireland Act 1949, 71, 73
Irish, in Britain (non-IRA), 15,
  17, 88, 229–32
Irish Free State, punishment of
  IRA, 5
Irish government
  and Bogside 1969, 113
  helps IRA 1969, 122–3
  and British government/IRA
    talks, 310
  contacts with British
    government, 334, 339
Irish National Liberation Army
  (INLA), 152
Irish Republican Army (IRA)
  quiet in the later 1930s, 4
  violence in Britain 1939, 1–2,
    8–11
  punished by Irish Free State,
    5
  bomb-making lectures, 10
  declaration of war 1939, 11,
    14
  bombings 1939, 12–13,
    15–22
  'S Plan', 16
  personnel in Britain, 16
  trials 1939, 28–33, 38–9
  Coventry bomb 1939, 41–6

martyrs, 47
men in British prisons, 47–8
proscribed in Ireland, 48
and the Nazi Party, 48–50
and outbreak of the Second
    World War, 50, 51–4, 57
hunger strikes, 54
declining during war, 56
and Northern Ireland, the
    Second World War, 56–8
postwar disillusionment and
    schism, 62–3, 72
revitalized, 72–3
not to fight new Republic of
    Ireland, 74–5
'The Green Book', 75, 351
politics in Sinn Fein, 76
attack in Northern Ireland, 76
raids on arms depots, 78–82
'Operation Harvest' launches
    violence 1956, 84
more raids, 86
Brookeborough police
    station, 86
not targeting UK 1950s, 88
Blandford Army base, 90
internment, 91–2
end of campaign 1962, 92
central dump of arms set up,
    95
recruitment in UK, 96
and civil rights movement, 99
attributed bombings, 98–9,
    104
and the breakdown 1969, 107
in Lower Falls 1969, 116–17
not the gainers from 1969
    violence, 118, 120
protection of Catholic areas,
    122
guns seized, 128–9
attrition policy, 131

losing to the Provisionals, 133
violence, post-internment,
    141
starts campaign against
    Britain, 146
attack on Parachute
    Regiment, Aldershot,
    147–52
pressure for peace, 154–5
talks with William Whitelaw,
    155–8
prisoners want political status,
    155
truce 26 June 1972, 156
killings reviewed 1972, 160
blamed for killings, 160
demands, in talk about
    ceasefire 1974, 191
new London campaign 1975,
    198
belief in eventual amnesty,
    210
cells in London, 211, 233–5
capture of group in London,
    and of materials, 223
'England Department',
    224–9, 272
agents in London cells, 243
campaign 1980s/1990s, 264ff
reasons for bombing, 271
attitude to Brits, 277–82
campaign, 1990s, 282ff
keepers and sleepers, 283
Nottinghamshire centre,
    284–5
objects of the exercise, 293,
    296–7
Gateshead and North Shields
    bombs, 294
more bombs in London 1993,
    295
scale-down of operations, 295

Irish Republican Army (IRA)
(*continued*)
talks with British
government, 301–2
and Sinn Fein talks 1990,
307, 309, 313–14
ceasefire hoped for, 311
campaign of violence must be
over, 316
violence suspended, 324
and Downing Street
Declaration, 343, 345–6
spokesmen, 345
see also Provisional IRA; Sinn
Fein
Irish Republican Army
(Northern Ireland branch),
93–4, 190
takeover of IRA 1976, 210
Irish Republican Socialist Party,
founded 1974, 152
Irish Special Branch, *see* Special
Branch, Irish
Italy, contacts with Provisionals,
164

Jenkinson, Noel, 148–9, 151
Johnston, Dr Roy, 94, 99
Joint Security Committee, 142

Kane, George Brendan, 28, 31,
39
Kavanagh, Paul, 212–13, 214
Kelly, PC Alexander, 273, 275
Kelly, Gerard, 166, 168, 171,
172, 173
hunger strike, 177
at talks, 317, 319
Kincora Boys' Home, 257
King, General Frank, 179–80,
193
King, Tom, 270

Kinsella, Denis, 285–9
Kinsella, John, 285–6, 289–90
Kitson, Brigadier Frank, 131,
136, 139, 144
Knightsbridge 1982, 217

Lamb, Ethel, 234–5
Lancaster, bomb 1939, 16
Larkin, WPC Susan, 275–6
Lee, Arthur, 12
Leicester, bomb 1939, 16
Lemass, Sean, 92
Lenadoon, 158–9
Libya, IRA links, 186, 212
Light Infantry, 3rd, 116, 119,
124
Liverpool
bomb 1939, 12, 16
bomb warning 1993, 291
Logue, Jack, 32
London
bombs 1939, 12, 15–16, 20
bank bombs 1939, 18–19
cell discovered 1939, 26
more bombs, 1939–40, 48, 52
IRA unit, 1972, 147–8, 151
Provisional targets 1972, 166
car bombs 1973, 167–75
railway stations 1973, 175
Harrods 1973, 175
Westminster Hall 1974, 176
Tower of London 1974, 176
long-term resident team
1974, 184–92, 198
bombs 1975, 198
Kensington Church Street,
198
Hilton and Portman Hotels,
199
Sir Hugh Fraser, MP, 199
Locketts' and Scott's
Restaurants, 200, 201, 202

Balcombe Street siege, 203–5
death of Army careers officer,
265
death of Ian Gow, 265
cell 1975 (Balcombe Street
Four), 202–9
bombs late 1970s, 210–11
Chelsea Barracks 1981, 213
Knightsbridge 1982, 217
Regent's Park 1982, 217
Rubens Hotel, 221, 222
1990s campaign, 266–72
railway stations, 270–1
Baltic Exchange 1992, 272,
310
Staples Corner 1992, 272
Camden Town, 290, 317
Bishopsgate, 292–3, 321
Finsbury Park 1993, 294
Harrods 1993, 346
King's Cross 1993, 294
Heathrow Airport 1994,
297–8, 342
London Underground, target
1970s, 189, 190
Long Kesh camp, 53, 141
Long War, begins 1972, 162
Lotte Continua, 164, 186
Lough Swilly port, 2, 3
Loughran, Seamus, 196
Lower Falls district, Army in,
128–30
Loyalist terrorists/paramilitaries,
138, 308
relationship with Intelligence,
240
Loyalist, bombings apparently
by, 161
Loyalists, see also Unionists
Lynch, Detective Inspector, 37
Lynch, Jack, 113–14
Lyons, James Michael, 28–9, 31

M60 Gang, 274
M62 coach bomb 1973, 176
MacBride, Sean, 4, 5, 6, 68,
73–4, 81
McCann, Danny, 227
McCann, Eamon, 123
McCarthy, Daniel, 32
McCormack, Leo, 79
McCormick, James (alias James
Richards), 43–4, 45, 46–7
McCullough, Mr Justice, 289
McDonnell, Gerard, 222
McFarlane, Brendan, 196
MacFhloinn, Pairic, 284–6,
287–9
MacGiolla, Thomas, 99
McGuinness, Martin, 141, 154,
157, 196–7
and talks, 306–7, 309,
314–16, 317, 319
and Downing Street
Declaration, 344
McKee, Billy, 191
McLarnon, Liam, 166, 168,
173, 174
McNearney, Roisin, 166, 168,
170, 172–3, 174
MacStiofain, Sean, 78–9, 159
Chief of Staff Provisional
IRA, 125, 153–4, 155
meets William Whitelaw,
157–9
British campaign, 163, 166,
168, 177
MacSwiney, Alderman Terence,
47
McWhirter, Ross, killed, 201
Magazine Fort, Phoenix Park, 50
Magee, Patrick, 212, 215–16,
218–21, 222
Brighton Grand Hotel,
218–19

Magee, Paul 'Dingus', 273–7
Maidstone (Kent), bombing, 199
Maidstone, HMS, 137, 141
Major, John
  target for IRA, 265, 269–70, 283
  and Downing Street Declaration 1993, 298–9
  and IRA contacts, 306, 318, 326, 328–36
  and Albert Reynolds, 335
  denial of talks, 336–7
  seriousness of Irish policy, 347
Mallie, Eamon, 336
Manchester
  IRA bomb 1939, 12, 146
  cell discovered, 23–5
  more bombs 1939–40, 48
  bomb 1974, 176
marching season, Northern Ireland, 109
Mason, Michael Joseph (alias Cleary), 27–9, 30
Matthew, John and Sheila, 203–4
Maudling, Reginald, 128, 137, 140
Mayhew, Sir Patrick, 313, 318–19, 320–1, 338–9
  denies Sinn Fein negotiations, 336
MI5, 180–1, 185, 241–3, 244–6
  and Balcombe Street, 203
  rivalries, 237, 238–9, 241, 242–3
  not sharing information, 257–8
  in charge of intelligence, 257–63
  and supergrasses, 261–2

  loses 1000 lb bomb, 262–3
MI6, 161, 180, 216, 240, 256–7
  rivalries, 237, 241, 242–3, 256–7
Midlands, IRA arms dumps, 211
Military Reconnaissance (Reaction) Force (MRF), 161
Ministry of Defence, and Intelligence, 181
Mitchell, John, 32
Moberley, PC Brian, 172
Morrison, Danny, 195, 196
  and talks, 306–7
mortars, 267–8
  and Downing Street, 268–70, 308
  and Heathrow Airport, 297–8

Napier, Lieutenant-Colonel, 119
nationalists, *see* Irish Republican Army; Social Democratic and Labour Party; Welsh Nationalists
Nazi Party, and IRA, 48–9
Nelson, Brian, 246–7, 250, 252–4, 256
  sentenced, 254–5
Netherlands, IRA in, 216
News Chronicle, on 1939 bombs, 13
News of the World, 1–2
no-go areas, Belfast, 120, 122
North Atlantic Treaty Organization (NATO), 70–1
North Shields (Northumberland), 294
Northern Ireland
  and IRA 1930s, 7

conscription feared by Eire,
51
IRA, World War II, 56, 57–8
some prosperity postwar, 62
confirmed 1949 as part of
United Kingdom, 71
elections February 1949, 71–2
Northern Ireland Civil Rights
Association (NICRA),
99–100, 102
Northern Ireland Executive,
178, 180, 190
Northern Ireland government
(Stormont)
against IRA, 58, 81
against Irish reunification, 70
and UK troops, 106–7
and Derry Apprentice Boys'
march 1969, 110
and Army in Belfast, 118,
121, 123
resignation of Cabinet, 145
Northern Ireland Labour Party,
72
Nottinghamshire, centre for
IRA activities, 284–5

O'Bradaigh, Rory, 197
O'Brien, Dr Conor Cruise, 293
O'Brien, Michael, 273, 275–7
O'Connell, Daithi (David),
153–5, 156, 197
meets William Whitelaw, 157
and campaign in Britain, 163,
166, 177
London campaign reactivated,
197–8
O'Connell, Martin Joseph, 182,
185, 187, 189, 191, 198,
199–200, 201
at Balcombe Street, 205
O'Donovan, Jim, 9

O'Donovan, Seamus, 49–50
O'Dwyer, Ella, 222
Offences Against the State Act
1939 (Eire), 17, 48, 52
O'Flaherty, Peadar, 14
O'Hanlon, Fergal, 87
O'Hara, Brigid, 44
Oldfield, Sir Maurice, 256–7
Omagh barracks, attempt on,
81–2
O'Neill, Captain Terence, 97,
98, 101
defeat, 104
Operation Demetrius, 137
Operation Harvest, 84
Operation Snowball, 253
Orangemen, 66, 71–2, 82–3
marches, 82–3, 100, 109, 135
O'Shea, Michael, 28, 31

Paisley, Revd Ian, 98, 101, 103
and Anglo–Irish talks, 336
Palestine Liberation
Organisation (PLO), 186
Pangbourne (Berkshire), arms
cache, 213
Parachute Regiment, 1st,
142–3, 146, 147–52
Parliament, British, little
discussion of Northern
Ireland in 1960s, 97
Parry, Tim, death, 291–2, 319
partition of Ireland, still an issue,
344
'Paxo', 37
Peacocke, Anthony, 106, 113,
114
People's Democracy movement
(PD), 102–3, 138
Pfaus, Oskar (alias Eion Duffy),
49

police, 40
  regional, intelligence, 237
  see also Anti-Terrorist Squad;
    Royal Ulster Constabulary;
    Scotland Yard; Special
    Branch
ports, Irish, for use of Britain, 2
Preston, Michael (alias
    Flemming), 14, 28, 29, 30,
    31
Prevention of Terrorism Act
    1939, 20–1
Price, Dolours, 164–6, 167,
    169, 170, 173, 186
  hunger strike, 177
Price, Marion, 164–6, 168, 170,
    172, 173, 174
  hunger strike, 177
Prince of Wales' Own
    Regiment, in Derry, 115,
    116, 119
proportional representation, 66
Protestants, 7, 9
  favoured in Northern Ireland,
    63–5
  and education, 66–7
  rampage 1969, 116
  in Shankill, 123–4
  weapon-holding 1970s,
    136–7
  see also Unionists
Provisional IRA ('Provos')
  background to, 8, 94, 108–9,
    122
  creation 1970, 124–5
  rise, 130, 133
  bombs, 131
  warned about internment,
    137
  violence, 141
  campaign against Britain, 146
  support in Derry, 141, 153

post-Whitelaw talks, 158–9
killings 1972, 160
bombing team for London
    1973, 165–7
the London car bombs,
    167–74
still working in England, 175
hunger strikes, 177
further campaign, 181
use of longer-term residents
    in UK, 184
contacts with Wilson
    government, 189
worried about 1975 ceasefire,
    195
changed, 196
campaign 1990s, 232
attitude towards British, 302
and British government,
    302–3, 324–6, 330–2,
    337–9
and Downing Street
    Declaration, 344
Provisional Sinn Fein, 124

Qadhafi, Colonel Muammar,
    212
Quarrex gelignite, 170
Queen's Regiment, 118
Queen's University, Belfast, and
    civil rights, 102–3
Quigley, Thomas, 212–13

Rees, Merlyn (later Lord
    Merlyn-Rees), 179, 192–5,
    328
Regent's Park 1982, 217
regional police, intelligence, 237
republicanism, and Clann na
    Poblachta, 68–70
republicans
  Britain, 89

Northern Ireland, 7
reunification of Ireland, 3,
    69–70
Reynold, Jimmy Joe, 39
Reynolds, Albert, 299, 347–8
    and John Major, 335, 339
Ribbentrop, Joachim von, 59
Richards, James (alias James
    McCormick), 43–4, 45,
    46–7
Roche, Dr, 36–7
Rooney, Patrick, 117
Ross, Albert, death, 13
Rowlands, George, 41–2
Royal Irish Regiment, formed,
    257
Royal Regiment of Wales, 118
Royal Ulster Constabulary
    (RUC)
    against IRA, 7, 51, 81, 84,
        230–1
    hit by IRA, World War II,
        56–7
    re-equipped 1951, 77
    1950s, 86–8
    and Derry civil rights march
        1968, 101
    student march to Derry 1969,
        103
    and Apprentice Boys' march,
        Bogside, 112–13, 116
    and West Belfast violence
        1969, 117, 120
    not in control of the Army,
        121
    disarmed, 125
    border duties, 133
    relations with Army, 133
    and internment, 137
    to replace Army, 194
    rivalry with Army, 241

alleged shoot-to-kill policy,
    241
E4 department, 241–2
rivalries with other
    organisations, 242–3, 248
and Stalker inquiry, 243
and Stevens inquiry, 257
relations with MI5, 257–8
and supergrasses, 261
Rubens Hotel, 221, 222
Russell, Sean, 4–6, 7–8, 9, 14
    and Germany, 49, 59
Russia, IRA contacts, 90
Ryan, John, 32
Ryan, Mick, 152

'S Plan', IRA sabotage 1939, 16
St Helens (Lancashire), bomb
    1939, 27
Salcey Forest
    (Northamptonshire), arms
    dump, 213, 214
Sands, Bobby, MP, 177, 216
SAS (Special Air Service), 193,
    240, 242, 273–4
    Gibraltar killings 1988, 255,
        265
Savage (Gibraltar victim), 227
Scotland Yard
    and bombs 1939, 13, 14, 21,
        24
    inaccurate information,
        229–30
    and MI5, 258
    see also Anti-Terrorist Squad
sectarian violence, late 1960s,
    106–7
Semtex explosive, 176, 219, 264
Shankill district, 116, 118, 124
Sherry, Peter, 221–2
Shillington, Graham, 112

Shoreland armoured vehicles, 117
Sinn Fein, 76, 93
  successes in General Election 1955, 82
  ineffective in 1970s, 190
  incident centres, 194
  possible talks 1990–2, 307, 309
  British government wish for talks, 312–14, 317
  told of new IRA campaign, 314
  peace initiative 1993, 295
  talks with British government 1993, 319–21, 323–4, 326–31
  British denial of talks, 336–7
  and Downing Street Declaration, 345
Smith, (Sir) Howard, 136
Social Democratic and Labour Party (SDLP), 133–4, 141, 144, 190
  Sunningdale Pact 1973, 178
  and Merlyn Rees, 195
  talks with Sinn Fein, 321–2
  see also Hume, John
socialism, and IRA, 92, 94–5
Solihull, bombs 1973, 175
South, Sean, 87
Spain, IRA contacts, 90
Special Branch, Irish Republic, 6–7, 50, 58, 91
Special Branch (UK), and IRA, 10, 12, 15, 39–40, 90
  Coventry bomb 1939, 43, 47
  1960s, 96, 100
  1970s, 185
  rivalries, 241, 258
Special Branch, RUC, 133, 137, 139, 243, 259

Special Powers Act 1922, and internment, 91
'Stages theory', 95, 108
Stalker, John, inquiry, 241, 243, 245
Staples Corner 1992, 272
Stephen, Sir Ninian, 312
Stephenson, Sean, see MacStiofain, Sean
Stevens, John, inquiry, 250–7
Stockhausen, Commander von, 59
Stoker, PC Mark, 286–9
Stormont, see Northern Ireland Government
Stuart, Peter (alias Peter Joseph Walsh), 27, 28–9, 30, 39
Sunday Times, reports of 1993 talks, 332
Sunningdale Pact 1973, 178
'supergrasses', 260–1
suspicion, of IRA membership, Second World War, 52

Tadcaster (Yorkshire), death of police officer, 273, 275
Task Co-ordinating Group, and intelligence, 259
taxi bombs, 293–4
Taylor, Jan, 346–7
terrorists
  anonymity in UK, 233–5
  and Government, 300–1
Terry, Sir Peter, 265
Thatcher, Margaret
  and hunger strikes, 54
  at top of hit list, 216, 266
  Brighton assassination attempt, 217–19
  and Northern Ireland intelligence, 256–7
  and IRA, 303

possible strategies on talks, 304–5
'The Green Book', 75, 351
'The Third Force', set up by Ian Paisley, 142
Thompson, Detective Sergeant, 151
Thompson, Detective Inspector, 30, 32
'Timmins, Michael', 284–9
trade unions
    IRA work in, 96
    activists interned, 138
treaty ports, 2–3, 55, 57
troops, see Army
Tuite, Gerard, 212, 214,
Tuzo, General Harry, 132, 135, 136–7, 142
    and interrogation, 139
    and Bloody Sunday, 142
Twoomey, Seamus, 157, 158–9, 190, 191

Ulster Defence Association (UDA), 142, 158–60, 246–7
    murders by, 160
    and Stevens inquiry, 250–4
Ulster Defence Regiment (UDR), 133, 196, 246, 249
    merger into Royal Irish Regiment, 257
Ulster Freedom Fighters (UFF), 246, 249
Ulster Special Constabulary (B Specials), 56–7, 58
Ulster Volunteer Force (UVF), 98, 104, 138, 160
Ulster Workers' Council (UWC), strike 1974, 179–80

Unionism, Northern Ireland, 63–4
Unionist government, end of rule, 144–5
    see also Northern Ireland government
Unionist Party, 65, 178, 195
Unionists
    and Eire's neutrality, 55
    and de Valera, 61
    and Northern Ireland, 62, 71
    triumphalism 1955, 82–3
    and IRA 1960s, 98–9
    counter-demonstrations, 101, 103, 107
    and Northern Ireland Executive, 178–9, 180
    and Anglo–Irish talks, 349
The United Irishman, 76, 85, 151, 152
United Nations, and Bogside 1969, 113
United States, 70
    IRA sympathizers, 9, 91

Walker, Joseph, 28
Walsh, Roy, 166, 168, 171, 173
'Walsh, Roy', 219–21
    see also Magee, Patrick
Ward, Judith, 176
warnings, see bomb warnings
Warrington
    gasworks bomb, 284, 286–9, 317
    Bridge Street bomb, 291, 319
welfare state, IRA against, 77
Welsh Nationalists, purchase of IRA arms, 96
West Belfast, place of strife, 115–16
Westmacott, Captain Herbert, 274

Weston, Captain Gerry, 150
Wharton, Gerard Francis, 32–7
White, Sir Dick, and
    interrogation, 140
Whitehouse, PC Mark, 275
Whitelaw, William (later Lord
    Whitelaw), 145, 155
  talks, 155, 159
Williams, Tom, 58
Wilson, Harold (later Lord
    Wilson), and Government
  not concerned with IRA, 96,
    98
  and Derry civil rights march
    1968, 101
  and collapse of Unionist
    government, 104
  and Derry Apprentice Boys'
    march 1969, 110, 113–14
  leaves Ireland to the Army,
    126
  and the Price sisters, 177
  and Northern Ireland 1974,
    179
  contacts with Provisionals,
    189, 304–5
  almost achieves ceasefire, 304
Wood, Vincent, 283–4
Woolwich bombs 1974, 188–9
Wright, Lee, 288–9

Young Socialists (Trotskyite), 96